DESTROY

THE DEFINITIVE HISTORY OF PUNK

Alvin Gibbs

BRITANNIA PRESS PUBLISHING

Copyright © 1996 Alvin Gibbs.

First published in Great Britain by Britannia Press Publishing, 1996.

This edition published in 1996 by Britannia Press Publishing, a division of Britannia Crest International Limited.

The right of Alvin Gibbs to be identified as the author of this work has been asserted by him in accordance with the Copyright, Designs & Patents Acts 1988.

British Library Cataloguing in Publication Data. A catalogue record for this book is available from the British Library.
Gibbs
DESTROY - *The Definitive History of Punk*
ISBN 0-899784-00-4

Printed and bound in Great Britain by WBC, Bridgend.
Distribution: Bookpoint Ltd.
Sales: Amalgamated Book Services Ltd.

Cover photograph: Rex Features Ltd.

This book is dedicated to Lisa Von Hasenberg.
"I couldn't help it... It's all your fault!"

About the author

Born in Croydon, south London in 1958 - the year of the dog - Alvin Gibbs swapped his dream of playing outside right for Crystal Palace Football Club to that of a professional career as a musician after catching a vital and inspiring Marc Bolan performance of 'Jeepster' on Top Of The Pops in the early 1970's - an experience he describes as *"Satori like"*.

Learning the rudimentary skills of bass playing and composition with his first Glam rock band Marionette, the author saw New York's New Wavers the Ramones during their first UK tour in 1976. *"Shell shocked and seized"* by this exposure to the new music genre, he embraced the sounds and style of the Punk culture and joined one of the first English Punk rock outfits, the Users.

Eventually unimpressed with the Users wasted-horizontal method of playing and conducting business, Alvin left the 'near-legendary' Cambridge Combo for a stint with ex-Damned, future Lords Of The New Church guitarist Brian James, during which time he toured extensively across the UK and Europe, mainly as support act to the Sting-led, highly successful Police. This in turn, led to his appointment as Thunderbird welder extraordinaire for that most British of Punk rock bands, the UK Subs.

After four years of global touring and substantial recording/chart success with the group - four Top Twenty albums, seven Top Thirty singles and the first Punk outfit chosen to play behind the Iron Curtain in Poland during the winter of 1983 - the author terminated his membership of the UK Subs and traded London for Los Angeles in search of the rock 'n' roll dream.

He found it in the guise of bass player to the rock legend and Godfather of Punk, Iggy Pop. Touring the world with his idol, Alvin made this wild, roller coaster experience over six continents the subject of his first book Neighbourhood Threat - On Tour With IGGY POP.

Though no longer working with the man he considers *the* seminal figure in rock 'n' roll, the author continues to stay in touch with Monsieur Pop and the two have been known to share a glass or two of fine claret together, post show, whenever the Baudelaire-esque singer comes to town.

Returning to London after a five year absence in 1990, Alvin took to recording and touring in Japan with ex-Hanoi Rocks guitarist Nasty Suicide in the rock outfit Cheap And Nasty. After two albums and many miles travelled, the author took time off from playing to complete his first book and lead a more varied life - *"Hedonism"* he insists, *"is a full time occupation."*

Alvin Gibbs is the proud owner of a classic Gibson Les Paul bass guitar, an autographed copy of Charles Bukowski's 'Erections, Ejaculations, Exhibitions And General Tales Of Ordinary Madness', and a black belt in the Japanese martial art of Shorinji Kempo.

Index

"History is hard to know because of all the hired bullshit, but even without being sure of 'history' it seems entirely reasonable to think that every now and then the energy of a whole generation comes to a head in a long fine flash, for reasons that nobody really understands at the time... that sense of inevitable victory over the forces of Old and Evil. Not in any military sense; we didn't need that. Our energy would simply 'prevail'. We had all the momentum; we were riding the crest of a high and beautiful wave..."

Hunter S. Thompson,
'Fear And Loathing In Las Vegas' (1971).

1
SAVAGE MESSIAHS
THE PUNK ROCK PROTOTYPES

"Music is a sum total of scattered forces."
Claude Debussy (1862-1918).

"I did like the New York Dolls a lot - their ambiguity and also the racket they churned out. I was very impressed by their ordinariness and how bad they were."
Sid Vicious (1976).

In the foul winter of 1974 I recall sitting on the top-deck of a blood red London Transport bus as it crawled its way in rush-hour traffic through the concrete and glass heart of the suburban south London town of Croydon. It was a viciously cold day with a merciless wild wind cracking cue-ball size hailstones against the bus windows.

As passengers took refuge from the cold and solid ice missiles aboard the barely moving vehicle, some would curse the sky and others would talk of the coming of a new ice age. I'd been hearing this kind of feverish discourse all winter. Doomsday soothsayers and apocalyptic visionaries all over the Goddamn place. It was a sign of the times.

The weather hadn't been the only thing causing the antipathy and discontent welling up from the deep, chattering underbelly of the United Kingdom in late 1974. Politically, things had been stormy too.

That year, Britain had seen a protracted and bitterly fought strike by the National Union of Mineworkers, resulting in the fall of prime minister Edward Heath's Conservative government, with the opposition Labour and Liberal parties establishing a necessary but uncomfortable pact to form a precarious administration. Instability and the resulting lack of investment, by those who had no wish to support a socialist run government anyway - will of the people or not - were driving the country's finances deeper into the red, and price rises by the oil producing countries (OPEC) had resulted in a reduced working week and recession. Add to this the accelerated level of unemployment, race hate via the increasingly high profile marches and activities of the fascist National Front party, and a new wave of bombings/ assassinations by the IRA, and you had the perfect recipe for a year of fear and loathing in the UK. The operatic nature of the weather that evening only added to the feel of a country in terminal decline.

Across the Atlantic, the USA was suffering a social and political hangover of similar proportions. In contrast to the stable, confident and affluent nineteen fifties and sixties, 1974 had produced America's imminent withdrawal from Vietnam and a contracting economy. These factors, along with the exposure of the Dark and Dirty Watergate deeds of Richard Milhous Nixon and his cronies, followed by the moves towards the presidents impeachment and eventual resignation, had led to a climate of insecurity, cynicism and despondency.

But these were mere droplets in my river of concerns.

As a young hound on the make, sitting impatiently on that slow, slow ride to the future, neither the political machinations of the day nor the weather were of any great consequence to me. My thoughts that evening were on more important things, for that was to be the glorious, promise filled night that I participated in my first ever rehearsal with a rock 'n' roll band.

Yeah, no more furtive, un-amplified strumming at home so as not to disturb the rock-hating neighbours, or endless sad jams on bad acoustic guitars with bores who wanted to play the Crosby, Stills and Nash back catalogue. It was going to be *The Real Deal*. A full-out drum kit pounding, ear stinging, amps cranked up *high*, blow out of a rehearsal with like minded and enthusiastic teenage-music-missionaries who wanted their music written in napalm, as I did.

With only a couple of stops left before the double-decker reached my destination, I made a final check that I had all the requirements for that evening. Guitar lead, heavy-duty picks and spare bass guitar strings in my black 'Granny Takes A Trip' crushed velvet jacket... Check!

In my left hand I held my bass guitar. It was a cheap Korean copy of an out-of-my-price-range Rickenbacker bass; a hideous monster of an instrument with feeble, rattling pick-ups and an action you could have driven the bus under. It was a piece of junk, but at the time I thought it was super cool.

In my right hand I held six vinyl records. Six favourite LP's of mine that I was taking along to provide inspiration and give direction to what would become our search for a *sound*, a noise of our own, during our first and future rehearsals. At the top of the pile of records was the self-titled maiden album by the New York Dolls.

Right: New York Dolls - Old Grey Whistle Test (1973) / Photograph © Hoffmann Ltd.

LIPSTICK KILLERS
THE NEW YORK DOLLS

The year or so before that first night of rock 'n' roll rehearsal nirvana I'd happened to catch a late broadcast BBC TV show with the fashionably surreal, seventies title of 'The Old Grey Whistle Test'. I didn't often get the approval of my parents to watch this particular programme (I was fifteen at the time), as it consisted of *"twisted, long-haired weirdos making a nasty racket"* as my father would have it, but after making the case that there was simply nothing else worth watching on the other channels I finally got their less than enthusiastic go-ahead.

I'd seen this show a couple of times before after making the same argument and had caught gems like Alice Cooper performing 'Under My Wheels', and David Bowie coming on like some kind of extraterrestrial life form with suspect tendencies laying down 'Queen Bitch', among the show's usual grey staple of pompous, progressive rock acts. That night, there was to be another such gem.

First the camera caught a painted death-head motif on the back of a shoulder shrugging, beat-up leather jacket. Quickly it panned to... *"Was that an Amazon woman with the Fender bass, twelve inch platforms and lipstick sneer or could it really be...?"* Quicker still, before I could make a full evaluation the camera turned on the gum-chewing lead singer, clapping in time to the infectious dirty rhythm, looking like Jean Harlow in 'Public Enemy' and dressed to kill in polka-dot blouse, tight, Tight, TIGHT ski-slacks and court shoes. The camera moved again, this time pointing its TV eye at a pouting lead guitarist who resembled a wigged out, high camp version of Keith Richards; a mass of raven hair defying gravity as he careered around the TV studio on stiletto heels, wind-milling at his low slung, tear drop axe.

As the images on the screen started to register, my father and I simultaneously laughed out loud. We were of course both laughing for very different reasons. My laughter did not contain a trace of the mocking tone of my father's, it was a reaction born of a stunned admiration and a real sense of karmic discovery - the song was 'Jet Boy', and this was my introduction to the debauched, deviant and divine New York Dolls.

As I sat transfixed, sucking in their performance, it seemed to me the Dolls were everything you could wish for in a rock 'n' roll band. They were musically and visually exciting, evidently degenerate, and authentically sleazy. They were perfect. Not since my first exposure to the musical sea of possibilities via a T. Rex performance on 'Top Of The Pops' some months earlier had such a sense of revelation prevailed.

I wasn't the only future punk to be turned on by the New York Dolls that night, there were others. Others who would utilise the audacity and energy of that performance to mutate, create, inflate into a style, a similar construction of musical self expression of their own. But first, lets deal with these inspiring Dolls.

If you were able to breathe the New York Dolls in, *deep*, into the intuitive backwaters of your mind, you would have caught the dank smell of hard drugs, hard liquor, hair-spray and failed ambition... They were *born to loose* motherfuckas!

Their saga begins at the roads end of 1971 at a hip Manhattan pick-up joint called Nobody's, where the women liked their men in eyeliner, leather and cock-crushing tight strides, and where androgyny and sexual ambiguity were all the rage. It was at this club for hedonistic peacocks that the four members of NY City rock band Actress decided they needed a singer/front man to take the strain off their lead guitarist who had been reluctantly handling the vocal duties. It just so happened they came across a promising candidate downing drinks at the Nobody's bar - a snake hipped pretty boy by the name of David Johansen.

Johansen had some experience of singing rock 'n' roll, having worked with two groups previously: the Vagabond Missionaries and Fast Eddie and the Electric Japs. He liked the androgynous, deviant look of the band and agreed to a rehearsal.

The androgynous deviants were Johnny Thunders (formerly Johnny Volume and born John Gonzales) - lead guitar, Sylvain Sylvain (born Sil Mizrahi in Cairo, Egypt) - rhythm guitar, Arthur Kane - bass and Billy Murcia on drums. All were tough and street wise "NOO YAWK" ex-hoods and hustlers who had served time with such notorious gangs as the Hell Burners and the Phantom Lords, real crazy outfits where blood-violence and blood-brotherhood were a way of life/death. Somewhere along the line though, Thunders, Kane, Sylvain and Murcia decided to swap guns and knives for guitars and drums and formed their own rock gang.

Figuring the way to score the cool chicks was to have an effete/ stud image of a band like the Rolling Stones, they instigated their own unique version of Anthony Burgess' 'Clockwork Orange', malchick 'chic', with gang style leather jackets and tattoos, blended with a daring combination of spiked heeled shoes, make-up and selected items of women's clothing. It was this Yin-Yang element to their look, machismo and fey, glamourous but tough, that appealed so to Johansen's sensibilities.

At Kane's suggestion, to mark the admission of Johansen into their gang, they changed the band's name from Actress to the New York Dolls and began rehearsing with their new singer in a spare room at a bike store off Columbus Ave. and 82nd St. Having cut their teeth on a couple of Johansen's songs, they worked hard on achieving a sound that was a blend of influences such as the Stones, MC5, the Kinks and Chuck Berry, and saw it metamorphose into a trash rock, drag-'chic' combination.

Their first show was played for a bunch of welfare cheque recipients at a run down, seedy hotel across from the bike shop after the group originally booked to play failed to materialise. After this dubious debut they secured some more prestigious gigs, and eventually gained for themselves a weekly residence at the Oscar Wilde Room, located in downtown Manhattan, where they soon attracted a twisted but loyal following. The furore caused by some of those early Dolls performances led certain members of the switched-on American music press to take up the musically sloppy but visually stunning, cross dressing Dolls as a 'cause célèbre' which eventually, in turn, brought them to the attention of one Marty Thau.

Having had solid experience of record promotions and A & R, Thau recognised a commercial commodity when he saw one. He realised that the earnest idealism of the sixties was dead, having been replaced in the seventies by a *"let's get fucked up and to hell with politics"* hedonism/cynicism, and saw in the Dolls the perfect standard bearers for the new attitudes. Pulling in business associates Steve Leber and David Krebs to form a management company - Dollhouse Productions - Thau signed the band and set about hustling them up a record deal.

They were sold to A & R departments as the house-band for the decade, but there was a small problem - the major labels were having trouble coming to terms with the Dolls image. Lipstick and eyeliner, nail polish and leather hot pant numbers worn with ripped-up glitter pantihose were all very well for appealing to the hip rock intelligentsia in NY or LA, but who the hell was gonna go for a look like that elsewhere in the country?

To counter these concerns Thau organised a high profile tour of the UK for the group in 1972. There, he hoped to hook up the Dolls to the thriving British glam rock movement where make-up wearing, androgynous acts such as David Bowie, Roxy Music, T. Rex and the Sweet had already gained acceptance and chart popularity. As support act to Rod Stewart's Faces and fellow American Lou Reed, the Dolls became an overnight sensation attracting the cream of the English rock aristocracy to their shows and were feted by the UK's bold and beautiful. Bowie quickly became a fan as did certain sections of British rock journalism. Nick Kent, star writer for influential music weekly 'New Musical Express' as an instant convert went so far as to herald them as the future of rock 'n' roll, as did Melody Maker's Roy Hollingworth in his numerous glowing reviews.

As the highly successful UK tour ended, Thau was not in the least bit surprised to have found himself in negotiations with the Who's record label Track, on the cusp of securing for the Dolls a lucrative, multi-album deal.

The Dolls were moving up, their wider fame and fortune seemed imminent... Then, fate showed its hand... All ace's... All spades... The Death Card.

On November 6th 1972, Billy Murcia went to a party in south London where he swallowed a bunch of Mandrax washed down with copious amounts of booze. This wasn't unknown territory for Billy, all the Dolls indulged in drug taking and heroic drinking, but that star crossed fall night Billy badly miscalculated and paid for it with his life. In an attempt to bring him out of his chemically induced coma, some party-goers inadvertently drowned poor, dumb, beautiful Billy with the coffee they anxiously poured down his throat.

With news of Murcia's death, Track records immediately dropped their offer. All pending shows were cancelled and the band found themselves back in the Big Apple, drummerless, penniless and back at square one. Down but not out they secured themselves a new skin beater in Jerry Nolan, who had the right credentials having played with rock's most dedicated female impersonator, Wayne County. Then Thau pulled a new deal out of the bag with the Mercury record label which though offering a much smaller advance to the one they would have received on signing with Track, never the less provided adequate funds to record their self-titled first LP.

Produced by idiosyncratic rocker Todd Rundgren, the Dolls' debut turned in a fine collection of comic book, trashy teenage anthems wrapped in street-wise and sassy rock 'n' roll. It had humour and verve and it polarised rock enthusiasts from the day of its release. You either loved it or hated it - you either loved or hated the New York Dolls.

Nick Kent knew the importance of this mutant masterpiece and summed it up for us in the opening lines of his 'NME' review of 25th August 1973...

"The New York Dolls are trash, they play rock 'n' roll like sluts and they've just released a record that can proudly stand beside Iggy & the Stooges stupendous 'Raw Power' as the only album so far to fully define just exactly where 1970's rock should be coming from."

I loved that record, I loved The Dolls. On my way to that maiden rehearsal in Croydon I had full confidence in the guys I was about to play with, attitude wise, because they had each passed 'The Dolls Test'. This evaluation simply relied on a straight answer to a straight question - "*Do you dig the New York Dolls?*". If the reply was yes, you were dealing with a switched on aficionado of cool and vibrant rock 'n' roll, if the answer was negative, forget it, the knucklehead was probably of the opinion that tired and lame farts like the Doobie Brothers and Jethro Tull were the future.

The Dolls first LP sold a hundred thousand copies, which was a chicken shit sales figure compared to the likes of Alice Cooper and other acts who had the coveted glam tag at that time, and despite another shot of reviving their fortunes with a tour of Europe and that 'Whistle Test' appearance in 1973, the Dolls were looking more and more like a band on the slide.

Their second and final album, the appropriately titled 'Too Much Too Soon', was released a year after their debut and sold even less, but to the press and punters alike, the image and sexual orientation of the group continued to fascinate. Johansen dealt with the question of the Dolls sexuality while on the 1973 Euro-Tour...

DAVID JOHANSEN: "*Kids are finding out that there isn't much difference between them sexually. They're finding out that the sexual terms, homosexual, bisexual, heterosexual, all those are just different words in front of sexual. I'm always asked am I gay, am I bisexual?... I just say I'm trisexual which means I'll try anything!*"

As eminently quotable as this explanation was, the real truth is that the Dolls were in fact insatiable womanisers and the "*What the hell are they?*" image was just that, pure image.

By 1974, the lack of hard success, hedonism and constant touring were taking their toll. Kane had become a stumbling, staggering drunk no longer capable of playing his bass on stage or contributing anything but problems to the band. Despite numerous attempts at cleaning him up at rehab, he would always bounce back with a spectacular fall from grace. Meanwhile, Thunders and Nolan had got themselves a little problem too, it was called Heroin. That same year, the Dolls were voted best and worst band in America's 'Creem' magazine.

A drunk and two junkies do not make a stable unit, and the disintegration kicked into overdrive. The management walked, their once supportive record company now viewed them as expensive

---

Right: The debauched and deviant Dolls - (1973) / Photograph © Hoffmann Ltd.

trouble and refused to put more money into the band, and the promoters who had witnessed the effects of excessive alcohol and drug consumption refused to give them gigs. It seemed the Dolls fifteen minutes were well and truly up.

But even as I held their killer first album under my arm on that south London bus journey, a rescue bid was under way.

Malcolm McLaren, the owner of a London retro rock 'n' roll clothing store, had met and become friendly with the Dolls while on a business trip to New York in 1973, and had been informed of their desperate situation by his friend Nick Kent. Determined to help, McLaren sent the word that he wished to take on the management of the band and relaunch their careers with his own money. This was an offer the Dolls simply couldn't refuse. The result was the infamous 'Red Leather' tour - the Dolls last stand.

After paying for Kane, Thunders and Nolan to detox, McLaren sent them out on the road in the guise of rock 'n' roll revolutionaries dressed in red leather outfits and complete with a huge soviet flag as a backdrop. Small wonder then that this was treated as outright treason by some of their perplexed American audiences, especially in the southern states where the commie hating rednecks would put a lynch-mob together for them after a show. It was all very well for their English manager to use them as a vehicle for his anarchic-politico ideas, but he wasn't the one getting into fist fights and receiving death threats night after night.

Eventually Thunders and Nolan had had enough, and midway through the shambolic 1975 Red Leather Relaunch, jumped ship. Returning to NY City to score some Chinese Rocks (a potent brand of Heroin), they eventually put together a new outfit, the Heartbreakers, with a future mover and shaker of the American punk scene, Richard Hell.

Though Johansen continued the tour with a replacement guitarist and drummer - he dryly refers to this line up as *"the Dollettes"* - this was effectively the end. After a visit to Japan, Johansen dissolved the band and took up a solo career... The Dolls were dead.

McLaren's rescue bid had failed, but his first experience/experiment as a rock 'n' roll manager would not go to waste. A short time after the break up of the Dolls he was to become interested in helping another band. This time an unknown British group who McLaren would drag up from the bottom rung of the steep and slippery rock 'n' roll ladder to achieve notoriety and controversy far outstripping even that attained by the Dolls. That band would eventually be unleashed on an unsuspecting world as the Sex Pistols.

So, how did these New York Dolls figure in the development of that particular brand of modern music known as punk rock? Well, apart from their direct connection to British punk via their association with the future manager of the Pistols and mentor of the movement, Malcolm McLaren, the Dolls more importantly provided the inspiration for a new generation of gunslingers through demonstrating that self belief and attitude could count for more than technical ability and skilled musicianship. The idea that you could learn to play - as the Dolls did - as you performed, went entirely against the grain of accepted practise in the mid-1970's, where virtuosity was God and technically advanced bands such as Pink Floyd and Genesis ruled the day.

This was what the Dolls taught us. It was a belief that what you said and the way you said it was of far greater importance than self indulgent techno expertise and polished but tedious musicality. It was a return to rock's roots. After all, neither Chuck Berry, Gene Vincent nor Jerry Lee Lewis gave a damn for virtuosity. They played their songs straight from the heart, simply, directly with passion and unencumbered by considerations of advanced technique.

The Dolls were also influential in their choice of subject matter. Most bands at that time were dealing in far out, Acid/Sci-Fi inspired lyrics - early 1970's Yes and Genesis LP's - or bad Tolkien 'The Hobbit', mystical babble concepts - Led Zeppelin, pre-electric T. Rex.

Teenage angst - 'I'm Looking For A Kiss', throwaway culture - 'Trash', and the alienation and deprivations of city life - 'Subway Train', were what the Dolls considered appropriate subjects for their wry pieces of poetry, and their contents had real value to me. They were talking my anxious language, and they spoke and gave lyrical direction to the future songwriters of such outfits as the Ramones, Pistols, Damned, Generation X and the Clash.

They were also one of the first bands of the 1970's to be associated with the name punk. Though the term had been used for some time to describe a range of underground psychedelic, surf music and garage rock of the 1960's, notably collected on a album for Electra Records in 1972 by the future Patti Smith Group guitarist Lenny Kaye and titled 'Nuggets', a review of the Dolls first album in the 'Hope College Anchor' (a small circulation American paper) as far back as 1973, had firmly tied the band to this particular musical brand name.

Under the headline 'DOLLS SUCCEED AT BASIC PUNK ROCK' the reviewer, Bill DeBlock, after panning new LP's by Humble Pie, Procal Harum and Jethro Tull, seized on the Dolls record as the sound of the future and following an ecstatic review he had this to say about them...

"Any action taken will usually cause a reaction and so music buffs are again looking to small, steamy clubs for a source of pulse and direction in 1973. Small clubs in New York City like the Oscar Wilde Room and Max's Kansas City are providing the places to dance and new bands like the New York Dolls are providing the good vibrations. The music is again 'Brass Tacks' rock and the crowds are loving it and dancing themselves silly again. Maybe rock music is just young kids 'punk music'. The floundering of bands like the Rolling Stones is perhaps because Mick Jagger just can't be a 30 year old 'punk' but lead 'Doll' David Johansen at age 19 is. Johansen fits the image perfectly as he struts the stage and belts the songs out. Punks never go out of style and this new salvo of 'punkitude' may be just what rock needs."

There it was, for the first time, allied to the Dolls particular formulae of music, in black and white - PUNK. If we get rid of a couple of phrases like *"good vibrations"* and *"brass tacks"*, replace the name Rotten for Johansen, change the city from New York to London and the year from 1973 to 1976, DeBlock's piece could have easily been written about those inheritors of outrage the Sex Pistols, rather than those doyens of scandal the New York Dolls.

Yes, the Dolls did play a leading part in shaping the sound, values and attitudes of that music of the near future, but they were by no means the only prophets and prototype for Punk. The second record in my rehearsal collection of LPs was by another native of the city of New York. Titled 'Transformer' - a delicious selection of Big Apple atmospheric pop/rock - the artist was Lou Reed, one time songwriter and collaborator for the Velvet Underground.

EXPLODING PLASTIC INEVITABLE
LOU REED AND THE VELVET UNDERGROUND

Even at that time of immense change in the musical landscape of the mid-late 1960's, the Velvet Underground were indeed something decidedly unique, something decidedly revolutionary. Their tale begins with two men.

Lou Reed, Brooklyn born and bred, recorded his first record while still a teenager with a high school group called the Jades. At Syracuse University, he played guitar and sang with various R & B and rock 'n' roll outfits but his wider musical influences took in all forms of black music, with a special interest and admiration for the cool jazz players such as John Coltrane, Miles Davis and Charlie Mingus.

After college he worked at Pickwick Records, based in Staten Island, as an assembly-line songwriter. Reed's brief was to come up with commercial material that hastily put-together groups of musicians could promote under a Pickwick chosen collective name. It was from one such counterfeit outfit, the Primitives, that Reed was to meet our second man, John Cale.

Cale was a Welshman, who having been educated in classical music at London's Goldsmiths College, became fascinated by the works of 'avant garde' composers John Cage and Stockhausen, and had obtained a scholarship to study modern composition in the USA.

Staying initially with Aaron Copland in Massachusetts, he headed for New York in 1964 after being informed by the composer that his pieces were too destructive and Cale's heavy handed trashing of his piano would no longer be tolerated. Once in NY, he immediately hooked up with a group of less precious musicians on a project entitled the Theatre Of Eternal Music. It was with the T.O.E.M. that Cale experimented and perfected the use of an electric viola; an instrument that would become an essential ingredient of the future Velvet's sound. It was also at this time, as a possible means of making some much needed cash, that he accepted a role in the bogus Primitives.

The song they were to promote was a Reed composition called 'The Ostrich', but that attempt at chart success proved more of a turkey (sorry, couldn't resist!) than a 'struthio camelus', and the Primitives disbanded almost as quickly as they had been formed. Despite the failure of the project, Reed and Cale never the less discovered they shared the same interests and started rehearsing and rooming together.

Reed already had some songs prepared for this new collaboration, notably 'Heroin', 'Sister Ray', and the eternally divine 'Venus In Furs'. All of these compositions had a radically dark edge. 'Heroin' for instance, dealt with the realities of addiction to that insidious opiate bluntly with its graphic descriptions of the user spiking his veins and its accepted understanding that a junkie constantly walks a thin line between life and death. In 1965 this was both rare and reckless subject matter for a pop song, though Reed didn't see it that way...

LOU REED: *"People were offended because we did a song called 'Heroin' but there's plenty of stuff about that in literature and no one gives a shit but it's rock 'n' roll so we must be pushing drugs or something. So what was the big deal? It was like talking to pygmies. I mean, they had it in the movies in the forties - 'The Man With The Golden Arm', for Chrissakes!"*

To give new impetus to this material, Reed - vocals/guitar, and Cale

- bass/viola, recruited drummer Maureen Tucker and a second guitarist Sterling Morrison. After Reed clocked the cover of a book depicting a stiletto shoe, a leather whip and a bondage mask, he took the book's title and made it his/their own. It will come as no surprise then that this cheap paperback with its sensational revelations of the hidden, seedy world of masochism, bondage and deviant sex was entitled 'The Velvet Underground'.

In late 1965 the Velvets played their first gig at a New Jersey high school, where their performance produced non-comprehension, disbelief and outrage in equal measure. This was in fact just the reaction that the Velvets desired, and they continued their policy of challenging the expectations of audiences at a series of audacious appearances at the Café Bizarre in the heart of Greenwich Village.

The patrons of the Bizarre were totally unprepared for what the band had in store for them. That part of the City was the preserve of Bohemian, sandal wearing, folk-music-freaks, and as the Velvets kicked in like some bad psychotic hallucination, with their endless excursions into distortion, painful wailing feedback and white noise, few stayed and fewer returned. One of those exceptions was Andy Warhol.

Warhol was indisputably the leading and most controversial artist of the 'avant garde', Pop Art movement. His outsize depictions of everyday objects such as the legendary silk screen Campbell's soup cans, and day-glo Coca-Cola bottles had caused a sensation in the Arts World and made him a global household name.

This famed New York artist had been searching for some time to find the right combo to sign to his 'Factory' - a workshop for visual and audio arts - to position his underground movies in a rock 'n' roll context. The Velvets fitted the contours of Warhol's desire perfectly.

On getting the band to join the Factory roster - a wonderful collection of drag queens, cracked actors, hustlers, users, doomed dreamers and the just plain deranged - his first suggestion was the addition of the Hungarian, moon pale beauty Nico to their line up. Warhol argued that she would add a charismatic edge to the group, and after discussing the proposal, Reed, Cale 'et al' agreed. Reed immediately wrote 'Sunday Morning' and 'I'll Be Your Mirror' for her to sing with the band.

With their new 'chanteuse' in place and with Warhol as their mentor, the Velvets set about performing what would best be described as a series of 'Happenings' rather than rock 'n' roll shows in the conventional sense. Playing in front of black and white movies, utilising exotic dancers, strobe lights, oil wheel projections and slides, these multimedia events were given the title, by Warhol, 'The Exploding Plastic Inevitable'.

Right: Lou Reed (1973) Photograph © Rex Features / BMO

DESTROY

STERLING MORRISON: *"We just played and everything raged around us without any control on our part."*

Having amassed a solid body of original material, Warhol took the group into the studio in 1966 to produce their first record. The result was 'The Velvet Underground And Nico'.

Almost thirty years after its release on the Verve Label, this record still retains the ability to shock the listener with its freshness of approach, innovations, lamentations and hypnotic darkness. It's a rock 'n' roll classic containing songs of supreme quality like 'Black Angel's Death Song', 'All Tomorrows Parties', 'European Son' and 'Heroin', but despite its brilliance, the LP generated poor sales and audiences were still finding it hard to grasp the harsh, radical sound of the band live. The West Coast audiences particularly just couldn't get a fix on it.

STERLING MORRISON: *"The West Coast music scene was then a very strong force trying to predominate within the music industry. We knew it would be hard to please these people on their own turf."*

JOHN CALE: *"Our attitude to the West Coast was one of hate and derision."*

Like the Dolls, the Velvets found it very hard to translate outside of their City environment. They flourished on the constant hum of the subway train, the incessant human beat of 42nd St., the sprawl, the Gomorrah that is New York City. Without that urgent Metropolis back drop, the Velvets proved a very strange fish out of water indeed.

Their second LP, 'White Light/White Heat' released in 1968, sold even less than their debut. The sound was simply too advanced... A fatal error!

Parting from Warhol and dropping Nico from the band that same year, Reed's solution to the Velvets lack of success was to compose more accessible material with a melodic, pop orientated sound. Cale hated this attempt at commercialisation and considered it a betrayal. He saw the Velvets ability to alienate audiences and the mainstream music buyer/biz as a virtue, and not as a failure. He quit the band in 1969 to be replaced on bass by Doug Yule.

Reed's desire for acceptance was dashed on the rocks of indifference after the Velvets third, self-titled album, failed to increase sales and widen interest. That same year Verve Records dropped the group.

Surprisingly the Velvets got the chance to give it one last vinyl shot via a final LP for Atlantic Records, titled 'Loaded'. But despite this deserved last chance at achieving universal understanding following a series of shows at the famed NY night club Max's Kansas City in 1970, Reed quit the band and made his solo move to higher (commercial) ground. The sands of time had finally run out for the Velvet Underground.

Lou Reed's sublime world wide hit 'Walk On The Wild Side', taken from the big selling 'Transformer' LP, brought him the wider audience he had been seeking with the post John Cale Velvets. His seventies solo albums 'Berlin', 'Coney Island Baby' and 'Rock 'n' roll Animal Live' consolidated his success and exposed both Reed and his former Velvets to a new generation of impressed and appreciative music recipients. Their legacy provided inspiration throughout the 1970's and beyond.

Punk-wise, a wide assortment of bands derived their manifesto and mandate from the Velvet Underground. Siouxsie and the Banshees bass player Steve Severin took his adopted name from a character in 'Venus In Furs', and elements of the Velvets sound are easily identifiable in their music. The Modern Lovers, Suicide and the Only Ones also took note of their sonic approach, as did singer/guitarist Knox of the Vibrators...

KNOX: *"Their music was so descriptive... the aggression and attack of the Velvets was a huge influence on my approach to lyrics and general songwriting."*

The Velvets music contained glorious chunks of pain, pleasure, horror, guilt and nostalgia. It was a dark, dark mind fuck of a sound, and it proved to be a potent catalyst for many of the Destroy Generation.

* * * * *

Of all the records I clung on to as the bus finally managed third gear and the scenery picked up speed, my favourite, the one I most wanted to effect my fledgeling band's direction, was an LP by the legendary Detroit firebrand Iggy Pop and his Stooges. Its title was 'Raw Power', and as far as I was/am concerned it's one of the finest collection of napalm-hearted, in-your-face rock 'n' roll ever committed to vinyl, bar none.

This I knew without a shred of doubt, but what I couldn't have known at the time was that I would one day perform those self same, venom-laced songs alongside Iggy as his bass guitarist, playing the venues of the globe as a latter day Stooge. It's a mysterious world alright, full of twisted karmic paths and weird destiny, but before I get too hung up on the nature and workings of fate, and other esoteric philosophical matters, let's cut to the chase...

THE NIGHT BECAME A REPTILE
IGGY POP AND THE STOOGES.

Born in the resort town of Muskegon on the eastern shore of Lake Michigan, Iggy Pop (real name James Osterberg Jr.) spent his formative years growing up in the low rent trailer parks of Ypsilanti and Ann Arbor: small, slow paced towns close to the Michigan-Ohio state border. Despite the cultural wasteland reputation of these communities, Iggy, who's father was a school teacher, was academically adept, an avid reader who received top grades at high school and looked set to escape his claustrophobic, provincial existence through scholastic pursuits.

In 1965 after graduating from high school, he attended the university of Michigan to study anthropology, and the arc of his future life started to take on a predictable shape. But Iggy had a hidden desire.

While playing the drums in a high school band the Iguanas - hence the reptilian nickname - Iggy had acquired a taste for performing and making music, which slowly hardened into the dream that he could one day be a professional musician. He dug the Stones, the Kinks, and blues legends like Howlin Wolf and Muddy Waters. Loved their earthy, sweat stained sound and took it to his heart. He became hooked on rock 'n' roll.

Like any junkie looking for that big fix he gambled with his future, his life, in pursuit of his passion, quitting college, to the horror of his parents after just a semester, to beat the skins in a local white blues band, the Prime Movers. This audacious move provided his introduction to a pool of equally enthusiastic young players in the Ann Arbor music scene. These included Wayne Kramer, who went on to make a particularly fine noise with Detroit band the MC5, along with Iggy's Stooges-to-be Ron and Scott Ashton.

Iggy's special interest in R & B led to his departure from the Movers in 1966 and a trip west to Chicago in search of authentic blues music and musicians. He had hoped he would learn directly from the masters of the style, but instead his Chicago sojourn led to a belief that no white boy could ever play the blues

---

Right: James Osterberg Jr. aka Iggy Pop / Illustration © Adam Cansino

---

IGGY POP: *"When these black men played the music, it almost dripped off their fingers - like honey. It was just oozing out of these guys. It wasn't a studied thing at all".*

This understanding led to Iggy's return to his home town in the spring of 1967, where a 'phone call to the Ashton brothers, in turn, led to the formation of the Stooges.

IGGY POP: *"At first The Stooges were what you might call an experimental outfit. An instrumental three piece with Ron and Scott on bass and drums and with me playing a loud Hawaiian steel guitar and occasional vacuum cleaner... people thought we were weird!"*

Only after Iggy had caught a Doors show featuring a crazed and loaded Jim Morrison playing with his dick and coming on like Baudelaire on speed, did he decide to make the switch to lead singer. The Morrison performance had been an awakening. It had demonstrated to Iggy that the stage could effectively be used by a skilled and fearless front man as a place for psychic exploration and erotic, dramatic, self-expression. With every intension of following in the Lizard King's footsteps, Iggy got Ron Ashton to switch to guitar and recruited local boy Dave Alexander on bass.

This left Iggy free to blow minds across his home state with some of the most intense, shocking and brilliantly twisted performances any audience had witnessed from a singer on a rock 'n' roll stage.

Iggy and his Stooges came out of nowhere like a heat seeking missile determined to search out and destroy the complacent witness with their blistering metallic sound and no-bullshit attitudes. Iggy walked on hands and took on vicious biker gangs. He fucked, bragged, drank booze and scoffed drugs in heroic quantities, following the path of excess in the Baudelaire-ian belief that it would provide the way to wisdom... or his destruction.

Sensational press coverage was accorded to the band wherever they played, and within just seven months of their formation (spring of 1968), the Stooges found themselves signed to New York based Elektra Records. The following two years saw the recording and release of their self-titled debut album and the follow-up 'Fun House'.

These records were the antithesis of the laid-back, Acid-influenced vibe of the popular West Coast sound of the time. Instead of wasting their time on writing some immature, utopian, peace 'n' love fantasy or wigged-out, LSD-inspired travelogue, Iggy and the Stooges focused on the real concerns and experiences of middle American youth. Their music talked of violence, boredom, sexuality, riots and war. It spoke of trash culture, terrorism and nihilism, and it spoke directly to the television generation.

Nick Kent got to grips with the appeal of these two pieces of vital vinyl in the opening paragraph of a retrospective article on the Stooges for 'New Musical Express' in 1974...

"While everyone else was all duped up, dousing themselves in patchouli oil and getting themselves back to the garden, the Stooges had the collective ear right down on the beat of the street like some thoroughly realistic 'Clockwork Orange' manifestation - sans all that ultra-violent nonsense but still toting an attitude of rampant boredom defined perfectly in track titles like 'No Fun' and 'Real Cool Time'."

It's no wonder then that these records along with that final testament to the Stooges wayward greatness 'Raw Power', caught the imagination and entered the creative bloodstream of punk rockers. No wonder then that the pre-punk John Lydon - the future Johnny Rotten - would play and replay 'Funhouse' as a schoolboy, and his eventual vehicle for notoriety and stardom, the Sex Pistols, would perform Iggy's 'No Fun' and 'I Wanna Be Your Dog' as a live homage to that Stooges influence.

JOHN LYDON: *"'Funhouse' by Iggy and the Stooges was my kind of music. Our sound was pretty damn close to that."*

During the years those Stooges albums found their release the Vietnam war was being waged. Iggy beat the draft by beating his meat and acting like a drooling maniac in front of the draft board. He may have escaped the fire fights and napalm nightmares of south-east Asia, but during the endless touring to promote those records he discovered another kind of Charlie in the feverish chemical jungle and fell into a grim, drug-induced hell. During my time as his bass guitarist he told me a story indicating just how far he fell...

IGGY POP: *"I remember one party back when I lived in LA with the Stooges. I woke up on a couch with people around me and felt a terrible pain in my left leg. Looking down, I saw the cigarette I'd been holding had burned a half-inch hole in my thigh. There was smoke and the smell of burning flesh and everything. But I was too fucked up to care and those around me were too fucked up to notice, so I just went back to sleep."*

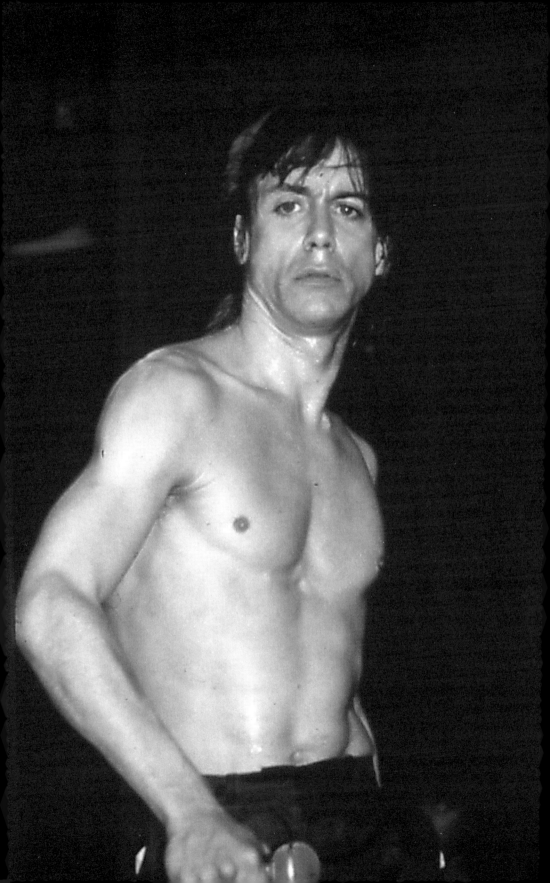

That destructive, unsustainable, close-to-the-edge lifestyle, despite a heroic David Bowie rescue attempt, led to the inevitable break up of the band in late 1974.

As a solo artist for the remainder of the decade, Iggy Pop continued to inspire the punk fraternity. His music was constantly adapted or straight covered by the mid/late seventies new wave outfits, and he became, by common consent, embraced as the 'Godfather of punk' by those in the movement.

A true new wave icon.

* * * * *

The New York Dolls, the Velvet Underground, and Iggy Pop and the Stooges constitute the proto-punk rock triumvirate - The Big Three.

These bands are mentioned as heavy influences time and time again by those who would eventually detonate the punk rock explosion. Each appealed to a different sensibility, and each were in their own way cutting against the grain of the musical trends of the time. These three outfits had no interest in mellowing an audience out or making it feel cool and part of the Aquarian age. No, they were the sonic equivalent of nose burning, brain trashing, amphetamine sulphate - bad assed, confrontational, troublesome, unconcerned and dangerously assured.

One of my teenage rock 'n' roll fantasies concerned the intriguing proposition that Iggy and the Stooges and the Velvet Underground had turned up at Woodstock to replace the Jefferson Airplane and Joan Baez at that overblown festival of futility. I'd imagine Iggy covered in peanut butter - a favourite, early-days, affectation of Monsieur Pop's - high on mandrax, singing hate and retribution, threatening and loose, followed by the Velvets playing an intense, droning, white-noise-laden fifty minute version of 'Black Angels Death Song'. What a savage and brutal mind-twister those two performances would have provided for hippie bad Acid casualties.

So, what else unifies these three bands and pulls them out of the pack? Well, they were all American and commercially unsuccessful with relatively short life spans considering their profound importance on the new generation of music waiting in the wings.

America and Britain have continually influenced each other in music, fashion and art throughout the twentieth century, and that interchange of styles and trends has transparently applied to rock 'n' roll and youth culture. American blues and artists such as Robert

Left: The down 'n' dirty Godfather of Punk - Iggy Pop (1980) / Photograph © Pat Enyart

Johnson, Muddy Waters, Elvis and Chuck Berry gave rise to a whole generation of imitators and admirers in Britain in the early to mid-1960's: Eric Clapton, Yardbirds, the Beatles and Rolling Stones, who put their own cultural spin on the music, exported it back to its country of origin, and in turn influenced contemporary music and musicians in the USA. This sustained exchange of influence and ideas between the two nations proved an essential ingredient in the birth of punk rock in the mid-1970's.

That combination of darkness, raw guitars, swagger and street savvy shared by the Velvets, the Dolls and Stooges spawned new attitudes and music on both sides of the Atlantic. The New Wave picked up these attributes like a soldier who picks up a relic from a fallen comrade - a transfer of power.

The transfer of power in America would indeed pass to a new breed: the Voidoids, Television, Patti Smith, Ramones, Dead Boys, Talking Heads and Blondie - inciters and 'agent provocateurs' of the USA punk rock revolution, and (unknowing) allies to the UK's Sex Pistols, Clash, Damned and Buzzcocks in the attempted overthrow of the staid and stagnant music status quo.

Though it was the big, Proto-Punk Three, who played gurus to the majority of these fresh faced gunslingers, there were others, some of whom deserve a major decoration for their services to punk rock's development, while for the lesser influential artists it's a mention in dispatches.

MAJOR DECORATIONS.

Detroit's kings of sonic mayhem THE MC5 (Motor City Five) are certainly due a more than casual mention for motivating punk/ new wave outfits on both sides of the Atlantic divide. Formed in 1964, The Five played as a covers band for the first two years of their existence. By 1966 though, Rob Tyner - vocals, Wayne Kramer and Fred 'Sonic' Smith - guitars, Dennis Thompson - drums and Michael Davis - bass, had shifted to original material of a free form, improvisational nature.

Their manager, the American music journalist and political radical John Sinclair, saw in their music the possibilities for a more confrontational, revolutionary sound, and pushed them in a direction that would produce such blistering chunks of bare-boned rock 'n' roll as 'The Motor City Is Burning' and the MC5 anthem 'Kick Out The

Jams'. Sinclair had no doubts as to the political importance of this change of approach, and articulated the MC5's strategy to the American music press in 1967...

JOHN SINCLAIR: *"The MC5 is totally committed to the revolution. With our music and our economic genius we plunder the unsuspecting straight world for money and the means to carry out our program, and revolutionize its children at the same time. We don't have guns yet - not all of us anyway - because we have more powerful weapons - direct access to millions of teenagers is one of our most potent, and their belief in us is another. But we will use guns if we have to. We have no illusions."*

In 1968, they signed to Elektra Records and released a live album, a passionate take-no-prisoners document of a two day stint in front of a rapturous audience at Detroit's Grande Ballroom. Titled 'Kick Out The Jams', the record was immediately banned from certain American record stores for the use of the word 'motherfuckers' on the title song, and a subsequent argument with Elektra over censorship of future pressings of the LP led to their move to Atlantic Records in 1969.

'Back In The USA' was their final failed stab at success, and the mid-west underground garage rock scene took a huge dive with the break up of the band in 1972. From behind bars - for giving away marijuana joints to an undercover cop - their ex-manager, angry at a the MC5's failure to spark a counter-culture 'coup d' état', bitterly summed up their demise: *"Those guys wanted to be bigger than the Beatles and I wanted them to be bigger than chairman Mao."*

Failed revolutionaries they may have been, but as a role model for the new wave this band was a definite success. The MC5 was a name that cropped up regularly in punk rock circles as a motivator, with their explicit, stripped down sound providing a useful blueprint for the new breed to build from and follow. The future front man of London punk outfit Generation X was certainly impressed...

BILLY IDOL: *"Once I saw the MC5 at this place called Phun City. They had these two guitarists dressed in spangled jackets who twirled around and jumped in the air. Here was this one blastoid rock 'n' roll band in among all this hippie shit!"*

An award for a decisive contribution to punk rock goes to the jam kicking Motor City Five.

The UK has its prize winners too. David Bowie and Roxy Music both turned on many of the future kings and queens of the British punk aristocracy with their flamboyant sense of style and futuristic imagery. Bowie's biggest contribution in this respect was his 1972 release - another album from my first rehearsal half dozen - 'The Rise And Fall Of Ziggy Stardust And The Spiders From Mars'.

This concept LP fired the imagination with its guitar led hymns of apocalyptic desolation, alienation, and its intrinsic theatricality. Bowie also had the distinction of working with two of the big three proto-punks: Lou Reed and Iggy and the Stooges, having produced Reed's superb 'Transformer' solo record and mixed the Ig's 'Raw Power' album. His personal image also had an impact.

At a time when the uniform for rock acts consisted of long, lank or corkscrewed hair, denim flared jeans and jackets, loon pants, Afghan coats and cheap Indian tat, Bowie rejected convention and played the Aladdin Sane in short feather cut, red dyed hair, make-up, space age fantasy creations and gangster style wide lapel & peg trouser suits. This alternative style would find its way into new wave fashion, just as Bowie's musical approach would emerge in its sound.

During his first UK radio interview, Sex Pistol Johnny Rotten had the DJ play Bowie's 'Rebel Rebel' as an indication of his regard for Bowie's music and as a metaphorical salute to Ziggy's sway on his own musical development.

Roxy Music also attracted admiration with their distinct image and sound. Looking like a Twenty First Century Elvis, Bryan Ferry, backed up by the colourful Eno and a bunch of rock stars from outer space, brought both glamour and sophistication to the early 1970's music scene with their singles 'Virginia Plain' and 'Street Life', and the compelling, popular LP 'Music For Pleasure'. Siouxsie Sioux and Steve Severin of the Banshees were fans and followers, as was Billy Idol; all three belonging to that collection of style shapers and opinion formers who would pass into punk mythology as the Bromley Contingent.

Those Sex Pistols also had an esteem for Roxy Music's dash and flair, swopping their collective name the Swankers for the Strand, a Roxy Music album cut, before new manager, Malcolm McLaren, convinced them that a more provocative group title was called for.

Though there is little evidence that Roxy Music had much of an impact directly on what would emerge as the punk rock sound, they never the less inspired many a future mover and punk rock shaker to turn to music as a form of self expression with their stylised art school rock and 'chic' dress codes which, during the staid and musically stagnant mid-1970's, provided a glittering and glamorous oasis in an otherwise insipid and barren desert.

MENTION IN DISPATCHES.

ALICE COOPER: 'School's Out' single and album provided some thrills, and Alice's horror movie rock image and lyrical content certainly rubbed off on some: Dave Vanian and the Damned, the Doctors Of Madness and the Dead Boys among them. Considered a little too premeditated and comic book for most, especially with those other Detroit providers of metallic mayhem, Iggy and his Stooges and the MC5, doing it for real.

THE MODERN LOVERS: Fuelled by his admiration for the Velvets and the Stooges, singer/songwriter Jonathan Richman formed the Modern Lovers in the early 1970's to perform his simple, romantic songs of teenage frustration and childlike optimism - totally at odds with the subject matter and approach of his influences. Had more of a impact on the American new wave, CBGB's scene than on the British version, though their self-titled album and the excellent singles 'Roadrunner' and 'Modern World', were well liked and were played aplenty in the London punk clubs, as well as being covered and reworked by more than one UK new wave outfit.

WAYNE COUNTY: Transvestite, and soon to be transsexual, who took the New York Dolls 'gender bender' approach to it's ultimate conclusion. With back up band Queen Elizabeth - later changed to the Electric Chairs - County both horrified and entertained NY audiences with his bawdy, inept rock songs and twisted humour. A large dildo, a 'come gun' and a toilet bowl out of which County would eat dog food, were essential parts of his act. His wicked theatricality and raw courage in dealing with sexuality in such implicit terms, earned him a cult following at both ends of the Atlantic and a welcome from the punk fraternity. His most popular song was titled 'Fuck Me Or Fuck Off'.

SUICIDE: New York duo Alan Vega - guitar/vocals and Martin Rev - synthesizer, took the psychotic elements of the Velvets and Stooges attitudes/attack and adapted them to create their own form of dangerous performance and discordant musical aesthetic. Considered far too unstructured and radical for early nineteen seventies consumption, the pair found it increasingly difficult to find gigs until a glowing endorsement from the impressed New York Dolls got them shows at CBGB's, Max's Kansas City and home to the Oscar Wilde Room, the Mercer Arts Centre, where in 1972 they performed an intense piece of black poison titled 'A Punk Music Mass'. Suicide was never a name that cropped up too often in answer to the *"who influenced you punk?"* question, but despite their limited appeal, they played their part in challenging the conventional, mainstream musical styles. A spirit and attitude that would become the cri de coeur of the punk movement.

T. Rex: After a hippie-dippy acoustic phase in the late sixties, Britain's Marc Bolan swapped his hollow-body guitar for an amplified solid-body Les Paul, his hip, underground status for superstardom, and turned in some of the finest pop songs of the 1970's: 'Jeepster', 'Telegram Sam', 'Twentieth Century Boy' and 'Children Of The Revolution' were pieces of catchy teenage music par excellence, loved and paid homage to by the new children of the revolution, who acknowledged Bolan's disdain for serious musicianship and techno expertise. All T. Rex songs were three, at most four, chord wonders. Simple to play and accessible to budding musicians, many of whom would use the Bolan formula combined with a amphetamine driven tempo for their future punk compositions. Bolan showcased new wave talent on his own weekly TV show 'Marc' - both the Boomtown Rats and Generation X got their first small screen exposure this way - and felt a great affinity with the movement which he explained to 'Sun' newspaper journalist Bob Hart during an interview in 1977.

MARC BOLAN: *"I have been sitting around waiting for the pop climate to change, for something like punk rock to come along. I consider myself to be an elder statesman of punk, if you like. Under this veneer of brilliantine, and behind this perfect profile lurks a lad who understands what the punk movement is all about. And I think it is what we all need. The glam rock thing was all right for the early 1970's, but by 1974 I was bored. But 1977 will be different. With the arrival of the punks there is suddenly more energy in the business."*

As a gesture of solidarity with the emerging movement, Bolan took the star-struck Dammed as his support band for a UK tour just before his tragic death in 1977.

MOTT THE HOOPLE: Not an obvious one, but worth a mention never the less. Put together by the legendary producer and Island Records talent scout Guy Stevens, and named after one of Stevens' cheap crime fiction paperbacks, Mott soon forged a reputation as a live band that could produce both brilliant performances and disasters,

---

Right: Punk advocate Marc Bolan / Photograph © Unknown

as the mood took them. This charming inconsistency endeared them to a cult following that included the future guitarist/songwriter of the Clash, Mick Jones, and bass player of Generation X, Tony James. After parting with Stevens and Island at the beginning of the nineteen seventies, David Bowie provided them with a song that would prove a world wide hit for the band - 'All The Young Dudes'.

At the forefront of the glam rock movement, Mott achieved a degree of success and recognition before lead singer and main songwriter Ian Hunter, split to form a band with ex-David Bowie guitarist Mick Ronson. Mick Jones explained their appeal during one of the Clash first interviews in the punk fanzine, 'Sniffin' Glue'.

MICK JONES: *"They're the most important English band. Like Mott The Hoople's Ian Hunter always spoke to the kids straight and even when they went to the States and they were getting a bit flash and a bit dopey he still used to sing about the dole and he had to translate for the Americans and say... look this is really the welfare"*.

The Clash even went on to use Mott's mentor Guy Stevens as their producer for their 1979 album release 'London Calling'.

I agreed with Mick Jones about Mott The Hoople. In fact, the fifth album in my *"check this out"* collection, was Mott's 'The Hoople' LP, from which my fledgling band took the name 'Marionette' - the title of one of our favourite tracks off that particular record - at the conclusion of our first rehearsal together.

The last album of my Croydon six was something of a rogue, punk influence wise. 'Sticky Fingers' by those perceived old fart, rock dinosaurs the Rolling Stones, would be a record that no self-respecting punk could admit to possessing and being turned on by in the early new wave years. In reality though I'm not so sure. Elements of the Jagger-Richards sound appear in dozens of punk rock recordings, and after all it would only be a few years from the commencement of the new movement that the band that sang *"No more Beatles or the Rolling Stones in 1977"*, the Clash, would earn for themselves the dubious title of 'The Rolling Clash' for the unavoidable similarity between those once radical rockers and the very band they once claimed to disdain.

But punk was not created by music alone. The sons and daughters of the proto-punks did not build their movement solely out of the sounds and attitudes of the Dolls, Velvets and the Stooges.

There were other forces at work - for the Destroy Generation there was also the considerable influence of Art, Anarchy and Commerce.

2
ART, ANARCHY AND COMMERCE
A TALE OF TWO CITIES

"If it is art it is not for all, and if it is for all it is not art."
Arnold Schoenberg (1874-1951).

"Il se faut réserver une arrière boutique... en laquelle nous établissions notre vraie liberté."
"We must keep a little back shop... where we may establish our own true liberty."
Jean-Baptiste Molière (1622-73).

A movement, in its truest sense, requires an attitude, a stance, a collective and agreed view of the world that finds its release in artistic, political and commercial expression. What is true for all movements was also true for the punk/new wave revolution.

Though punk is primarily associated with a particular brand of outlandish music and fashion, there were other forces at work, both at its origins and during its development; a collection of ideas, perceptions and attitudes woven together from diverse sources into a loose, but never the less, recognisable and distinct commodity.

These ideas came from the arena of radical politics and modern art concepts - reformed, revitalised and sustained by individuals who could see both the creative, as well as the commercial possibilities in upsetting the apple-cart and seeing which way the apples would go a-rolling.

In the UK, the two most important figures in the vanguard of the London chapter of that movement were to become the eventual proprietors of a small clothing store on a street that had become synonymous with English pop style and fashion. The street was 'swinging' Chelsea's Kings Road, and the proprietors were Malcolm McLaren, and his sometimes lover and business partner, Vivienne Westwood...

SITUATIONISTS AND SEX
MCLAREN AND WESTWOOD.

Born in 1946 to a Scottish father and a Jewish mother, Malcolm McLaren had a flair for rebellion from an early age. Considered antisocial and withdrawn at school, his early working life consisted of a series of superficial temping jobs which he would inevitably be fired from in short order, for attitude problems and general tardiness.

To escape from his less than satisfying working situations and the pervasive parental control of his home life, McLaren embraced the clothes, the music, the pop culture that was finding its way from the USA to an enthusiastic postwar generation in Britain. Rock 'n' roll styles, Bill Haley, Elvis... the discovery of an exciting alternative approach to life than that exhibited by his staid and conservative fellow worker drones.

In 1964 he took some positive steps to change the mundane routine of his existence by studying life-drawing and graphics at London's St. Martin's College, and by applying for a full time course at Harrow School of Art for which he was accepted and attended from the autumn of that year. It was a decisive move.

UK art schools throughout the nineteen fifties, sixties and seventies were the citadels of radical politics, of Bohemian lifestyles, sexual liberation, drug experimentation and the testing grounds for new trends and movements. McLaren, with his instinctual, anti-establishment tendencies, flourished in this environment and was delighted to discover other like minded, angry, young individuals.

MALCOLM McLAREN: *"I learned all my politics and understanding of the world through the history of art."*

Out of all those he was to meet at Harrow College though, the student who was to have the most impact on his future life was the then twenty four year old, Derbyshire born and bred, Vivienne Westwood.

Westwood was born in 1941 in a small, rural village in the north of England, where she lived a sheltered early life with her parents and two sisters until, on the family moving to Harrow in the late 1950's, she discovered the teenage delights of dressing up, making out with boys and going to night clubs.

After leaving school she took a bunch of low-paid jobs until her

Right: The mentor of the movement - Malcolm McLaren / Illustration © Adam Cansino

Malcolm McLaren.

love of the nightlife led to the meeting and eventual marriage to club owner, Derek Westwood. The marriage was an unhappy one and Westwood showed the first signs of a fiercely independent nature by leaving her husband to forge a life on her own, despite the fact that she was heavily pregnant with their son Ben at the time.

Westwood's passion for painting took her to Harrow Art School in 1965, where, among the misfits, radicals and assorted mid-sixties Warriors Of Change, she met McLaren and found herself attracted to his notions of art as lifestyle, and his romantic, flame-haired Bohemian looks and attitudes. A relationship soon developed and the two became lovers. In 1967 they had a son, Joseph.

For McLaren and Westwood, art school not only provided a liberation from the sucking mud of their repressive and grey backgrounds - an important factor in their personal development - but also, an opportunity to redefine art and to discover and play a part in the evolution and expansion of radical political ideas and action that had been growing among the student class, world widem, since the early 1960's.

VIVIENNE WESTWOOD: *"Looking back, the whole process was about trying to confound the establishment, even though I really wanted to be a part of it. More than anything we wanted to be in rebellion. It is very, very, healthy to be angry."*

In the USA, opposition to the Vietnam war had galvanised students to protest and take unified action. The University of California-Berkeley led the way in demonstrations and confrontations with the authorities - 'The Forces of the Old and Evil' - and organised the burning of draft cards and the American flag. Revolutionary 'youth' parties and organisations sprang up across the nation: the Yippies (later corrupted to Hippies) were back to the garden, anti-materialistic, *"do your own thing"* peace-nics. The White Panthers had a more radical agenda. They were pro-violent action and advocated the overthrow of the government by armed insurrection - the white middle-class 'Yin' to the Black Panthers 'Yang'. The Weathermen were counter-culture bombers with a world to change and the Diggers, a ultra-left wing, anti-government, Yippie offshoot.

The leaders of this new American revolution: Abbey Hoffman, Jerry Rubins and John Sinclair - that very same manager of the MC5 - declared a jihad on the establishment and called on the counterculture to be the foot-soldiers of decisive change. Many heeded the call.

Unarmed kids took on Chicago's self appointed Baron-Of-Reaction, mayor Richard Daly's brutal private army of police and national guardsmen, each one armed to the teeth with CS gas, skull breaking batons and bullets, outside the Democratic party's convention in 1968. Their defiance and courage was allied to a belief that the world could be reformed for the better and that the time was right for action.

'Street Fighting Man', by the Rolling Stones became the soundtrack to a series of protests, riots, street battles and confrontations around the globe. By the late 1960's there was the tangible taste of rebellion in the air and the momentum was with the young and idealistic.

In Japan, masked, highly organised and motivated left wing students had taken to the streets of Tokyo and other Japanese major cities in anti-American and anti-government policy demonstrations. Echoing the radical views of their western counterparts, they demanded changes to the political 'status quo' and backed it up with violent action where they deemed it necessary, unafraid to confront the powers that be.

Europe had its young revolutionaries too. Left wing extremists were organising themselves into paramilitary units, such as Italy's Red Brigade (Brigade Rosse) and their German equivalent, the Red Army Faction - better known and feared worldwide as the Baader-Meinhof Gang. These outlaw organisations represented the dark side of the youth rebellion - murder and terrorism as a means of change.

But for McLaren (especially) and Westwood, the most influential of the various international youth revolts of the time, was the student uprising in Paris in 1968. These anarchist French students were known to a horrified nation - who watched them night after night on their TV sets, manning the barricades and taking on the savage Parisian riot police in an attempt to destroy and replace the fifth republic - as 'Les Enragés'. Inspired by their ideas and courage, McLaren sought out the source of les Enragés' particular form of political radicalism in books and pamphlets, and in the process discovered the Situationists.

MALCOLM McLAREN: *"I'd heard about the Situationists from the radical 'milieu' of the time. You could get their pamphlets from Camden's Compendium Bookshop. The text was in French but there was also these wonderful pictures to break the whole thing up."*

The Situationists were a loose-knit group of European artists who earned their collective title by endeavouring to transform the mundane and ordinary aspects of modern life into something notable and extraordinary, through constructed encounters and happenings, or as those behind their strange projects liked to put it - *"Situations"*. Their politics were anarchistic, with a firm rejection of dogma, an avoidance of organised political systems and an emphasis on individual choice, judgement and expression. They were true anarchists and they spread their non-conformist ideology through their artistic output: painted wall slogans, pamphlets and those unique situations.

Their example gave rise to spin-off organisations in the latter part of the1960's with similar views and aims, such as the UK's prankster driven, Kim Philby Dinning Club and King Mob.

King Mob were named after Christopher Hibbert's excellent book on the eighteenth century Lord Gordon riots, and their simple manifesto consisted of confrontation, chaos and anarchy. McLaren, recognising the spirit of the Situationists - a movement he had become fascinated with - became a active member participating in at least one of their happenings, which on one notable occasion involved various King Mob members dressed up as father Christmas handing out broken toys to bewildered children in the toy department of a famous London store. Their pranks also entailed spray painting anarchist slogans on as many London walls as possible, and that stalwart of 1960's student/rebel expression, sit-in's.

After moving to Croydon School of Art from Harrow in 1968, McLaren himself organised a sit-in after a list of student demands were pronounced *"impossible"* by the college governing body. The central demand called for an end to the oppressive lecturer/student system. McLaren took on the role of a suburban Che Guevara with relish, and held the rebellion together 'till the summer recess had the students drifting off to take holidays and prey on their parents, leaving Malcolm no choice but to change college once again; this time to London's Goldsmiths where he dropped painting in favour of photography.

Westwood, meanwhile, was supplementing the meagre income from their government grants by making jewellery and selling it on a stall in west London's Portobello Road. While McLaren played wayward revolutionary, it was left to his lover to make ends meet, to look after the children, and be supportive of Malcolm's latest radical wheezes. He always seemed to be instigating some kind of anti-establishment craziness, seeking to be the centre of attention, avid for rebel credentials.

When he took up with South African dwarf and fellow Goldsmiths student, Helen Wallington-Lloyd, for both companionship and romance, the strain on his relationship with Westwood reached crisis point with several break-ups and reconciliations. But, despite the instability and difficulties, the relationship was sustained. The adverse political climate at the end of the 1960's/early-1970's then conspired to push McLaren to take on a new identity.

By 1970 the forces of authoritarianism had rallied and engaged in a counter strike. Following the tragic assassination of Robert Kennedy, Nixon had made it to the White House.

The blanket bombing of Vietnam was increased, spilling into Cambodia, and the body bags of the American dead continued to heap-up despite the assurances of the politicians and generals that the brutal and divisive war against Asian communist expansion was all but won. At Kent State University that year, four anti-war protesters were killed, one crippled for life, and many injured when the National Guard opened fire with live ammunition on the unarmed students.

In America, at the start of the new decade, protesting against your government could get you killed.

However, it wasn't just the government doing the killing.

Over one weekend in the summer of 1969, members of the Charles Manson family commune ritually slaughtered the occupants of two Los Angeles houses. Among the five dead bodies they left behind was the pregnant wife of film director Roman Polanski, the actress Sharon Tate.

In December '69, a young black man, Meredith Hunter, was stabbed to death in front of the Rolling Stones as they played 'Sympathy For The Devil' at a free concert at the Altamont Speedway outside San Francisco. His killers were those counter-culture hero's and ultimate outsiders, the Hell's Angels - hired by the Stones to provide security for the concert as a *"hip"* alternative to those *"fascist pigs"* from the Californian State Police. Altamont and the Manson murders shattered the hippie assertion that a brave new world of peace and love could be achieved if the counter-culture were able to run things. It had been demonstrated that even those who had taken Dr. Timothy Leary's (guru to the LSD generation) advice to *"Turn on, tune in and drop out!"* had as much capacity for murderous acts and brutality as any hated policeman or national guardsman from the straight world. The spirit of Woodstock was drowned in the blood of Meredith Hunter, Sharon Tate and the La Bianca's - America's second revolution had failed.

A clampdown in the UK had been under way since the establishment had sent out the word in the late sixties, that the perceived leaders of the Youth Movement: the Rolling Stones, the publishers of 'International Times' and 'OZ' magazines (house periodicals to the UK's counter-culture) and political radicals such as Michael X, were to be harassed and brought to book. In fact, the concerted efforts of the British constabulary to nail the Stones on drug charges led, in large part, to the destruction of the group's once beautiful and talented guitarist Brian Jones, and even brought condemnation of the police tactics and motives from that organ of the British establishment 'The London Times'.

By 1970 then, the UK radicals, Hippies and subversives were on the run. Some fled the country, some learned to conform and joined the old enemy, while others were hounded, imprisoned and alienated... forced to the fringes of society where they nursed their paranoid sores.

With this backlash in savage momentum and the political pendulum swinging firmly back to the political right, McLaren and Westwood decided a more subtle form of revolution was required for the future and looked around for a suitable HQ - an emporium of new ideas and style, with capitalism as its camouflage. In 1971, McLaren and Westwood looked around for premises to establish a clothing store. They had always been interested in fashion and design and found just the location they were looking for at 430 Kings Road - the Worlds End section of London's affluent Chelsea.

MALCOLM MACLAREN: *"Fashion is important. It's real everyday culture - a simple, accessible part of all our lives. Without fashion we probably would never dress up."*

VIVIENNE WESTWOOD: *"There is nothing young people like more than having people against them and knowing they look good."*

Four hundred and thirty Kings Road was the location of Paradise Garage; a pale imitation of that famous and classic early-1970's store to the pop and rock aristocracy, 'Granny Takes A Trip'. The owner Trevor Miles had gone bankrupt, so, with a mixture of Westwood originals and retro rock 'n' roll styles, Malcolm and Vivienne restocked the shop and opened for business as 'Let It Rock'.

Within months the store became a mecca for Teddy boys, rockers and all seekers of the expensive and hard to find classic clothing associated with fifties rock 'n' roll: velvet trimmed drape jackets, thick soled brothel creeper shoes, string ties, gaudy gold and silver 'lame' waistcoats, drainpipe jeans and 1950's leather jackets. McLaren had clocked an opening in the nostalgia market and with his love for early rock 'n' roll modes and singers - especially Billy Fury who he considered the archetype star - was more than happy to cater to the quiffed, tough and tattooed fashion sharp's who flocked to his new store.

Made up almost entirely of working class 'lads', Teddy boys, so called because of their Edwardian style long side-burns and velvet collared coats - the fashion of the late 19th/early 20th centuries - were a subculture with their own intrinsic value structure and easily identifiable look. They were rock 'n' roll fundamentalists, freeze framed in the era of Eddie Cochran, the Big Bopper, Jerry Lee Lewis, Bill Haley and pre-army Elvis. They also shared with the other alternative, British proletariat subcultures of the early nineteen seventies - skinheads, soul boys, rockers and bikers - a hatred of the student/middle class, long haired, hippie culture with its liberal attitude to immigration, race mixing and homosexuals and its unpatriotic, 'smart arsed' irreverence towards Queen and Country. The ultraconservative and down right racist opinions of the bulk of this clientele often enraged McLaren and Westwood who came to regard them as dumb and reactionary. It became apparent that these were not to be their Children Of The Revolution.

In 1973, a decision was made to move the style of the clothing away from the retro rock 'n' roll garments, to a harder, leather and studs, biker look - less Ted, more Rocker. Westwood elaborated and exaggerated the perceived fetish, kinky, sexual connotations of the leather biker gear by adding zips and metal studs to black leather trousers, skirts, jackets and T-shirts. To commemorate this change of design emphasis, McLaren had one of his biker customers paint the legend 'Too Fast To Live Too Young To Die' on the front of the store. Four hundred and thirty Kings Road now had two names.

Later that year, McLaren and Westwood widened their horizons with a trip to one of the most vibrant cities on earth - New York. It proved a seminal journey.

Staying at the seedy and famous Chelsea Hotel in SoHo, the partners set about exhibiting their clothes and making connections. They met the New York Dolls and immediately hit it off with those Sultans of Sleaze, taking note of their theatrical look, juxtaposed with their gang bred toughness and street smarts. On their return to London, they caught the Dolls at their famed 'Bibas' performance and were introduced to music journalist and energetic advocate/admirer of the Dolls brand of rock 'n' roll, Nick Kent.

New York City, the Dolls and Nick Kent all had a huge effect on McLaren and Westwood. Each had, in their own way, turned Malcolm and Vivienne from the past to the future, from retro to the modern. For them both, something began orbiting inside.

Shutting up shop in the spring of 1974, they revamped the building. Some months later, with the store now stocked with Westwood's new line of rubber wear, slogan emblazoned and zipped sleeveless T-shirts, and close to unwearable twelve inch high-heeled women's boots, the metamorphosis was complete. No longer a shop with two titles, 430 Kings Road reopened, fully equipped to play a decisive part in the history of the punk rock movement.

Where once 'Let It Rock' had defined the aims and aesthetics of the McLaren/Westwood venture, large pink sponge letters now spelled out the new name... 'SEX'.

* * * * *

'SEX', was a result of McLaren and Westwood's experience of a new attitude and aesthetic in New York City, joined to their own intrinsic politics and notions of art as lifestyle. With their finely tuned radar for the NEW and RADICAL, they had detected the raw energy and momentum of a potentially, important movement, coming up from the streets (where else!) in NY and desired along with a small, equally aware, group of pulse feelers to play a part in its development.

MALCOLM McLAREN: *"Plagiarism is what the world's all about. If you didn't start seeing things and stealing because you were so inspired by them, you'd be stupid."*

The net result was that 'SEX' became the headquarters of the UK branch of that movement, while back in New York the musicians, writers and artists found their creative home on a street famous for its drunks, low-lifes and bums. That street was the Bowery, and that home was CBGB's.

NEW YORK RENDEZ-VOUS
CBGB'S AND 'PUNK' MAGAZINE.

By 1973, the Mercer Arts Centre, the maiden venue for the Dolls and Suicide, was finished as a showcase for untried raw talent. Max's Kansas City meanwhile, had become the preserve of high profile acts with record deals leaving the unsigned and urgent New York foot-soldiers of the New Sound looking for a suitable Manhattan venue to introduce themselves.

A stone's throw from the Canton beat of Manhattan's China Town, sitting on the corner of Bowery and Bleeker Streets, a Hell's Angels bar called Hilly's was being reconstructed by its owner, Hilly Kristal, to accommodate country music and blues acts. With this in mind, he re-christened his club Country, Blue Grass and Blues. A name that would eventually be shortened to the more compact CBGB's.

Despite Kristal's initial ambition for the club to become *the* venue for

Left: Cheeks out for 'SEX', (from left to right) Unknown, Chrissie Hynde, Vivienne Westwood and Jordan (1976) Photograph © Rex Features

country music in New York City, Hilly allowed two *very* un-country outfits in shape of Suicide and Wayne County to perform there that year of 1973.

ALAN VEGA: *"We had done a gig at CBGB's in the early seventies... This is the really early seventies, he didn't even have a stage. He had a pool room in the back where the stage is now. You could buy a whole pitcher of beer for twenty five cents, so it had nothing but Hell's Angels and the bums from the Bowery."*

He further broke his own policy during the early months of 1974 by giving the largely unheard of, experimental outfit, Television, a gig there after the band managed to convince him that there were trace elements of both country music and the blues in their unique and disobedient sound.

Television went down somewhat better than Kristal had anticipated and were awarded a Sunday night residency. They continued to attract good size audiences, in comparison to some of the poor attendance figures at the straight country/blues shows and taking into account the undesirable nature of the venue's location.

Sensing a buck to be made, Kristal turned over his stage to the likes of new outfits Blondie and the Ramones with the result that the club acquired a reputation as launching pad for the variety of bands and artists that would soon be classified as American punk/ new wave. The front man of another important outfit to emerge from the Bowery, Talking Heads, describes how easy-going a venue CBGB's was to play in its early days...

DAVID BYRNE: *"CBGB's was the kind of place where you'd sit at the bar and when your time came you'd just casually walk over and get on-stage. When you were done you'd walk off, wipe the sweat, then walk back to the bar to have a beer."*

In the same way that London's Marquee Club had showcased the fresh faced, breaking new English groups during the 1960's R & B boom, and Liverpool's Cavern Club had been a must-play for aspiring Mersey beat acts in that same decade, so CBGB's came to be seen as the important club for purveyors and consumers of New York's newborn sound in the middle portion of the 1970's.

In the summer of 1975, Kristal hosted a rock festival with over thirty bands of the new style participating. Attending these shows as enthusiastic members of a growing CBGB's audience were two high school buddies, Legs McNeil and John Holmstrom - two, turned on, natives of the adjoining state of Connecticut.

Excited by the energy and variety of this burgeoning new scene, they decided to give birth to a magazine devoted to groups, artists and subjects that embraced the inflammatory and provocative style, attitudes and sound of their CBGB's favourites. After playing around with various titles for their proposed publication - 'Teenage News' was one suggested but eventually rejected name - McNeil and Holmstrom decided on a monicker, that for them, summed up the spirit of the music and look of this new wave. Influenced by the generic name used for the music of a rag-bag collection of sixties, underground, garage and psychedelic groups and a disparaging term for toughs and degenerates in American gangster movies, they called their magazine 'Punk', and in so doing inadvertently gave the movement a collective name.

JOHN HOLMSTROM: *"Punk was a dirty word at the time. Us putting punk on the cover was like putting the word fuck on the cover. People were very upset. It was a very controversial thing."*

'Punk' magazine's first edition featured a cartoon drawing cover of Lou Reed along with an interview with the ex-Velvet, as well as with those standard bearers of bare knuckled, speed punk, the Ramones. There were also articles on Marlon Brando (old punk) and the pros and cons of dating girls - two subjects that McNeil and Holmstrom figured would be of interest to the new breed.

Over the first few months of its publication, 'Punk' defined the movement, put it all together, packaged it, and became a propaganda sheet and pamphlet for its intrinsic style. It embraced the modern world, reached out to the fast food, nihilistic, unsophisticated American TV generation, and marked an end to the *"back to the garden"* Hippie mentality which had disdained modern urban life, and had been the hallmark of the counter-culture of the previous decade.

The future new wave sex icon and Blondie lead singer, Debbie Harry, gave the musicians' perspective of 'Punk' magazine...

DEBBIE HARRY: *"'Punk' became an organic part of the whole scene, as it was the most interesting magazine in the world when it came out. It was very cool to be in too."*

In New York, as in London, the stage was set for a new performance - a changing of the guard.

3
LET'S TAKE IT OVER
THE CHILDREN OF THE REVOLUTION

"To produce music is also in a sense to produce children."
Friedrich Nietzsche (1888).

"You have to destroy in order to create, you know that!"
Malcolm McLaren (1976).

My first rehearsal with my fledgling band Marionette had proved loud and excellent fun. By the summer of 1975 we had honed our sound down to a guitar murdered, glam, trash rock noise complete with Dolls/Stooges sound alike originals and a double speed, feedback laden cover of Simon and Garfunkel's 'Sound Of Silence' which, with a few choice lyrical changes of our own, we re-titled 'The Sound Of Violence'.

We played a few local gigs - pubs, church halls and the like, opening up for a bunch of hard rock outfits riffing their way through the Led Zeppelin set list (all the rage in 1975) and with our Dolls inspired, self conscious, satin and tat meets leather and studs image, acquired the reputation of being a very peculiar item.

This was fine by us. As far as we were concerned, the music scene had reached an all time low; full of aimless and introverted guitar technicians and pretentious, synthesizer bores. We hoped our anti-muzo, pro-raw power stance would help, in its own small way, to alter the dire state of the rock nation. Delusions of grandeur to be sure!

These were the ugly, pop related facts for that year of 1975. The British charts were filled with novelty records and vile pop songs from the likes of Telly Savalas - the bald headed, lolly sucking star of Kojak! - ham comedy actors Windsor Davis and Don Estelle, one hit wonders Pilot and Typically Tropical and for the wet knicker brigade, a couple of slices of sugar coated nonsense from the Bay City Rollers.

The American charts were hardly better with white boy, funk monstrosities from the likes of the Average White Band and KC and the Sunshine Band sitting alongside Barry Manilow's inane 'Mandy' and John Denver's insipid 'Thank God I'm A Country Boy' - a truly hideous state of affairs.

By nineteen seventy five, glam rock greats like Marc Bolan and Sweet had creatively taken a dive and Slade had been chewed up and spat out by the USA in their attempt to gain acceptance in that holy land of rock 'n' roll. Bowie had killed off his colourful Ziggy Stardust and Aladdin Sane alter-egos, having replaced them with the anaemic Thin White Duke. While across the Atlantic, Alice Cooper was living an alcoholic nightmare, the New York Dolls were on the (Chinese) rocks and after the wretched break up of the Stooges, Iggy Pop had committed himself to a Los Angeles psychiatric institution... gone, gone, gone on his own riveting brand of perversity. This was a year for both stagnation and disintegration.

Those bands and artists that did thrive and survive had developed lifestyles that were totally remote from the mundane, workaday realities of the vast majority of their audience - they had become out of touch, aloof and insensitive.

Hardly a week went by without the UK music press gossip pages giving a report, in full decadent detail, about a champagne and caviar record launch party for Elton John, Queen or the Rolling Stones, complete with attending royalty and high profile establishment figures, 'dilettantes' and the jet-set cocaine crowd, while out in the real world, jobs were scarce and money too tight to mention.

I became increasingly pissed off to read these Rabelaisian accounts of the latest tax exiles extravagants while queuing up to sign on for unemployment payments at Croydon's bleak labour exchange on leaving school that same year.

Those progressive rock bands that had not attained the tax exile, super league status, had become more pompous and indulgent than ever; bands such as Barclay James Harvest, Greenslade, Camel and Gentle Giant - synthesizer led, art school groups of supreme indulgence and dullness.

The only items of new musical interest to me in 1975 were a couple of the rootsy outfits emerging from the London pub rock scene. Dr. Feelgood were a cool Canvey Island four piece, playing no-nonsense R & B from their hearts, in razor sharp sharkskin suits, skinny ties and scuffed winkle picker shoes. Mop topped lead guitarist Wilko Johnston, cut a fine dash careering around the Marquee stage like some outta-control, renegade robot, laying down some super speed, stylish fret work with his unique 'splayed hand' method of connecting with the strings of his battered Fender Telecaster. I came away from their show that night thinking that all was not lost. There was still hope for the survival of rock 'n' roll.

In the same way that groups like the Ramones, Suicide and Television had provided a fresh option to an equally staid scene in the USA, UK pub rockers such as the 'Let It Rock' dressed Kilburn and the High Roads, Eddie and the Hot Rods, the Stranglers, Vibrators and 101'ers featuring Joe Strummer on lead vocals and guitar, offered a palatable and low cost alternative to the remote, money spinning rock dinosaurs who toured once a year, as standard practise, in cavernous stadiums for small fortunes and the progressive, long haired college bands who had badly lost the plot.

Despite this glimmer of hope it became obvious to many that a more radical cure was necessary for what was less a malaise, more a cancer in the body rock 'n' roll. 'Sounds' journalist, Jonh Ingham wrote a prophetic piece decrying the state of contemporary music and calling for a comprehensive change and renewal that same year.

The continuing bleak political and social conditions certainly helped reinforce this view. In 1975 the fact that New York had become a crime ridden, financially bankrupt city had proved an important factor in developing the mind set and emergence of the new wave/punk CBGB's groups. Midway through that year, the UK's chancellor of the exchequer had introduced public spending cuts totalling billions of pounds. Unemployment was at a post war high, inflation was at twenty six percent and prime minister Harold Wilson introduced a wage increase limit with a complete freeze on salaries over £8,500 per annum. The IRA had targeted the teeming pubs of Birmingham for its latest blood and death mainland bombings and reaction against the libertarian, permissive 1960's, had gained its full momentum with a political swing to the right and the election of Margaret Thatcher to the leadership of the conservative party - to the devil a daughter!

Life then, for the majority of the British population, was running hard and mean and people were starting to get *angry*. But anger is an energy that can be tapped and exploited, and the largest disaffected and enraged group in the UK in 1975 was its working class youth.

School leavers were becoming resigned to a life on social security payments, of violent streets, bleak council estates, and a 'no future' mentality. Many looked again to the youth tribes for their sense of belonging and purpose, and a second wave of skinheads, Teds and soul boys emerged to fill the void.

Others blamed minority groups for society's ills, taking their resentment and bigotry out to the streets, joining and marching with the thuggish Nazi National Front and British Movement parties, and getting their kicks from red bating and ethnic hating. Some saw the extreme left wing dogma of the Socialist Workers Party as a panacea for the state of the nation and counter marched, looking to do battle with their right wing enemy

Along with this renaissance of subculture identification and extreme right wing/left wing political agitation, a different breed had emerged that felt no affinity with either far right, far left politics or the various diverse youth sects on offer. They owed no allegiance to the past and had a nihilistic view of the present and future. They were a section of British youth without a collective name and without leadership.

But that would soon change.

In the fall of that foul year of our lord 1975, the ex-manager of the New York Dolls and co-owner of Chelsea's strangest clothing emporium, had talked a rag bag collection of young non-musicians into changing their group name. They had originally been called the Swankers, later the Strand. At Malcolm McLaren's insistence they became the Sex Pistols.

DE-GENERATION
The Birth Of The Sex Pistols And London SS..

McLaren, on setting off to the USA on his failed mission to save the loudly disintegrating New York Dolls, had given orders to his friend and sometimes creative collaborator Bernie Rhodes - together they had devised a slogan T-shirt bearing the legend *"you're gonna wake up one morning and KNOW what side of the bed you've been lying on!"* - to look after 'SEX' and help out the light fingered *"wanna-be"* guitar hero of a less than polished rock outfit called the Swankers.

The wanna-be was Steve Jones, an ex-skinhead, football thug who hailed from the Shepherds Bush area of London. Together with fellow school mates Paul Cook - drums, and Warwick 'Wally' Nightingale - guitar, Jones - vocals, had formed a band dedicated to the task of playing covers and writing original material in the style of his musical heroes Rod Stewart and the Faces, David Bowie, the Dolls and Roxy Music.

Jones already had a string of convictions for shoplifting, car theft and burglary, and he came to see the band as a way to escape an otherwise inevitable life of prison time and villainy. Still, his skills in that direction proved helpful to the group when he masterminded the acquisition of amplifiers, drums, guitars, etc., from the back of parked tour trucks, rehearsal rooms and recording studios. On one notable occasion, he acquired the whole of David Bowie's PA system from the stage of one of London's leading rock venues, the Hammersmith Odeon, which with Cook and Nightingale's help, he dismantled the night before a performance and drove off in a stolen van.

Having hung out at 'Let It Rock', Jones struck up a friendly familiarity with McLaren and on clocking an article by Nick Kent in 'New Musical Express' titled 'The Politics Of Flash' - a piece that pinpointed the alliance between fashion, style and rock music that featured Malcolm - embarked on a policy of bugging him at every conceivable opportunity to manage the Swankers. At first, McLaren wasn't interested but eventually, worn down by Jones' persistence, he reluctantly agreed to attend a rehearsal.

Jones, Cook and Nightingale served up bad covers of Bad Company, the Faces and a never ending, painfully inept and shambolic version of the Troggs 'Wild Thing'. The raw truth was that the band was fucking awful, but despite reaching this evident conclusion McLaren couldn't help but admire their courage and enthusiasm and felt sympathy for what they were setting out to achieve. Figuring they desperately needed a bass player, he introduced them to a shop assistant who had made claims of bassist ability and had worked for McLaren since the 'Let It Rock' days, Glen Matlock.

GLEN MATLOCK: *"Over the course of a year Steve and Paul came into 'SEX' and I struck up a relationship with them. It wasn't really like a friendship thing, it mainly involved stopping them from nicking things!"*

Matlock shared with Jones a love of the brand of rock 'n' roll performed by the Faces, and after playing through one of that particular band's songs as an audition piece at Nightingale's house, copped himself the gig as the Swankers full-time bass player.

Though this was certainly a step in the right direction, McLaren felt they still required a more charismatic and forceful front man/singer to make them a serious proposition. While in New York as manager without portfolio at the destructive conclusion of the Dolls 'Red Leather' tour, he set about trying to find the right prospect.

Catching one of the budding CBGB's groups Television, at that club of the NEW, he became duly impressed with the visually stunning Richard Hell and did his utmost to talk the Kentuckian into splitting to London with him to front Jones' fledgling outfit. Hell would have none of it. He was too caught up in a leadership contest with fellow Television member Tom Verlaine, for control of the soul of the group, to warrant following an ex-manager of the fatigued and failed New York Dolls to the UK on some lick and a promise.

RICHARD HELL: *"McLaren wanted me to go back to England and start a band with me being the singer, but I didn't want to do that. So he used everything that was transportable... you know, the spiky haircut and the ripped-up clothing style, the mode of the material, and transplanted it to London."*

Meanwhile back in London... The Swankers had changed their name to Roxy Music inspired Strand and Bernie Rhodes had helped them along to the point where they had been able to play their limited and non-musical set to an unappreciative, at best, mildly amused set of revellers at a Kings Road party. Loud in the worst possible way, and staggering drunk to boot, Steve Jones well remembers that first public performance as being *"a fucking nightmare"*.

Within days of his return to London and the affairs of 'SEX' in 1975, McLaren worked on convincing Jones, Cook and Matlock that the spec wearing, ineffectual Nightingale had to go. They eventually agreed. Wally was told the news and defiantly walked off into obscurity with Jones taking over on guitar and McLaren redoubling his efforts to find that elusive front man. Sylvain Sylvain of the Dolls was approached as was Nick Kent, but both declined - rock history had chosen another.

John Lydon was a working class Arsenal supporter of Irish decent, a product of the tough neighbourhoods of North London's Finsbury Park council estates. He had a affinity for the music of Bowie, Iggy and the Stooges and Roxy Music along with a taste for the eccentric creativity of more left field outfits such as Captain Beefheart and the German band Can.

Lydon had a friend - a fellow student at Hackney Technical College and teenage victim of a unstable and unhappy childhood, turned big-time Bowie admirer, by the name of John Ritchie. Lydon insisted on calling him Sid, after his pet hamster who sported a similar spiky hair style to Ritchie's Bowie-esque cut, and sometime later added the cartoon surname Vicious in recognition of his surly, sometimes aggressive nature. In 1975, under Sid's influence, Lydon chopped off his shoulder length hair, dyed it green and got chucked out of his family home for his trouble, ending up squatting in an abandoned building with Vicious in the up-market Hampstead area of North London.

Now, Sid had a flair for the dramatic and the unorthodox, and his clothing choices certainly reinforced this impression. 'SEX' had been a particularly favourite store of his and with Lydon tagging along they would check-out the new Westwood rubber and leather masterpieces and on odd occasions even buy a garment or two. While shopping there one weekend Sid introduced Lydon to McLaren who amazingly saw just the kind of front man he had been looking for in this bizarre looking geek with the green hair and matching teeth. At Malcolm's insistence, a meeting was set up at the Chelsea pub-cum-group hang-out, the Roebuck, to introduce Lydon to the less than enthusiastic members of his soon-to-be outfit.

Jones especially took a dislike to McLaren's potential lead singer. Not only did he not look anything like Rod Stewart or David Bowie, but he also noted the green haired one had a hefty attitude problem. *"He seems like a real prick"* Jones told his manager. Still, Jones agreed along with Cook and Matlock to take Lydon to 'SEX' to give him an audition, of sorts, in front of the store jukebox where John was asked to sing along to the Alice Cooper song 'Eighteen' while manager and band sat back and assessed his performance - a nerve ripping situation for the reticent Lydon.

Despite his natural anxiety, Lydon managed to pull off a successful if somewhat surreal performance, adding his own improvised and savagely funny words to Cooper's original lyrics, and entertaining his small audience with his bizarre dancing.

PAUL COOK: *"John just started going into spasms in front of the jukebox and singing and doing the act that later everyone would know and love. I knew right away that he was our singer, and that he would be the one."*

Equally impressed, McLaren announced they had found their man, and made arrangements for the now complete band to get together for their first rehearsal later that week. However, when Lydon turned up at the specified rehearsal room in bleak Rotherhithe, he found the place deserted and despite kicking around in the vain hope that the others would eventually turn up, took off two hours later, angry and hurt. This was not a promising start.

Lydon phoned Matlock the next day with threats of extreme violence for each of the no-shows. Matlock apologised and pleaded with Lydon to give it another shot, eventually calming the would-be singer down and getting him to agree to a rehearsal later that week. This time the session was fully attended and proved fairly successful.

The band went on to rehearse in all manner of pubs and hired rooms until after some pressure from Matlock, McLaren agreed to invest £1000 on a rehearsal room/office for the group, amongst the music stores, guitar shops and tin pot, Tin Pan Alley offices of Denmark Street, in the heart of London's West End. Having now put money into the project and therefore giving greater weight to his pronouncements, McLaren declared that the outfit sorely lacked a second guitar player and placed an ad in 'Melody Maker' in the late summer of 1975 which read...

WHIZZ KID GUITARIST. NOT OLDER THAN TWENTY. NOT WORSE LOOKING THAN JOHNNY THUNDERS.

But, despite dozens of auditions, and much to Steve Jones' delight, not a single axe welder who turned up at their rat infested rehearsal room fitted that particular bill and Malcolm was eventually forced to drop the advert and leave the line-up as it was.

With their new rehearsal facility, the group took to practising their expanding set every day. They continued to play Faces covers along with a couple of Who classics, but as their collective confidence grew, added some original compositions to the list. Matlock brought along a song entitled 'Pretty Vacant' which Lydon re-worked some of the lyrics too, while a Jones effort originally called 'Scarface' was rearranged and re-titled 'Did You No Wrong'.

The future classic 'Seventeen' was also written and rehearsed at their Denmark Street HQ, and it was also at that point in time that Lydon was given a new and disparaging name by Jones, who still felt that he was less than right for the band. Inspired by the horrible state of the lead singer's teeth, Jones followed by Cook and Matlock, took to calling Lydon, Rotten. The name stuck.

By the Fall of that year, Matlock had sorted out a maiden show for the new line-up. As a part time student at St. Martin's School Of Art, he had talked the entertainment's secretary into putting his band in the support slot for a gig headlined by local rock outfit, Bazooka Joe. With just days to go till their performance, McLaren once again showed the Machiavellian edge to his character by insisting that the band changed its name to something more controversial and memorable before they took to the stage for the first time. The band now dependant on their manager for the rehearsal facilities and his financial support, had no choice but to agree.

McLaren, of course, already had a suitable name in mind. His aim was not just to unleash this wild synthesis of loud, amateurish musicality, nihilistic anger, raw desire and anti-style on a predictable and empty music scene, but to firmly harness and associate this lightning seed with the fashion revolution in progress led by Westwood, Rhodes and his good self at 'SEX'.

Start an uprising on two fronts and then sell the uniforms of the revolution to it's children - a wonderful blend of naked greed and rebellion, of capitalism and insurgency. To this end he anointed the band the Sex Pistols and at once tied his band and business together in unholy matrimony. As McLaren was to observe some time later about the name change: *"I was out to sell a lot of trousers!"*.

MALCOLM McLAREN: *"The idea of the name Sex Pistols was sort of sexy young assassins. Pistol meaning a gun and pistol meaning a penis. Rotten said 'why can't just have the name Sex?' And I thought well, the name Sex... you're just not saying it all boy, you know, get it out! Sex, that could mean anything, Sex Pistols, and your active immediately."*

That first gig on November 6th 1975 proved to be the shape of things to come. Rotten stalked the stage snarling and berating the increasingly hostile audience for being *"fucking boring"*, while Jones, Cook and Matlock tore through the set at maximum speed and maximum volume, increasingly nervous at the response they were provoking. When Rotten took out his frustrations on the main band's equipment, the guitarist with Bazooka Joe climbed onto the stage and engaged in a fist fight with the Pistols singer. Shortly after, the whole band fled from the stage to the sounds of wailing and gnashing from the art student contingent.

Their debut had been far from successful in any conventional sense but McLaren was delighted at the results. For him, the main aim was to elicit a reaction. He had set his sights on shaking up the city, the country, the whole straight and boring world.

He wanted to *destroy*.

By nurturing the Sex Pistols he had forged his hammer of destruction and his day was at hand.

* * * * *

During his caretakership of the Strand, while McLaren was in the USA overseeing the final chapter of the New York Dolls story, Bernie Rhodes had acquired a taste for rock band management and wanted more. Via his contacts at 'SEX' he got to hear of a suitable little outfit dedicated to the look and sound of the New York Dolls, and with more than a passing admiration for the Stooges and the MC5. These seemed the right kind of credentials to Rhodes, and after attending a group rehearsal in Paddington, West London, he became convinced he was on to a winner.

London SS was the brain child of guitarist Mick Jones and Bassist Tony James, two capital city glam rock fans with serious intentions of bunking the rock 'n' roll train to stardom. Unlike McLaren's Pistols, SS membership required long hair, a Dolls style dress sense, and as well as a thorough knowledge of the metallic Detroit sound, the works of the UK's glam finest, Mott the Hoople and T. Rex.

Despite Rhodes' help though, nothing much came of the band. No gigs were played and the only recording achievement of the SS was a demo tape which according to James was a fine example of *"raw rock 'n' roll... it drives like fuck!"*. Though the general ingredients were sound, the main problem seems to have been the fluidity of the line up with Jones and James having to deal with a constant stream of half-hearted musicians, joining then leaving, to pursue other opportunities. The result was constant personnel changes and an overall membership of London SS that reads like a Who's Who of British punk rock.

Jones would soon jump ship with Rhodes, SS drummer Terry Chimes and one time vocalist Paul Simenon to form those Hate & War rockers, the Clash. James went on to play a low slung Thunderbird for first Chelsea and then later Generation X. Among the collection of guitarists who could claim membership to this not-so-exclusive-club were Brian James who along with sometime SS drummer Chris Miller (later Rat Scabies) would become founding fathers of The Dammed. Matt Dangerfield, with ex-SS keyboard player Casino Steel put together his own outfit, the Boys. And last, but by no means least, short stay guitarist/vocalist Chrissie Hynde, who would surface a few years down the line with her own, high quality creation, the Pretenders.

*   *   *   *   *

As well as these London town discoverers of the Wondrous Power Of Noise, there were additional future players of the new wave in the city that year of 1975, who were discovering other talents and situations that would have an eventual impact on a slow but perceptibly forming movement.

At the end of that year, one of the avidly read and opinion forming papers of the UK's weekly music press, 'New Musical Express', advertised in their back pages for *'HIP YOUNG GUNSLINGERS WANTED'* - a fresh and switched-on new breed of journalist to join the papers roster of established writers such as Nick Kent and Charles Shaar-Murray. The result was the recruitment to the publication of a tongue-tied and hopelessly shy, West country girl and an Essex teenage firebrand, who precociously had his first novel 'The Kids' published while he was still only sixteen.

Julie Burchill and Tony Parsons would become literary discoverers, energetic advocates and propagandists for the emerging movement, virtually turning the 'NME' into the British house magazine of punk, and both confronting and alienating its detractors at the paper and putting the fear of God into the weekly's aloof editor Nick Logan. At the same time, Burchill and Parsons brought a new attitude and style to rock writing that mirrored the savage energy and attitude of the music they were about to bring to the attention of the UK's rock readership.

Back in the 1970's, these papers were of great importance to the rock music fan and industry. A band's reputation could be enhanced or ended by a glowing or brutal review, new record releases given the seal of success or failure, sales won or lost - who was *hip* and who was *not* decided in their influential pages.

I was one of these music press junkies. Every Thursday from the age of fifteen I would buy 'NME', 'Melody Maker', and (the now defunct) 'Sounds', 'Record Mirror', to read the reviews and check out the state of play in the rock 'n' roll scene. When the likes of Jonh Ingham wrote about the stench of decay and loss of direction in mid-seventies rock music I agreed, and like him sought out an alternative to the rehashed, generic and lukewarm fare served up by both the majority of the regularly gigging outfits of the day and the rarely seen stadium rock, Masters of the Universe. Burchill and Parsons aggressively pointed the way and we followed. Some were already on the march.

In the suburbs of London, a group of Roxy Music and Bowie admirers had originated a look of their own based on the dress codes of their musical heroes, and blended with the styles they saw exhibited at gay clubs and discos. Great admirers of the movies 'A Clockwork Orange' and 'Cabaret', they had formed an attachment for a band that mirrored their own innate sense of theatricality - a pub rock, pre-punk oddity called the Doctors of Madness, featuring a Transylvanian count look-alike lead singer Richard Strange, a bassist with a taste for macabre Halloween costumes named Stoner, and a manic lead guitarist, Urban Blitz.

The head peacock and self-styled dominatrix of this following was a trainee Soho masseuse and a daughter of southern England suburbia, Susan Ballion, who having caught the name change bug from the Mad Doctors, re-invented herself as Siouxsie Sioux. Her fellow style seekers followed suit with good friend Steve Bailey changing his pedestrian surname to the more glamourous Severin and fellow suburbanite William Broad opting for the heroic Billy Idol.

Siouxsie Sioux, Severin, and Idol liked to dress in leather, 'SEX' style rubber wear, and wide 1940's demob suit trousers with crazy colour dyed hair and heavy make-up. They found their regular visits to the London gay clubs didn't provoke the violent reactions that were usual in the straight pubs and discos, and gay fashions seeped through into their own aesthetics and became a major influence in what would shortly become known as the Punk look.

As a regular and colourful fixture at Roxy Music, Bowie and Doctors of Madness shows, these three, plus supporting players, earned themselves the collective title of the 'Bromley contingent' after the quiet suburban town they emanated from. On the street grapevine they heard about a new group that seemed to embody the spirit of their clique, a band that would prove a catalyst for their transition from sideline cheerleaders to players of authority in punk's evolutionary tale.

The Bromley Contingent decided to go to see the Sex Pistols, but meanwhile, across a rollin' ocean...

Out of the CBGB's/Max's Kansas City/New York vortex, came a host of new outfits looking to change the face of mid-seventies music, style and attitudes, with their own vision and sense of purpose. Preeminent among the pack was the band that had impressed Malcolm McLaren so during his Dolls Days in Manhattan, Television.

LOVE COMES IN SPURTS
TELEVISION.

Delaware school friends Tom Miller and Richard Meyers hung-out and made plans during their teenage years with a view to making their mark on the world via some unspecified creative and artistic endeavour. Meyers was influenced by the French poets, especially Rimbaud and Baudelaire, and made the journey in 1967 to New York to become a poet and make his way in the teeming artistic community of THE BIG CITY.

Miller meanwhile stayed behind, learned to play the guitar, and formed a band that baked an R & B cake with a free form jazz topping; a piece of confection that, to the Deleware-nese, proved a less than inviting proposition. Disheartened by the negative reactions to his first group and compositions, Miller bunked college in 1969 and set forth to NY to join his friend, where together they served up books in a Big Apple second-hand bookstore in-between experimenting with the various types of LSD available in that year of the summer of love.

The result was their first artistic collaboration, a book of surreal poetry titled 'Wanna Go Out?' which, despite high expectations, did not gain them entry into the Parthenon of the Poets. Bored and disappointed by what they saw as a smug and self satisfied poetry scene, a trip to the Oscar Wilde Room at Mercers Art Centre provided a 'satori' inducing exposure to the New York Dolls that confirmed their suspicions that new and exciting artistic bullets were being fired elsewhere. The Dolls performance turned Miller and Meyers away from poets and poetry, and ignited a passion in them for music that was both raw and confrontational.

In 1972 they started a band with Delaware buddy Billy Ficca on drums. Meyers picked up a bass guitar for the first time, and shared the vocal duties with Miller who provided the guitar parts, and together they took to rehearsing under the group title of the Neon Boys.

Meyers, a complete musical novice, had to be spoon fed the bass lines by Miller in easily digestible bite size pieces, but this, far from inhibiting the band, seemed to add an edge to their compositions and placed them clearly in the arena of the learn-as-you-play outfits such as the Dolls. Inspired by Miller's love of 1960's Beatles, Yardbirds, Who and Kinks singles, and by both Meyers and Miller's admiration for the Dolls approach and the brutal, vital noise of the Velvets and Stooges, a basic sound developed which proved too fast and uncommercial for the record companies that reviewed their six track demo tape in 1973.

This less than enthusiastic response led to Miller going solo, with Meyers taking up the role of manager. At a Miller performance at Reno Sweeney's nightclub, the guitarist and his manager were introduced to another axe player, a lover of the blues and new arrival to Manhattan, Richard Lloyd. At Miller's invitation, Lloyd stopped by the ex-Neon Boys apartment, and during the jam session that ensued, the musical sparks flew. Miller and Lloyd's playing meshed like twisted wire and a twin guitar attack became the feature of a new sound.

Ficca was recalled to drum duties and, despite his protestations that he wasn't up to the job, at Miller's insistence, Meyers eventually picked up the bass guitar again, and Television were ready for their first broadcast.

To mark the name change from Neon Boys to Television, Miller and Meyers likewise took on new names and re-invented themselves as Verlaine (Miller's French symbolist pretensions) and Hell (Meyers' pure rock 'n' roll attitude), cut their hair and stepped into the future. Their first show was played out in front of a wall of flickering TV screens in the spring of 1974 at the small capacity Townhouse Theatre located on NY's 46th St. to a handful of lukewarm spectators. A more conducive venue was called for, a kind of home territory from which to build a following and kick off a career.

TOM VERLAINE: *"There weren't even any other bands around then, apart from the leftovers from the New York Dolls scene. I was just complaining to a friend that there was no place for an unrecorded band to play in New York, because even Max's at that time was taking acts through the record companies. So he suggested we find a bar with a cabaret licence where we could play once a week, which is what we did."*

Having convinced Hilly Kristal to give them a gig at his renamed Bowery bar, they made their debut at CBGB's in March 1974, and became an instant club favourite acquiring a advantageous reputation with the art crowd and muzos that had begun to frequent the club. With cropped hair and ripped-up clothes, Television offered a new style alternative to the flared jeans, long haired, mid-seventies uniform, and set the standard for a radical, substitute NY City musician's look. Their sound was cutting edge too.

Their shows were amateurish but intense, with Verlaine and Hell providing a riveting spectacle of defiance and determination. Songs like 'Blank Generation' and 'I Don't Care' reinforced the nihilistic trend in lyrical composition and complemented the band's image and attack superbly. By 1975 though, things were starting to degenerate between Hell and Verlaine. The very names each had adopted point vividly to this difference of attitude towards their approach to rock 'n' roll.

The result was a power struggle between the two to decide the leadership and future direction of Television. With war openly declared, Verlaine began his take over bid by chipping away at Hell's confidence, pointing out his lack of ability on the bass guitar and continually deriding his overall musicianship. At first, the band's lead vocal duties were shared between the two, but slowly Verlaine worked the set so that by the end of 1975, Hell was left singing only two of his own compositions 'Love Comes In Spurts' and 'Blank Generation'. Despite Hell's efforts to meet the challenge, Verlaine, armed with the knowledge that he was the superior musician, convinced the remaining members of the band that Hell was not technically up to the job and forced a show down.

It was at this time that Malcolm McLaren did his utmost to tempt Hell away from America, to front Steve Jones' Strand in London, but Hell refused to leave the battle ground and lost - Verlaine's 'coup d'état' had succeeded, Hell was forced to leave the group.

Verlaine lost no time recruiting a new bassist in Fred Smith from another CBGB's fav' outfit, Blondie, and set about getting a record deal for Television mark II. Hell, down but not out, joined up with Johnny Thunders' Heartbreakers.

A number of Television admirers regretted this schism having severely dug the combination of the fiery Hell and the poetic Verlaine in tandem. Among them were two New York music journalists turned poet and guitarist, Patti Smith and Lenny Kaye.

DREAM SOUP
THE PATTI SMITH GROUP.

Patti Lee Smith, was born in that American city of the Valentine's Day Massacre and the Blues, Chicago.

Moving with her family as a child in the mid 1950's to New Jersey, Patti became interested in contemporary arts, music and poets and gaining a sense of direction and freedom from these sources made plans in her teenage years to go to New York City to live the life of an artist. Just as she was ready to make her main move, Smith discovered she was pregnant and had to postpone her trip to face the harsh realities of the birth and the adoption of her child. By 1967 though, she was ready to relocate.

With the intention of trying to get a job at the Brooklyn Pratt Institute Of Art as a life-study model, she met teenage art student Robert Mapplethorpe and the instant, mutual attraction that ensued led to a live in liaison. Despite her new lover's evident homosexuality, the relationship worked well and Mapplethorpe encouraged Smith in her sculpture and painting, giving her his blessing when she set off for Paris in search of artistic inspiration in 1969.

Her return, two months later, saw her shacked-up with Mapplethorpe once again, this time at that hostelry of the infamous, cracked and loaded, NY artist/Bohemian community, the Chelsea Hotel. At this home of the distinguished and deranged, Smith also struck up a relationship with ex-Bob Dylan sidekick Bobby Neuwirth, and followed that with an affair with playwright, future movie star and (then) Holy Modal Rounders (very weird and wonderful Benzedrine driven rock 'n' roll band) drummer, Sam Shepard.

Shepard left his wife to move in with Smith, and their intense and tempestuous association produced a co-written play 'Cowboy Mouth' along with the mutual understanding that they were slowly but surely driving each other insane. Shepard, moved right back in with his wife.

Patti dealt with the emotional turmoil of this failed love affair by writing poetry and prose for *the* American rock 'n' roll magazine 'Creem', and took to live readings in the clubs, where she found a manager in Mercer Arts Centre booker and face, Jane Friedman. In 1973 she added fellow 'Creem' journalist/musician Lenny Kaye as guest guitarist to her live performances, along with pianist Richard Sohl, and the rock 'n' roll elements slowly started to fuse with her poetry to produce an art-rock mutation.

By 1974, she was singing more and reciting poetry less, and with Friedman's encouragement and contacts and Mapplethorpe/Kaye's finances, recorded and pressed up a single - a superb, atmospherical piece detailing Smith's work experiences in the industrial heartland of New Jersey titled 'Piss Factory'. Released in the summer of 1974, Smith showcased the song during a residency supporting Television at Max's Kansas City, and followed this with a trip to the West Coast to play a series of shows to audiences who were completely un-attuned to Smith's poetry-rock combination, and to the emergence of the new movement and sound that had already made broad inroads into the East Coast scene.

PATTI SMITH: *"We were like Paul Revere's, riding through villages shouting wake up, wake up!"*

LENNY KAYE: *"Only instead of sleepy hamlets, we found armed and artful urban insurrectionaries just waiting for the word to strike."*

Returning to Manhattan, Smith, Kaye, and Sohl, decided to expand to a more traditional rock 'n' roll line up and added Blondie defector Ivan Kral on second guitar, bassist Leigh Fox and skin beater J. D. Daugherty to complete the formation of the Patti Smith Group in 1975.

A regular series of successful CBGB's appearances helped solidify the improved line up, and armed with her tougher sound Patti was ready to go surfing in earnest on the new wave.

DEBBIE, LEATHER, BLITZKRIEG AND BOP
BLONDIE AND THE RAMONES.

Like the band Television, the story of Blondie revolves around the desires and determination of two people, Debbie Harry and Chris Stein.

Debbie Harry, a native of up-state New York and one time folk singer, succumbed to the glamourous gravitational pull of Manhattan, and earned a living on that island of possibilities waitressing in Max's Kansas City. It was at Max's that Harry ran into Elda Stiletto, one time member of an all girl group called Pure Garbage, and with a little persuasion and the addition of Harry's friend Roseanne Ross, put together a Supremes/Phil Spector style music and dance outfit called the Stilettoes in 1973.

The trio took to gigging the usual dives and (alca)holes, and were checked out at West 28th St. Boburn Tavern by ex-School Of Visual Arts student turned guitarist/songwriter, Chris Stein. Chris was deeply attracted to Debbie and offered his services to the girls as a ploy to get close to her. The result was the withdrawal of Roseanne Ross and the addition of Stein on guitar, with local scene musicians Fred Smith on bass and drummer Billy O'Connor providing a rhythm section to complete a new look Stilettoes. This line up made its CBGB's debut in the spring of 1974.

As a regular support act to Television, the band attracted a growing following that would gather at Hilly's Hang Out to dance and move to their well liked covers - Stones and Disco hits - and accessible, original, catchy songs. Having two vivacious and attractive singers in Debbie and Elda didn't hurt their appeal either, but Harry and Stein had got close and made the decision to break company with Elda, who seemed only interested in using the group as a platform for her own theatrical ambitions.

Taking the band with them and adding backing singers Jackie and Julie, Harry and Stein returned to CBGB's later in 1974 under the new group name, Angel and the Snakes. When after two more shows Harry and the new girls showed up to a rehearsal with bleached hair, they changed the name one final time to Blondie.

During the dying embers of 1974 and into the burning torch of 1975, Blondie made the musical transition from covers and generic pop originals to a psychedelic influenced punk sound. This trip into new musical territory signalled the departure of the two J's followed by O'Connor who had decided to quit rock 'n' roll for law school. Replacement backing singers Tish and Snookie were added along with new drummer Clem Burke and second guitarist Ivan Kral, and things looked stable for a while. Inevitably though, setbacks were on the horizon.

After just one show with their new bassist, Fred Smith rejected Blondie's upbeat punk for the art school seriousness of the Tom Verlaine led Television, followed by Kral's defection to the Patti Smith Group, and the departure of Tish and Snookie who formed their own outfit, originally to be titled, Hot Boxes but later to be infamously renamed, Sick Fucks.

Un-phased by these snags, Harry and Stein pulled in Gary Valentine

to take over the bass duties and added keyboard player Jimmy Destri, securing in the process their newly discovered, punk/pop sensibility.

The Bowery had, by 1975, been responsible for churning out bands of varying shades of sound and style colours.

The poetic, art school rock of Television and Patti Smith. The radio friendly chunks of twisted musical candy offered by Blondie, and in a comic book dimension of torn denim and black leather, the blistering, Amphetamine driven assault on the senses delivered by those nerds with attitude, the Ramones.

The Ramones, were the product of a meeting of minds between four Forest Hills high school attendees of the late 1960's. Jeffrey Hyman (later renamed Joey Ramone) - vocals, John Cummings (Johnny Ramone) - guitar, Douglas Colvin (Dee Dee Ramone) - bass, and Thomas Erdelyi (Tommy Ramone) - drums, were fated to bring a stripped down, superfast form of mutant rock 'n' roll to the American new wave party. But first there were two.

Having been turned on to the possibilities for guitar led pop music and outrageous self expression by (inevitably) the Dolls, American heavy rockers Kiss and British glam leaders T. Rex, Slade and Bowie in the early 1970's, Tommy Erdelyi put together a band to emulate the glam sound and gave it the unfortunate name of Butch. Joey had a similar outfit with glam rock pretensions and ambitions, though with a slightly harder Stooges style edge called Sniper. Meeting up in the clubs and venues of common interest, Tommy and Joey quit their respective bands and joined forces as manager and drummer, seconding rejected Television bassist Dee Dee, and freelance guitarist Johnny to their project.

Writing and rehearsing songs that lasted no longer than two minutes maximum, the trio settled on the collective name of the Ramones and played an undistinguished debut - thirty punters were present - at NY's Performance Studio on E. 23rd St. They had been together only three months on the day of their first show, and the words inept and nervous would best describe this opening shot at stardom.

Freeing up Joey, to take on the front man/vocal duties, Tommy swopped his manager's hat for a drummer's, and as a musically crude but hard driving four piece, they copped some gigs opening for Blondie at the club on the Bowery. During this time the Ramones image made the transition from glam tat - Dolls style satin, 'lame' and flash - to sulphate driven street gang - biker style, beat up leather jackets, torn

---

Left: Debbie Harry - American Punk sex icon (1978) / Photograph © Sheila Rock

jeans and baseball boots - and earned good lines in the 'Village Voice' weekly paper for their power drill sound and *"fuck you"* approach.

With buzzsaw renditions of their original compositions such as 'Judy Is A Punk', 'I Don't Care' and 'Today Your Love (Tomorrow The World)', nihilistic and humorous anthems each, the band secured a following at CBGB's, some positive reviews in the rock press, and recorded a demo of their unique songs for record company consumption. Thing was though, just about every label that heard these tongue-in-cheek, two minute masterpieces hated them.

JOEY RAMONE: *"The fifteen-song demo, which we recorded for $2,000, we sent around to the record companies. When we got it back, you could see that they'd only played the first thirty seconds of it."*

Despite the almost universal loathing for the band by A & R departments, Craig Leon of Sire Records showed understanding and support for the Ramones' non-musical, tough, delinquent attitude and worked hard to convince his associates that the group were a serious proposition. Eventually they were swayed by his arguments and despite reservations a record deal was offered.

As 1976 fast approached, both in the Bowery and the streets of London, things were gathering speed.

Left: Joey & Dee Dee beat on the brat - The Ramones (1980) / Photograph © Rex Features

4
HIGH ON REBELLION
THE FILTH AND THE FURY

"... When the blast of war blows in our ears, Then imitate the action of the tiger; Stiffen the sinews, summon up the blood, Disguise fair nature with hard-favoured rage; Then lend the eye a terrible aspect."
William Shakespeare, 'Henry V' (1595).

"I'm mad as hell and I'm not going to take it any more."
Peter Finch, 'Network' (1976).

In the summer of 1976, I had my first, direct experience of the power and relentless energy of a punk rock band.

The Ramones were on their first tour of the UK as ambassadors of New York's New Wave, and had been booked for a gig at my local, Croydon rock venue, the Greyhound. It was at this particular place of worship, that I had first been exposed to live rock 'n' roll in the early 1970's - Mott The Hoople playing a set of straight ahead rockers and cool Dylan-esque ballads, T. Rex delivering their glam-pop masterpieces, and Slade, imploring us to *"Feel the noise"*. They had all been performances of verve and vitality, but nothing I had witnessed before came close to the jolting experience I received that night of the Ramones.

As was usual, I was late for the show, and as was also usual, I met up with my friends and fellow Marionette band members for beers in the downstairs bar before making my way up to the concert hall. For the first time ever, I felt uncomfortable and out of place in this familiar environment.

There we were in our NY Dolls inspired outfits; all crushed velvet and satin, six inch platforms and 'Thunders style' shoulder length hair, suddenly surrounded by cropped and dyed haired mutants in multi-zipped leather jackets, wraparound shades and tartan bondage trousers - their punk legs bound together by a mysterious series of buckles and straps. Some with safety pins through their snotters and cheeks with aggressive attitudes to match... A very disturbing invasion!

Being regular readers of the music press we had some knowledge of what kind of creatures we were dealing with. The emerging bands and their followers had been appearing in the rock rags for some months with 'NME' writer, Charles Shaar Murray, having filed a two pager covering the CBGB's scene featuring a glowing review of the Ramones, as far back as 1975. Names such as Television, the Voidoids, and the Heartbreakers had become familiar. Patti Smith's debut LP 'Horses' had been released to critical acclaim and the Ramones were in the UK that summer to promote their maiden, self-titled album, for Sire Records.

We had even become aware of a band called the Sex Pistols, via various articles detailing their chaotic performances, and had caught the drift from journalists such as Parsons and Burchill, Jonh Ingham, Caroline Coon and Nick Kent that the times were a-changing again and a new and vibrant movement was about to be unleashed on the land.

But this was my first 'in the flesh' exposure to the phenomena, and my initial glance at these self-mutilated storm-troopers of punk left me feeling queasy and none too sure whether to stick around for the show or to make a run for it. The BBC radio DJ and enthusiastic advocate of punk, John Peel, had similar feelings on his primal viewing of the new style...

JOHN PEEL: *"From the start, I think I was aware there was some kind of movement. But when I saw the first punk girls on the street, I thought they ought to be taken into care for their own protection. When I was in the army, there was a offence with which you could be charged for shooting yourself in the foot to escape service overseas, and I thought if there was some civil equivalent to that, then these people should be charged with it because they seemed to be wilfully disfiguring themselves."*

Despite the initial shock and apprehension, I downed my beer and headed on up to the concert hall which was separated from an upstairs bar by four heavy glass doors. As I reached this entrance, the muffled sound of the group at play could be heard and even before going inside I could tell they were super-loud. I held off going in for a second to light a cigarette, took a deep draw and walked into the room... *"Wah! What The Hell Was This?"*

A blast of hot air greeted me, really hot, like you get when you open an oven door to check on a roasting joint, followed by a electric rush of compressed energy - then the visual elements slowly registered.

Right: Storm troopers of Punk / Photograph © Rex Features

The hall was packed air-sucking-solid with the type of mutants I had seen downstairs earlier, sweat spraying off their bodies as they heaved up and down in leather unison, a crazed mass, a weird army, jumping as one to the brutal sound attack from up on the Greyhound stage.

And the attackers themselves, the Ramones, dressed in their uniform of fatigued leather jackets, ripped blue jeans and sneakers, silhouetted under the stage lighting - legs wide apart, guitars hung low, heads bowed, all except for Joey who gazed at his victims through weird insect shades while delivering words that lashed them like a wire whip.

I was mesmerised. It took me three numbers - this being the Ramones, less than four minutes! - to recover my senses and step into the belly of the beast where the atmosphere was super humid and charged. By the time I'd fought my way to the front of the stage through the punk legions, I was drowning in my own sweat and desperately fighting for my share of what was left of the oxygen in the building. But the effort was worth it, the Ramones were worth it.

Close up, I studied Joey Ramone and noticed the sleeves to his disintegrating leather jacket were held on to the main body of the garment by a series of steel safety pins which ran under his armpit and over each shoulder. His T-shirt was trashed, a ripped and torn mess that had the look of a flag which had been carried into too many battles.

To his right stood Johnny Ramone, his Prince Valiant haircut covered his face which dripped warm sweat, jeans were slashed at the knees, Mustang guitar hung crazy low, straight arming his way through a furious rendition of 'Teenage Lobotomy'.

Dee Dee, mimicked Johnny's impossible guitar etiquette just to the left of Joey's leather clad shoulders. He was wearing dirty sneakers, a metal studded belt and a wristband that cut deep scars into his instrument with each motion of his right hand.

And Tommy Ramone, a double speed drummer in black cutaway T-shirt, easy rider shades and shoulder length hair, drilling out a no-nonsense back beat on his shuddering kit. A primitive spine to straighten out the manic guitar onslaught of his amped up, ravenous brothers.

After each anthem came to an abrupt end, before the crowd could suck more air into their starved lungs, Joey would count *"ONE, TWO, THREE-FOUR"* in his NY, cartoon accent, and the band would power their way into the next two minute song. The pace never slackened, the attack was relentless, it was poetry on the pull. What at first glace I had taken to be a Dante-esque hell, I now saw as rock 'n' roll Nirvana, the stuff of rock dreams - before that Ramones performance, 'rock excitement' had just been a phrase in my mouth.

After the show, I followed the line of damp and spent bodies back down to the bar, ordered myself a cold beer and drank it down like my life depended on it; I was both roused and shell-shocked by the sights and sounds I had just witnessed. The keyboard player from my rock band, Marionette, noticed my stretcher-case demeanour and came over to talk.

"What do ya reckon then?" he asked.

"Fucking amazing!" I replied.

"Yeah" he echoed *"Fucking amazing!"*

We were converts to the new approach.

The next day I cut my hair, went to the Kings Road to buy the 'de rigueur' leather jacket, drainpipe jeans - flares were out for ever! - brothel creeper shoes and cat-sleeve, slogan T-shirt purchased from 'SEX' competitor Acme attractions, and made the transition from glam to punk rocker.

Though the incredible energy and freshness of that Greyhound/Ramones performance had proved to be the deciding factor in the switching of my own musical and stylistic allegiance, across the UK, McLaren's Sex Pistols were proving to be the major catalyst in converting a noteworthy slice of the adolescent energy of the nation to the new expression.

The Pistols' star had risen to new and unexpected heights since their shambolic unveiling at St. Martin's School Of Art, and during that searing hot summer of 1976 it was to reach even greater altitudes.

FROM NOWHERE TO EMI
THE CONTINUING ADVENTURES OF THE SEX PISTOLS

Following on from their maiden gig, the Sex Pistols had decided on a novel solution to the problem of the lack of interest from promoters and bookers and the dire lack of shows. Turning up at college gigs, the band would falsely claim they had been hired as the support act, quickly set up their equipment, and proceed to plough into their set before the real opening band turned up and the plugs were pulled on them.

These tactics, though crude, provided an opportunity for the gathering of a following that hinged around the Bromley contingent, who, having caught a particularly caustic and entertaining performance from the band at Ravensbourne College, had decided to swap their loyalties from Roxy Music and Bowie to McLaren's boys. This small but vivid contingent, helped to create an enticing, subcultural 'milieu' around the group, while at the same time giving the new and struggling outfit a confidence and focus for their performance.

A breakthrough gig of sorts, occurred on Valentine's day 1976 at Andrew Logan's studio in London's Butlers Wharf. Logan, a respected artist and sculptor, had invited a host of his influential friends and Bohemian, London art-set acquaintances to a party where the Sex Pistols were asked to provide the musical/visual entertainment. They did not disappoint.

Rotten, in a drug induced frenzy - a mixture of LSD and Amphetamine Sulphate - immediately assaulted the intrigued crowd, first verbally, then as the chemicals kicked in with more venom, using various pieces of the band's equipment. Excited by the events on stage, McLaren talked 'SEX' shop assistant and chief dominatrix Jordan into joining in the fun. On climbing onto the stage, Rotten ripped up her Westwood T-shirt and exposed and fondled her breasts while jaws dropped, cameras flashed and the band kept up their ear splitting rendition of the Stooges classic 'No Fun' for a full forty minutes.

The Pistols proved a sensation with the artist/journalist/ photographer crowd assembled. They loved it, and the following week various articles appeared in the music press from those writers who had been present, detailing the events and providing much needed publicity for the group.

This was coming off their first and only Marquee appearance, two days before the Logan bash, supporting *"good time"* pub rockers, Eddie and the Hot Rods. There the Pistols had provoked and raged in the now familiar fashion, and climaxed with the attempted destruction of the headliners' equipment before making a hasty exit from fist waving Rods' roadies and fans.

JOHN LYDON: *"Eddie and the Hot Rods to me were everything that was wrong with live music. Instead of fighting all this big stadium nonsense, it was all about denim and plaid shirts and long droopy hair."*

They received a great review for their troubles that same week from NME staffer Neil Spencer, under the headline *'DONT LOOK OVER YOUR SHOULDER BUT THE SEX PISTOLS ARE COMING'* - the Hot Rods didn't even get a mention.

Utilising this spate of press attention, McLaren contacted 100 Club booker Ron Watts and set up a headline gig for the group that very nearly ended in Rotten's departure from the Pistols. On stepping on to the stage of the sparsely attended club, Johnny decided to let his frustrations fly at bassist Matlock, firstly by picking arguments between songs, and when that failed to phase the bass player, by openly challenging him to a fight.

The truth was Rotten never liked Matlock, thought him too straight, serious, and squeaky clean, *"a mummy's boy"*, and his loathing finally found expression in a attempted physical showdown. But Matlock would have none of it. He refused to indulge Rotten in fisticuffs in the middle of a gig and turned his back on the fuming singer.

Utterly frustrated, Johnny stormed off stage and was about to leave the building when McLaren grabbed him and gave him the ultimatum of either rejoining the band and finishing the set or getting the sack there and then. Rotten returned to the stage.

With the Pistols' profile building nicely, McLaren decided it was time for some more traditional rock group activities and hired experienced rock photographer Ray Stevenson to take some publicity shots, and appointed Ray's brother Nils as his personal assistant and road manager to the band.

Despite this acquiescence to normal rock-biz procedures, McLaren found it was again *no* business as usual when the emphasis in the music press on the Pistols confrontational style and laser guided mayhem led to a reluctance by the rock club promoters to allow the band to play their venues.

Malcolm decided guerilla tactics were called for to keep up the press coverage, and dispensing with the traditional rock clubs, found an unusual venue for his boys' next gig.

The El Paradise, was a sleazy Brewers Street strip joint-cum-hookers hang-out in the heart of London's Soho. A perfect location for Rotten and Co. to deliver their anarchistic creed.

Alerting the growing Pistols following - and those McLaren considered worthy music press - to the gig by Xerox flyers, the band played a cranium crunching set and received some of their best press coverage, with 'Melody Makers' Caroline Coon giving a thumbs up report of the action, and a two page spread in 'Sounds' by Jonh Ingham who among his various observations of the event, had this to say...

The small, sleazoid El Paradise Club in Soho is not one of the more obvious for English rock to finally get to grips with the seventies, but when you're trying to create the atmosphere of anarchy, rebellion and exclusiveness that's necessary as a breeding ground, what better place?"

With inaudible lyrics the music is very similar from song to song, but a cranial trigger says that song is great (applaud), but that one is just okay (don't applaud).

Which annoys singer John Rotten endlessly. "Clap you fuckers. Because I'm wasting my time not hearing myself"

John is a man who likes to confront his audience, not to mention the rest of the band. It's this Stooges-like aura of complete unpredictability and violence that gives the Sex Pistols that extra edge. Paul (Cook) reckons the broken glass attitude will only disappear when they get as old as Pete Townsend (the Who guitarist) and just do it for the money."

Ingham's depiction of the Pistols in the Stooges mould, creating an atmosphere of anarchy, rebellion and exclusiveness reached and resonated with a UK wide group of young and bored teen droogs who had been searching for the right outfit to give their alienation and hostility a voice. A handful of these would turn up at each of the dates of the Pistols' first provincial tour from which a determined one or two would form their own bands based on the Pistols prototype.

Back in the UK capital, the band found favour with the promoters again in the shape of an offer of gigs at the Nashville Rooms and the 100 Club. True to form though, both appearances provided incidents that only confirmed promoters and club owners' worst fears about the group and their bizarre following.

At their Nashville Rooms show, Vivienne Westwood decided to slap the girl seated next to her, mid-performance, *"to liven things up"* which in turn led to the assaulted female's boyfriend retaliating. Unconcerned about who instigated these face slapping shenanigans, McLaren jumped in to land a blow, quickly followed by Jones and Rotten who, having left the stage to join the fracas, aimed a flurry of brutal punches at the hapless boyfriend's nose and jaw. A report of the incident, complete with an action photo of the guitarist and singer laying into the blooded boyfriend, appeared in the 'NME' the following week.

Then, just to confirm the violent tendencies of the Pistols and their entourage, a more serious piece of mindless brutality made an appearance at the group's 100 Club show. During the band's performance Sid Vicious decided to block journalist Nick Kent's view of the on-stage action by deliberately standing in front of him - Vicious being somewhat taller than the writer.

Despite Kent constantly moving to various new locations to escape this childish harassment, Sidney would always turn up seconds later to hinder his view again, eventually leaving Kent no choice but to confront the Vicious one.

Vicious' response to Kent's reasonable request to get out of his way was to pull out a rusty old bike chain from his leather jacket and proceed

Left: Glen Matlock/Johnny Rotten (Sex Pistols) preaching Anarchy in the UK (1976)
Photograph © Rex Features

to split open the journalist's skull with it. Spurting copious amounts of blood from a gaping wound, Kent finally got away from the demented thug and received medical attention at a local hospital. Once again, the music press had a Sex Pistols related crime of violence to report in their following issues, and once again McLaren took the view that any publicity, especially if it was of a sensational nature, was good publicity.

In fact, Kent later discovered that McLaren, with Rotten's help, had instigated the attack by winding Sid up, telling him that Kent had it in for the band and deserved a good kicking. When it came to getting his boys sensational press headlines, McLaren could be ruthless in his methods.

The gig ban was immediately reinstated by outraged promoters and the group's momentum was temporary halted, leaving Malcolm no choice but to make personal visits to the rock club bookers to argue the Pistols case for more shows.

On hearing that the Ramones were coming to the UK for their first tour, McLaren and his new assistant Nils, bombarded the Ramones British promoter, John Curd's office with 'phone calls, pleading for the support slot at their London, Roundhouse show.

Curd wouldn't speak to either of them, and eventually frustrated manager and assistant paid a surprise visit to the promoter's house, whereupon on ringing his bell, Curd's wife answered the door. Here's the ensuing scene, as remembered by Nils Stevenson...

McLAREN: *"We're here to see John Curd about a gig at the Roundhouse for the Sex Pistols."*
CURD'S WIFE: *"He's out."*
CURD'S INFANT CHILD: *"No he's not, he's having dinner."*
CURD'S WIFE: *"He's seen your band and he doesn't like them."*
McLAREN: *"It's not a matter of what he likes, It's what the kids want, he can't be an arsehole all his life!"*
NILS: *"Yes he can. Let's go."*

As McLaren and Nils made to depart, Curd suddenly burst through the door and leapt down the stairs throwing punches, knocking the startled manager to the hard pavement. Nils tried to intercede but ended up getting strangled and having his T-shirt fashionably ripped by the irate promoter. The Sex Pistols did *not* support the Ramones at the Roundhouse.

Though the gig drought continued, Granada TV offered the group

Right: Keep it up lads! Malcolm (Machiavelli) McLar en / Photograph © Rex Features

their first on-the-box slot playing live on a late broadcast music show titled 'So It Goes', that summer of 1976. The show's host was a Manchester journalist by the name of Tony Wilson, who some years down the line would start his own record company, Factory Records, and become the proprietor of the famous Mancunian club, the Hacienda.

The Pistols delivered a powerful, feedback laden rendition of a new song called 'Anarchy In The UK' and people began to take notice.

Record companies started to make enquiries, and McLaren decided to put together a bill of suitable outfits to support the Pistols at a gig specifically designed to showcase the group for A & R men. Sticking to his policy of finding his own venues when mainstream rock promoters refused to give the Pistols gigs, McLaren hired the Screen On The Green Cinema in Islington, north London and got Manchester's Pistols-inspired Buzzcocks, and the new Bernie Rhodes managerial concern, the Clash, to open proceedings.

McLaren's art school buddy, Jamie Reid designed the leaflets and posters for the show, and the record company types and music press, hoping for more blood and violence no doubt, duly turned up along with Siouxsie Sioux sporting bare breasts, leather mini skirt and swastika arm band, Sid Vicious with his bicycle chain stuffed into his leather jacket (just in case!), Sue Catwoman (feline hairdo, early Pistols convert), Idol, Severin, Berlin, 'et al'.

The Screen On The Green event, not only provided an opportunity for the record biz to check out three bands of the new idiom for musical and commercial viability, but also unveiled, for the first time, an inter-band rivalry for the affections and cheque books of the A & R men present, that took the form of old style shady one-upmanship. It was only when the Pistols had taken to the stage as the headlining act that the full power of the PA system was allowed - on McLaren's orders - to be turned up. Both the Buzzcocks and the Clash had to play their sets with inadequate volume. From the very beginning, mutual help and solidarity in the British chapter of the punk rock movement was in very short supply.

Rotten articulated his disdain for the attitudes of the leader of his rivals, the Clash, in a recent interview...

JOHN LYDON: *"There was a lot of nonsense and inter-band jealousies and I remember a Joe Strummer quote (at the time) that struck me as being really, really stupid of him. He said his ambition was to be bigger than the Sex Pistols. My God, talk about missing the point... SO sad!"*

A week after the Screen On The Green show, McLaren and the Pistols crossed the Channel for a bit of continental posing and hype, and a gig at the Chalet du Lac Disco situated in the centre of the Bois de Boulogne area of Paris. Designer Castelbaljac was in the audience, along with independent record company owner Marc Zemati, and large portions of the French music press. Billy Idol drove the Bromley contingent over from the London suburbs, and Jonh Ingham, Caroline Coon and Ray Stevenson turned up to cover the first overseas gig for the band, for the British media. Westwood dressed the quartet in her latest creations - bondage suit for Rotten, Anarchy shirts for Jones and Matlock, well aware that a famous Parisian clothes designer was present, and the city was after all the perceived world centre of fashion and style.

Another opportunity for the Pistols to add more French converts to the cause followed when McLaren received an invitation for the band to appear at the 'First European Punk Rock Festival', organised by independent record label, Bizarre, at Mont de Marsan, in the south-west of the country in August of 1976. Unfortunately though, having been fully informed of Pistols pal Sid Vicious' attempted brain surgery on Nick Kent, the promoters dropped the group from the bill and gave the top spot to Eddie and the Hot Rods instead. The Rods, as you can imagine, were delighted.

New-to-the-movement outfit, the Dammed, formed by ex-London SS guitarist and drummer Brian James and Rat Scabies, and managed by Vivienne Westwood's accountant Andy Czezowski, ended up being the only true punk rock band to make it onto that French festival's stage.

Un-phased by these censorial manoeuvres, and more convinced than ever that the Pistols were about to become the biggest group in Britain, McLaren made his final, canny, business preparations.

Having formed his own management company 'Glitterbest', he immediately had all the group members sign a binding contract giving him full powers of representation. McLaren's management fee would be twenty five percent of the Pistols earnings, the norm for that time being ten percent with even today's management commissions rarely exceeding twenty percent of a bands income. Then, still smarting from the Mont de Marsan ban, McLaren, in conjunction with Ron Watts, put together a two night British punk rock festival featuring the Sex Pistols, at the 100 Club in London's Oxford Street.

The Pistols would headline the first night of the 28th September 1976, thus formally crowning them as undisputed kings of UK punk, while groups such as the Clash, Vibrators, Buzzcocks and the Damned, Stinky Toys and Subway Sect vied for pecking order.

The 100 Club punk rock festival was billed as the festival of the 'Summer of Hate', the 1970's angry retort to the 1960's, Woodstock, 'Summer of Love'. It not only served the purpose of establishing McLaren's Pistols as leaders of the 'genre' but also impressed upon the cheque book waving, salivating, record company A & R departments, that this was indeed a movement that was gaining momentum and becoming unstoppable. British punk's first festival received maximum coverage in the music press and was portrayed as an event of great significance. The record companies pounced.

Newly established independent labels such as Chiswick and Stiff Records had been making overtures to the emerging outfits for some time, but McLaren wanted to unveil his band to the world in the most theatrical manner possible and that would required the money and machinery of a major record company. Both Polydor and EMI had been showing an interest in the Pistols for a couple of months prior to the festival. With the approving publicity and media buzz from the event ringing loudly in their ears, both labels decided to make serious plays for the band's signatures.

After personally convincing EMI A & R man, Nick Mobbs that the Pistols were the future of rock 'n' roll, McLaren had the Pistols sign a contract with the company on the 8th of October 1976 for a £40,000 advance with Polygram putting in an identical offer just after the signing party at EMI HQ, Manchester Square, London.

That bid had come just a heartbeat too late to prevent the Sex Pistols - *"all you need is hate"* - from joining forces with the former record company of the Beatles - *"all you need is love"*. The exorcism of the spirit of the 1960's was complete. The Pistols now had the corporate ways and means to inflict their nihilistic manifesto directly into the collective consciousness of the British nation, and beyond.

* * * * *

As punk rock stretched its limbs in the UK, growing interest in the movement led to the development of artistic and commercial ventures based on its doctrine of desire and expression, having precedent over technical ability and expertise. This, aligned with an emerging attitude of self reliance and enterprise, a developing reaction against the welfare state creed of successive Labour (socialist) administrations in the 1960's and 1970's, motivated individuals to start their own cottage industries of which, two have become synonymous with the advent of punk rock...

DIY
U K FANZINES AND THE RISE OF THE INDEPENDENTS.

Galvanised by the Ramones first record, Nick Kent, and the crude photostatted pamphlets he had seen on 60's rock music - 'Bam Balam', USA West Coast groups - 'Dark Star' - and country rock - 'Omaha Rainbow' - on sale in the specialist record stores, Deptford bank teller, Mark Perry conceived the idea of a similar DIY fanzine dedicated to the bands and related interests of punk.

Though aware of McNeil and Holmstrom's New York effort, Perry was suitably unimpressed with their 'Punk' magazine to believe he could produce a far better, in terms of content if not production, punk avocation piece. This is what he had to say about America's premiere new wave read, in issue five of his own controversial periodical...

MARK PERRY: *"This 'Punk' magazine has got nothing to do with anything. It's a kiddy's comic. This crap's actually selling well, it just shows you how dumb people are... fucking crap!"*

So, using his girlfriend's father's office Xerox machine, Perry produced his first issue and titled it 'SNIFFIN' GLUE' - after the cheap and popular way of getting high by teenage runaways and the delinquent unemployed - in the summer of 1976.

This first edition featured concert and record reviews of the Ramones, Flamin' Groovies - 1960's style, Byrds sounding outfit, touring with the Ramones that summer - and Blue Oyster Cult, who, oddly enough, were a long-haired American heavy metal group with no new wave credentials. There was also typing errors aplenty and an amateurish, felt tip scrawled front cover, but despite the grammatical problems and cheap presentation 'SG-1' conveyed a real sense of enthusiasm for its subject which gave it charm.

Within a short period of time, Perry's fanzine became a regular fixture at punk gigs and on the counters of the new wave record stockists, selling for a nominal fee and providing opinions and information for punks and other interested parties. As Sniffin' Glue's popularity and influence grew - both the Clash and Chelsea went to 'SG' to give their first interviews - Perry changed his editorial name to Mark P *"to confuse the unemployment office"*, and added a bunch of motivated, independent writers and photographers of no-fixed-abode to his 'SG' contributions list.

Danny Baker cut his journalistic teeth at Sniffin' Glue before rock

SNIFFIN' GLUE...
AND OTHER ROCK'N'ROLL HABITS,
FOR ~~PUNKS~~ GIRLS! ③ SEPTEMBER '76.

THE MAG THAT DOESN'T LIKE GIVING YOU 'UP TO DATE' NEWS ON THE MUSIC SCENE.

THE DAMNED ☆ SEX PISTOLS ☆ IGGY POP +
WITH

writing for 'NME', and much later selling Mars bars, soap powder and hosting his own talk show on British TV. Caroline Coon contributed along, with future name snappers Erica Echenberg and Jill Furmanovsky.

Following hard on the heels of Sniffin' Glue's success came an assortment of 'SG' rip-off, fanzines and publications from around the UK. Among them...

RIPPED & TORN: Assembled by two Scottish punk converts, Tony Drayton and his sidekick the Skid Kid. Considered by many at the time to be as good as, if not even better than Perry's 'SG'. Pistols, Clash and all the early punk fav's featured in its pages with the emphasis on atmosphere and style.

HONEY, THAT AIN'T NO ROMANCE: Ultra tacky and badly put together, presentation wise, and as a consequence great fun to read. Proto-punk enthusiasts - Dolls, Velvets with a special affection for Iggy and his Stooges.

JOLT: Edited by Lucy Toothpaste, Jolt dealt in feminist issues and gave excellent coverage to the emerging punk women such as Siouxsie Sioux and the Slits.

ZIGZAG: More mainstream than the rest but with plenty of punk representation. Proto-punk fanciers and NY/UK coverage. Edited by one time Mott The Hoople fan club secretary and fan, Kris Needs.

ANARCHY IN THE UK: Self produced broadsheet of the Sex Pistols dedicated to their (McLaren's and Westwood's) views, articulating anarchistic philosophy and featuring the photographs of Ray Stevenson and the drawings and graphics of Jamie Reid. Put together at Glitterbest's offices in Oxford Street, it was the closest that the UK movement got to a written manifesto.

Also highly rated... '48 Thrills', 'Pulp', 'London's Burning', 'Live Wire', 'Teenage Depression', 'White Stuff', 'Chainsaw', 'Strangled', 'Trash '77' and 'New Wave'.

The above are but a small selection from the proliferation of punk related fanzines that emerged across the nation during the years 1976 to 1977. Fanzines provided the means of direct participation and

Left: Brian James (The Damned) graces the cover of Mark P's Sniffin' Glue No. 3 (1976)

expansion of the movement for those who wanted to be a part of the revolution, but had no inclination to pick up a guitar or form a band. All you needed was a little time and enthusiasm, some ideas, and access to a photocopying machine to add your own voice to the growing chorus. Cheap but effective, the fanzine phenomena continued to flourish well into the 1980's.

Not everyone though was content to challenge the status-quo with a simple Xerox fan sheet. Some had the ambition and resources to take on the real Goliaths of the music industry - the major record companies. Considered out of touch, aloof and too conservative by many of the emerging outfits, the major labels such as EMI, CBS and A & M, had anyway, been slow to show interest in, and recognise the potential of the new bands. This lack of foresight provided an opportunity for the more switched on and adventurous independent record companies to tie the new wave colours to their masts with appropriate signings.

Small, pre-punk, indie labels were revitalised by their new association with the rising movement, and many labels were duly formed to cater specifically for punk tastes. Chiswick and Stiff were two of the former who, though initially providing releases for British mid-seventies pub rock groups, have become synonymous with the halcyon days of UK punk.

CHISWICK RECORDS: Roger Armstrong and Ted Carroll were traders who ran a Camden town record store and Soho market stall in the early nineteen seventies, stocking R & B and rock 'n' roll disc rarities. During the pub rock boom of the mid-seventies they started to receive requests for the harder edged R & B, as performed by the likes of Doctor Feelgood, and spotting a potential market formed their own back room record label.

Chiswick's first release in 1975, was an EP by basic rhythm and booze merchant, the Count Bishops, which included among the original material a cover of that old pub rock standard 'Route 66'. That same year, Joe Strummer's 101'ers had a love song released on the label - yes folks, radical, angry Joe sang a soppy love ballad before discovering his true nature with the Clash! - and Armstrong's and Carroll's pursuit of more pub acts to sign eventually exposed them to a new scene.

Catching a Damned performance in 1976 at that home of London pub rock, the Nashville Rooms, the two were knocked out by the energy and aggression of the performance and immediately made overtures to the group's manager Andy Czezowski regarding a record deal. They were to be denied.

Despite this failure to sign up the Damned ones, their persistence to add new wave groups to their roster led to the signing of Croydon's own Johnny Moped, Dublin's Radiators From Space, and hard-core skin-punk outfit, Screwdriver.

Chiswick had failed in their attempt to get the Damned's signatures on paper because another like-minded independent label had undermined their efforts with a better financial offer. Their reward for successfully snatching the group from their rivals was the kudos gained from being the first label in music history to release a record by a UK punk rock group.

STIFF RECORDS: Like Chiswick, Stiff was the brainchild of two pub rock enthusiasts - Jake Riviera and Dave Robinson. Forming the label in the summer of 1976, their first single release 'So It Goes' by ex-Brinsley Schwarz bassist, Nick Lowe, reflected these tastes and again 'à la' Chiswick, it wasn't until the jolting experience of the Dammed's performance at the Nashville Rooms (both companies were there on the same night) that Riviera and Robinson decided to change tactics and pursue new wave signings.

Beating their rivals to become the first label to secure the services of a British punk outfit they released the Damned's and the UK's Destroy Generation's debut record 'New Rose' in November 1976. Hot on its heels, a Nick Lowe produced LP 'Damned Damned Damned' followed, and by the tail end of 1977, Stiff were seen as *the* number one, new wave record company, with that year's signings, Elvis Costello and Ian Dury bringing the label artistic praise and substantial commercial success, while the more riskier propositions, the Averts, provided the all important street credibility. The labels motto, worn on T-shirts, badges and other promotional devices was *"If it ain't Stiff, it ain't worth a fuck"*.

Chiswick and Stiff's ascendancy led to the establishment of a plethora of small independent record labels determined to follow their profitable example. A few lines on each of the more relatively successful follows...

STEP FORWARD: Astute businessman Miles Copeland, swopped gig promotion for the role of record company boss. Using 'Sniffin' Glues' Mark Perry as an A & R front man for the operation, to give it authentic punk credibility, Step Forward got its contractual hands on first generation outfits the Cortinas, the Models and Chelsea. Later, Copeland switched operations to his ILLEGAL RECORDS label, which launched the career of brother Stewart's band, the Police, as well as financing Perry's own DEPTFORD FUN CITY label.

ROUGH TRADE: Starting life as a Portobello Road record retailers in 1976, Rough Trade became an important outlet for punk and independent record releases and selling point for fanzines from the UK and USA. Its owner, Geoff Travis' empathy with the musical revolution, led to the formation of a distribution network and record label the following year, releasing industrial punk soundsmiths, Metal Urban's first record 'Paris Maquis' and picking up the Fall and second wave Ulster rockers, Stiff Little Fingers (among others) thereafter.

BEGGARS BANQUET: Conceived in 1977, the label's first release was the single 'Shadow' by the Lurkers. Signed Australian oddity, Duffo (waste of vinyl) then came up trumps with Tubeway Army, featuring Gary Numan on synthesizer, who would establish the label's reputation and financial security with the monster selling LP 'Are Friends Electric'.

A bunch of less prestigious UK indies from the mid-late 1970's include...

NEW HORMONES: Manchester's Buzzcocks own label for their 'Spiral Scratch' EP, before moving to major record company United Artists.

RABID RECORDS: Manchester based label with 'Slaughter And The Dogs' providing the appropriate noise for their vinyl.

RAW RECORDS: Home of Cambridge's top punk act the Users.

THE LABEL: Presumptuous title for precocious juveniles, Eater.

PINNACLE RECORDS: Launching pad label for the UK Subs among others.

This proliferation of independents wasn't just confined to Britain. Both in America and Europe, the Do It Yourself record labels were providing vinyl opportunities for the bands of the burgeoning scene...

BESERKLEY RECORDS: Founded by Berkeley, California resident Matthew Kaufman, Beserkley Records aimed to revive the prominence of the 45 rpm in a decade that had seen the LP take over as the big selling format. To this end he signed the made for 45 new wave outfit, Jonathan Richman and the Modern Lovers, and consequently released two of the finest pop-punk singles of the period 'Roadrunner' and 'Modern World'.

BOMP RECORDS: Greg Shaw's USA label that not only provided American distribution for Stiff's new wave acts such as Devo, but also gave us such Yankee obscurities as the Weirdos and Chicano punks, the Zeros.

ALTERNATIVE TENTACLES: Would provide the means for American West-Coast hard-core's finest vinyl moment 'California Uber Alles', by the Dead Kennedys.

SKYDOG RECORDS: French company, started by Dolls/Thunders admirer Marc Zermati who's first release was a Flamin' Groovies EP. He got into UK and USA punk rock from its conception, being present at the Sex Pistols, Chalet du Lac, Parisian disco gig. Distributed American and British new wave records in France and the rest of Europe becoming a big Euro advocate and friend of the mid-seventies rock 'coup d' état'.

The birth of these labels provided the movement with an adventurous and philosophically sympathetic business partnership, giving punk outfits deals where the majors feared to tread. This sense of adventure and experimentation also led to a stylistic change in record presentation. Chiswick, Stiff, and Skydog took to using picture covers and special artwork for their single and EP releases; something the major labels only reserved for their LP's using plain paper jackets with, at best, the company logo on them for their 45's.

After the success of this trend from the indies was demonstrated in terms of increased sales, the majors followed, likewise, the independent's use of coloured vinyl. Manufacturing albums and singles in various day-glo shades along with the traditional black wax brought dividends for the small operators. With a desire to possess a particular record on all available colour formats, it soon became apparent that fans and collectors would be prepared to purchase up to six or seven copies of the same title, boosting sales and chart positions.

By the beginning of the 1980's, this indie innovation had also become standard procedure for the recording giants.

* * * * *

The roads end of 1976 may have been the start of a boom-time for the independents, but for the EMI signed UK punk point men, the Sex Pistols, things had got off to a shaky start and were about to get worse...

"HEY, HEY, WE'RE THE SEX PISTOLS"
ANARCHY AND OUTRAGE IN THE UK

With the ink still drying on the Pistols' EMI contract, McLaren moved his Glitterbest HQ to more conducive offices just off London's Oxford Street, and hardened plans with the label to record some songs with a view to releasing a first single. Lansdowne studios was agreed as a suitable location, and after some humming and harping from a sceptical EMI, the Pistols live sound engineer Dave Goodman was appointed as producer.

The Pistols and Goodman lasted just two days at Lansdowne. The mess and graffiti left by the band after forty eight hours of recording proved too much for the studio management and they were told in no uncertain terms to leave.

That same month (October) punk received more adverse media attention. During a Clash show at London's ICA, Shane MacGowan - later to front lightweights the Nips and Irish-folk rock, booze supping heavyweights the Pogues - bit the ear off fellow Clash fan Jane Crockford, providing more photos of blood splattered punks and concrete evidence of the violent nature of this new youth cult for the tabloid press.

Swiftly moving to Wessex studios, the Pistols behaved themselves well enough to record live and chaotic versions of originals 'No Lip', 'Did You No Wrong', and 'Anarchy In The UK', as well as their unique cover versions of the Who's 'Substitute', the Monkees 'Steppin' Stone', and the Small Faces 'What You Gonna Do About It'.

EMI though, were not impressed. At the label's insistence Goodman was axed and Roxy Music producer Chris Thomas was called in for a salvage operation. Using layers of guitar overdubs - twenty four in all - as the foundation for a powerful, overall sound, Thomas, in spite of Rotten's winging and sarcasm, produced an acceptable series of recordings for group and label, from which a debut 45 rpm could be chosen.

The record company wanted the added, Matlock written 'Pretty Vacant', but McLaren and the band were adamant that the first Pistols record should be 'Anarchy In The UK'. EMI eventually relented.

On November 26th, 1976, the first recorded offering from the Sex Pistols was unleashed on an expectant assortment of punk rock enthusiasts, musicians, journalists and the record industry. Though the Damned had beaten the Destroy combo to the release of the

Right: Anti-Christ and Anarchist (Johnny Rotten) / Illustration © Adam Cansino

first bona fide UK punk rock record by a margin of days, it was this debut that they all had held their breaths for and for most, the Pistols vinyl calling card did not disappoint.

Kicking off with a sneering *"RIGHT"* from Rotten over an intense bass-drum intro', 'Anarchy' shifted into fourth gear with the arrival of Jones' blazing guitars and smashed large rhythmic nails into the coffin of the Peace and Love generation with its opening verse/chorus...

"I am an anti-Christ, I am an anarchist,
don't know what I want but I know how
to get it, I want to destroy passers by
... 'cause I want to be, an anarchist"

... through to its screamed *"D-E-S-T-R-O-Y"* over rampant feedback conclusion.

This record, above all others, embodied the spirit and power of the punk rock revolution. It was a call to arms, an anthem and a warning - it was the fine noise of a generation.

Jamie Reid's promotional poster depicting a torn Union Jack flag held together by safety pins with the band's name and record title spelled out, ransom note style, from cut out newspaper letters, provided the perfect visual compliment for 'Anarchy'. A powerful visual statement for a powerful and emotive record.

The UK music press heralded the release of 'Anarchy In The UK' as the beginning of a new musical era. Melody Maker's' Caroline Coon, under a headline that ran *'ANARCHY, VENOM, OUTRAGE, FURY!'*, started her ecstatic review with these lines...

"It was obvious that if ever there was to be a single then this should be it. But it was difficult to imagine how the band could capture all that excitement on vinyl. They HAVE done it, though. The single is the epitome of their sound, at the band's most furious, venomous best. It's great. It's startlingly harsh, loaded with cynical irony and too concerned with urban reality to appeal to those settled into the thrill of romance."

'Sounds' writer Alan Lewis made 'Anarchy' his single of the week and, though playing down the revolutionary nature of the record, had this to add to the chorus of press approval...

"Thrashing guitars, a maniacal chuckle from Johnny Rotten, and we're into the most eagerly awaited single in ages. Single Of The Week? Has to be, and not just because Sounds was the first to feature the Pistols/Punk phenomenon. It explodes out of the pre-Christmas pile, and by any standards it's a great rock record".

Still scarred and indignant from his run-in with the Pistols' pet monster, Sid Vicious, Nick Kent was about the only reviewing rock journalist to slate the record - but even among the punk musicians, there were some who felt that 'Anarchy' was a missed opportunity.

Damned bassist, Captain Sensible explains his band's reaction on first hearing the Pistols single.

CAPTAIN SENSIBLE: *"I remember when copies of 'Anarchy in the UK' were brought down to Stiff records hot off the presses. We sat down to listen to it with bated breath. What are our rivals up to ... what sort of thing have they come up with? They were rough and ready on stage all right, but no one knew what they would sound like on record. When we heard it we all pissed ourselves with laughter. It sounded like some redundant Bad Company out-take with like, old man Steptoe singing over the top. I couldn't believe 'Anarchy In The UK'!"*

Despite the sniping in some quarters, the general consensus was that the Pistols had cut the mustard with their debut, and buoyed up by the enthusiastic response to the record, EMI got their powerful promotional department into action to fix up radio, press and TV interviews. During the meet the press part of the 'Anarchy' PR drive, Steve Jones reiterated the Pistols anarchic philosophy to journalist Neil Spencer...

SPENCER: *"What music are you into?"*
JONES: *"We're not into music."*
SPENCER: *"What then?"*
JONES: *"Chaos!"*

A prime opportunity for a graphic demonstration of this nihilistic viewpoint provided itself for the band when EMI had the Pistols replace label mates Queen - the embodiment of the kind of group the Pistols wished to destroy and replace - on December 1st, 1976, as guests on an early evening news and entertainment TV show called 'Today'.

The band, who were busy rehearsing for their imminent concert tour of the UK, told both the label and McLaren they didn't want to do it. Sensing a perfect occasion to unleash Rotten and Co. on the Great British public - 'Today' followed the national news and was watched by millions - the Pistols manager insisted that they make it and threatened to withhold their £25 weekly wage if they failed. Faced with this 'fait accompli' the band agreed and received as a concession, a Glitterbest paid-for Daimler limo to drive them from the rehearsal rooms to the TV studio.

On arrival at the 'Today' HQ in London's Euston Tower's complex, the group were met by McLaren along with Siouxsie Sioux, Severin and other Bromley contingent members, invited by Malcolm to appear with the Pistols - to make the point that punk was not just a particular brand of music or band, but also a movement. This colourful crew were looked upon as some kind of freak show by the programme's staff, especially by the 'Today' host, Bill Grundy.

Grundy, a sardonic and world weary, middle-aged TV journalist, didn't want to interview the Sex Pistols. They looked loutish and trouble and he argued long and hard to drop the report on the group from the show. Overruled by his bosses though, he headed down to the studio from the control room, angry at their decision and spoiling for a confrontation.

Meanwhile in the hospitality room, McLaren had made sure his band and their followers had consumed large amounts of the free beer available. He wanted them to be loose and leery, ready to explode on a million-plus TV screens. The resulting clash between the uptight and goading Grundy and the Pistols at their obnoxious best has entered rock mythology as The Punk TV Moment.

I am fully aware that the details of this confrontation have been duly recorded in numerous other publications dealing with this subject, but as the subtitle to my humble offering is, after all 'The Definitive History Of Punk' I have decided, on general principles, to record the action one more time for your enjoyment.

GRUNDY: *"They are punk rockers. The new craze, they tell me. They are heroes, not the nice clean Rolling Stones. You see, they are as drunk as I am. They are clean by comparison. They are a group called the Sex Pistols. And I'm surrounded now by all of them..."*
JONES: *"In action!"*
GRUNDY: *"...Lets just see the Sex Pistols in action. Come on chicks."*

A film clip taken from a documentary on the punk rock phenomena broadcast the previous week is shown. The cameras shift back to Grundy and the Pistols.

GRUNDY: *"I'm told that that group* (Grundy slaps his thigh with his sheet of questions) *have received £40,000 from a record company. Doesn't that seem...er...to be slightly opposed to their* (Grundy takes deep breath) *anti-materialistic way of life?"*
MATLOCK: *"No, the more the merrier."*
GRUNDY: *"Really?"*

MATLOCK: *"Oh yeah."*
GRUNDY: *"Well, tell me more then."*
JONES: *"We've fucking spent it, ain't we?"*
GRUNDY: *"I don't know. Have you?"*
MATLOCK: *"Yeah. It's all gone."*
GRUNDY: *"Really?"*
MATLOCK: *"Down the boozer"*
GRUNDY: *"Really? Good Lord! Now I want to know one thing..."*
MATLOCK: *"What?"*
GRUNDY: *"...are you serious or are you just making me, trying to make me laugh?"*
MATLOCK: *"No, it's gone. Gone."*
GRUNDY: *"Really?"*
MATLOCK: *"Yeah"*
GRUNDY: *"No, but I mean about what you're doing."*
MATLOCK: *"Oh yeah."*
GRUNDY: *"Are you serious?"*
MATLOCK: *"Mmm"*
GRUNDY: *"Beethoven, Mozart, Bach and Brahms have all died..."*
ROTTEN: *"They're all heroes of ours, ain't they."*
GRUNDY: *"Really? What? What were you saying sir?"*
ROTTEN: *"They're wonderful people."*
GRUNDY: *"Are they?"*
ROTTEN: *"Oh yes! They really turn us on."*
GRUNDY: *"Well, suppose they turn other people on?"*
ROTTEN: (whispered) *"Well that's just their tough shit."*
GRUNDY: *"It's what?"*
ROTTEN: *"Nothing. A rude word. Next question!"*
GRUNDY: *"No, no. What was the rude word?"*
ROTTEN: *"Shit".*
GRUNDY: *"Was it really? Good heavens, you frighten me to death."*
ROTTEN: *"Oh alright Seigfried..."*

Grundy turns his attentions to the Bromley contingent girls standing behind the band.

GRUNDY: *"What about you girls behind...?"*
MATLOCK: *"He's like yer dad, in' he, this geezer, or your Grandad."*
GRUNDY: *"...are you... er... are you worried, or are you just enjoying yourself?"*
SIOUXSIE: *"Enjoying myself."*
GRUNDY: *"Are you?"*

SIOUXSIE: *"Yeah."*
GRUNDY: *"That's what I thought you were doing."*
SIOUXSIE: *"I've always wanted to meet you."*
GRUNDY: *"Did you really?"*
SIOUXSIE: *"Yeah."*
GRUNDY: *"We'll meet afterwards, shall we?"*
JONES: *"You dirty sod. You dirty old man."*
GRUNDY: *"Well keep going chief, keep going. Go on, you've got another five seconds. Say something outrageous."*
JONES: *"You dirty bastard."*
GRUNDY: *"Go on, again."*
JONES: *"You dirty fucker!"*
GRUNDY: *"What a clever boy."*
JONES: *"What a fucking rotter."*

Grundy turns to face the cameras to close the show.

GRUNDY: *"Well that's it for tonight. The other rocker Eamonn* (Eamonn Andrews, the co-host of 'Today'), *I'm saying nothing else about him, will be back tomorrow. I'll be seeing you soon. I hope I'm not seeing you* (Grundy looks across at the band) *again. From me though, good night.*

The 'Today' show theme music is played and the credits roll while Jones stands up to do a bad impersonation of Elvis, gyrating his hips and quivering his upper lip for the cameras while Rotten looks at his watch and faints boredom.

The reaction was immediate. Thames Television's switchboard was inundated with calls from shocked and offended viewers for the rest of the evening.

By the following day the incident had become a national scandal.

As the historian Macauly sagely observed in a past century *"The English are prone to periodic fits of morality"* - the Pistols/Grundy clash provide the country with the perfect excuse for another seizure.

Unanimous condemnation of the band's performance came from every quarter, with the British press leading the way in the displays of moral indignation. *'THE FILTH AND THE FURY'* ran the front page headline of 'The Daily Mirror' with a full report on *"The pop group (sic) that shocked millions with the filthiest language ever heard on British television"*, and a companion piece titled *'WHO ARE THESE PUNKS?'* that portrayed the new movement as a violent and apocalyptic youth cult. Fellow tabloid newspaper 'The Sun', ranted in similar fashion under a 'ROCK GROUP START A 4-LETTER WORD TV STORM' headline, with 'The Telegraph', 'Daily Mail' and 'Daily Express' joining in with suitably mouth foaming headlines of their own.

The public at large, encouraged by this high grade bent and twisted journalism, joined the fray. A certain Mr. James Holmes (truck driver, aged 47) became a national hero of sorts when he related to the overjoyed 'Daily Mirror' how *"in a fit of rage"* he had destroyed his own television set *"with a boot to the TV screen"* to end the stream of filth and foul language the Sex Pistols were exposing his watching eight year old son to. When asked about his reaction to this heroic act by a 'Mirror' hack, Rotten cooly replied *"Ridiculous to hear of people kicking in their TV sets; haven't they heard of the OFF button?"*

JORDAN: *"It was the best publicity you could get really. It alienated the Sex Pistols from every ordinary, normal, God-fearing person in the country which immediately made every child of those God-fearing parents absolutely adore the Sex Pistols. There was a great influx of outrage on the one hand, and love on the other."*

By the end of that December week, EMI record packers had declared that they would no longer handle copies of 'Anarchy In The UK'.

Various politicians were decrying this new threat to our civilisation - always a vote winner - and churchmen (what a surprise!) had climbed into their pulpits to warn that membership to this new cult, was tantamount to dancing with the Devil. After all, had not Johnny Rotten declared himself to be an anti-Christ on their record?

For the vast majority of the UK, the 'Today' incident and its resulting negative publicity, provided the first realisation of the punk movement's existence. It's not surprising then that this new subculture was considered fiendish, subversive and detrimental to the health of its youthful followers by a large portion of the population.

The 'Today' fallout was to have serious professional consequences for all concerned. Bill Grundy was suspended by the Thames Televisions programme controller for his part in the affair - it was effectively the end of his broadcasting career. For the Pistols too, the price of new found infamy was to prove very expensive.

McLaren had put together a package tour to promote the 'Anarchy' single; a throwback to the Joe Meek/Larry Parne multi-band touring circuses of the 1960's. The Sex Pistols had the headline (naturally), with the Damned in the second spot, and ex-New York Dolls guitarist Johnny Thunder's Heartbreakers and the Clash in support. Titled the 'Anarchy In The UK Tour', the four bands were to share a coach, PA and lights, and spread the message to the masses nationwide, starting the nineteen date tour in Norwich on December 3rd, and returning to the capital on the 26th for what was expected to be a final, triumphal show at Harlesden's Roxy Theatre. But, as a result of becoming public enemy number one, the Pistols and Co. were to eventually play only a mere five out of the nineteen gigs McLaren had booked.

First, the University of East Anglia governing body cancelled the Norwich show, causing a sit-in by protesting students enraged at their reactionary decision. Then the second gig, in Derby, was abandoned after the town's council insisted the bands provide them with a private performance so they could check for lewd behaviour and obscenities before the public show. McLaren refused, and the bandwagon rolled into Newcastle only to find yet another cancelled gig.

Leeds came next, where the bands finally got to perform at the city's Polytechnic. Due to the 'Today' notoriety though, the majority of the audience seemed more interested in staring at the freakish foul mouthed yobs who had taken over the airwaves than reacting to the music and participating in the usual manner.

The following day's Bournemouth show bit the dust, and the coach did a quick U-turn heading due north to Manchester where prior to their Electric Circus performance the touring party were thrown out of two city hotels before accommodation could eventually be secured. It seemed the entire country had decided to treat these punk rockers as lepers, and as more and more gigs were cancelled and the backlash grew, the pressure began to show.

McLaren didn't rate the Damned too highly - *"They're no fucking good"* was his succinct evaluation of the band, and from the start he had clashed with Stiff Records supremo and Damned tour strategist Jake Riviera. Riviera looked upon McLaren as a jumped up clothes seller turned manipulator and self promoter with no understanding of the music business and for his part, McLaren saw Riviera as an oathish, uneducated and unimaginative beer swiller.

This clash of personalities led to the Damned travelling separately from the rest of the tour party on their own bus, a gross act of disunity as McLaren saw it, and reached crisis point after the Derby no-show - the Pistols manager discovered Riviera had advised the Damned to perform before the self appointed protectors of public morals there, despite his declaration to the council that the bands had unanimously decided against such a humiliation. Interpreting this as an unforgivable act of treason, McLaren threw the Damned off the tour, an action that only served to heighten the chaotic nature of events.

The national press didn't help matters either. Sensation seeking journalists from the tabloids followed the tour and would report every piece of riotous behaviour, every profanity uttered and each conflict with the authorities in magnified detail for the scandal hungry public.

Other organs of the media were not far behind the press in trying to dig up some dirt on these monstrous punks. Pistols photographer Ray Stevenson remembers the subtle approach of a journalist from the Yorkshire TV company...

RAY STEVENSON: *"In the foyer of the Draganora Hotel, Leeds, a TV interviewer asked me if I was anything to do with the Sex Pistols. 'I have been waiting here for over an hour. How can I get to the group or Mr. McLaren?' he asked. It's very unlikely I said. 'We cover a greater area than Thames TV' he remarked with a knowing smile. OK, I said, I'll tell Malcolm you're here. Shall I tell him you want some swearing?... He smiled again."*

'Anarchy' tour dates in Lancaster, Liverpool, Bristol, Cardiff, Glasgow, Dundee, Sheffield, Southend, Guildford, Birmingham, Torquay, and London were all cancelled. The bands returned to the UK capital on the 22nd of December, penniless and tired - angry at having their tour turned into a fiasco and having been made whipping boys for the British gutter press. In that winter of 1976, censorship and the forces of reaction were alive and well in the UK.

The results of the Grundy and 'Anarchy' tour debacles couldn't have been more destructive. Punk unity had been shown to be a mirage, the movement was now perceived - thanks to tabloid headlines - as a brutal and twisted cult by the majority of the public, and though the 'Anarchy In The UK' single had reached the top thirty of the pop charts, EMI, under pressure from the many raised voices of indignation, decided to pull the record from the stores.

By Christmas 1976 then, there seemed a very real possibility that the emerging movement would be pronounced Dead On Arrival and the status quo would survive and rule the day.

* * * * *

These developments disturbed me deeply. As I read and watched the concerted efforts of the media to destroy punk at its birth, I heard the echoes from another decade when prejudice and ignorance had informed the attack on rock 'n' roll music; the 1950's backlash against rhythm and blues and all other forms of Afro-American influenced expression, deemed and dismissed by the agents of simpleton as *"nigger music"*.

White Southern baptists hysterically declaring rock 'n' roll as the devil's toy and identifying the cause of Satanic recruitment as *"That jungle beat... the beat... The Beat... THE BEAT!"* Radio stations across the USA proudly boasting that they would never play Negro tinged music performed by whites, smashing R & R discs on air while Elvis, banned from appearing in certain states because of his provocative hip movements, could only, absurdly, be seen from the chest up on his TV debut.

A similar air of hysteria was prevalent during British punk's formative years, and it struck me as so dumb that those who loved the music of those original rock 'n' roll acts, and the new rock establishment as personified by the Rolling Stones, Aerosmith and Led Zeppelin - R & B influenced acts every one - joined in the abuse of punks and the punk movement without seeing this paradox.

Even within my own rock group, an antagonism had developed between that part of the band that had been converted from glam to punk rock by the power and energy of the Ramones - the keyboard player and myself - and the remaining members of Marionette who hated our change of image, the faster new wave songs we were writing and who had decided punk was but a one minute wonder.

Eventually we were given the ultimatum of either getting back with the glam rock programme or moving on. It was time to move on. Splitting from the group at the onset of 1977, I turned and looked to the future.

5
SURFERS OF THE NEW WAVE
BUNKING THE PUNK TRAIN
TO STARDOM

"And learn, my sons, the wondrous power of Noise,
To move, to raise, to ravish ev'ry heart."
Alexander Pope, 'The Dunciad' (1728).

"Don't accept the old order. Get rid of it!"
Johnny Rotten (1976).

The British summer of 1976 proved to be one of the hottest on record. Apocalyptic talk had been changed from the dawn of a new ice age to that of another paranoia, with the river Thames drying up to a trickle of its former self and a serious nationwide shortage of water. A drought bill was passed in the House of Commons for the month of August, with MP Denis Howell appointed as emergency minister of drought, delivering a stern warning from the government to cut water consumption or face the possibility of H_2O rationing.

England's green and pleasant land had become parched and brown, with trees, plants and the abundant grass withering and dying under the sun's relentless onslaught. To a population more used to gentle summers and rain swept streets, the intense heat and humidity seemed more of a curse, a climatic manifestation of Britain's social afflictions, than a welcome change in the weather.

But just as things can wither and die in such harsh conditions, so can others grow and flourish; mutant strains develop - spores and fungus, bacteria and the larva of new and weird insects. Up and down the UK, that blistering season, the musical and stylistic equivalent of this natural process was taking place in sauna-like rehearsal studios and sweaty back rooms - the ideal breeding grounds for transformation, mutation and metamorphosis, for a new and infectious strain of the rock 'n' roll virus.

Out of that muggy swamp came the children of the Sex Pistols, some taking up guitars for the very first time while other more experienced players changed styles, having made a Damascene like conversion to the new wave. Punk proclaimed that all were equal, that anyone with something to say and access to an instrument could and should produce music as valid as McLaren's Media crowned Monarchs of the Movement. That was the theory.

However it soon became clear that some were more equal than others. A hierarchy had emerged with its court in the UK capital, and with the Pistols at its pinnacle. Challenging their supremacy were two bands - one with fire, ideas and ambition, the other simply looking for a good time.

LONDON CALLING
THE CLASH AND THE DAMNED.

Both the CLASH and the DAMNED were the result of a two way split from the Dolls/Iggy loving London SS. Brian James and Rat Scabies left to construct their own high energy outfit while SS manager Bernie Rhodes, guitarist Mick Jones, and occasional singer Paul Simonon took off in the same general direction to piece together their own group.

As well as the proto-punk bands, Jones, an art school student, was heavily influenced by the Kinks, Mott The Hoople and the Stones, while the Brixton born and bred Simonon, who was also an art college attendee, loved the West Indian music he heard coming up from the streets in his home environment - reggae, ska and bluebeat. This mix of influences would emerge time and time again in the music they would make together.

At first the same problems that had beset London SS - unreliable musicians and short timers with little enthusiasm - plagued their attempts at forming a stable group and outfits with names like the Weak Heartdrops, the Mirrors, the Phones and the Psychotic Negatives came to nothing. Jones and Simonon wanted their group to be more than just another bunch of musicians playing some revved-up rock 'n' roll; they wanted a rock gang, in the mould of the New York Dolls.

Their ambitions were fulfilled when they ran into the ex-singer/ guitarist of pub rockers the 101'ers while waiting at a social security office to sign on for unemployment benefit in 1976. Joe Strummer would provide what others had so patently failed to add to their enterprise - ambition, energy, skill and glamour.

Strummer had also been to art school and had made his own

attempts at putting together a rock 'n' roll outfit he could be proud of, starting in the early 1970's with teen rockers Flaming Youth. Eventually convinced that Flaming Youth did not have the potential for greatness, he took off to Wales to live with a girlfriend, formed the Vultures and set about gigging the Welsh pubs and clubs till his fascination with both the environment and the women waned and he headed back to the smoke.

On his return to London, Strummer took to living in squats in Shepherd's Bush and Queensway - up to 35,000 people were estimated to be squatting in empty London properties at this time - where with fellow squatter/musicians, he put together the 101'ers, a name that derived from the door number of their squat.

Strummer and the 101'ers took their R & B sound onto the capital's gig circuit and became players in the pub rock boom of the mid-1970's, securing a one-off single deal with Chiswick Records, who released their self penned and against type love song 'Keys To Your Heart'.

Despite this progress, Strummer still felt hungry for a new kind of sound, and that craving was finally satisfied when a little known band called the Sex Pistols opened up for the 101'ers at a Nashville Rooms gig in the April of 1976. Joe dramatically recalled the effect this foursome had on him in an early interview...

JOE STRUMMER: *"Yesterday I thought I was a crud, then I saw the Sex Pistols and I became a king and decided to move into the future. As soon as I saw them I knew that rhythm and blues was dead, that the future was here somehow. Every other group was riffing through the Black Sabbath catalogue. But hearing the Pistols I knew. I just knew!"*

Finally convinced he had at last found in that Sex Pistols performance the elusive sound and attitude he had been searching for, Strummer left the 101'ers and looked around for some like-minded young bloods to join forces with. Meeting Jones and Simonon at his local dole office took care of that and Jones and Simonon had discovered the perfect front man for their rock gang.

MICK JONES: *"We went to Portobello Road once and there was this stall that had a pile of, like, fifty pence leather jackets. They were old ladies car coats in pinks and whites and things. We (Jones, Simonon and Strummer) all went in there - because we had been drinking and everything - and we picked up these fifty pence coats and we all put them on as we walked down the road and I knew we was a group - regardless if the people couldn't play or anything! It just felt so right because we all had the same leather jackets. It made sense. From that day it was a group really."*

Calling themselves the Clash as *"It seemed appropriate, considering our aims"*, Simonon picked up a bass guitar for the first time, having never played a note in his life, while Jones providing the lead licks, Strummer the stuttering vocals/machine-gun rhythm guitar and mild mannered ex-London SS skin beater, Terry Chimes, the solid backbeat. A third guitarist, Keith Levine sat in with them for a short while, but his reliability was somewhat questionable and eventually he moved on to rehearse with Sid Vicious's less disciplined first band the Flowers Of Romance, before copping the guitar gig with John Lydon's post Pistols enterprise, Public Image Ltd.

Rehearsing in a squalid room in Camden town, the band wrote themselves a set of songs that were angry, fast and furious, imitating the roar and tempo of the Westway overpass that sat eighteen floors beneath Jones' high rise tower block flat in west London. Early tracks like 'Protex Blue', 'London's Burning', 'White riot' and 'Hate and War', dealt with police brutality, boredom, bigotry, and justified the use of violence in personal self-defence, and when used by abused social groups to resist the forces of oppression.

Bernie Rhodes liked what he heard and encouraged the group to find a suitable hard-edged image to go with their burning sound. They came up with an uncompromising look of cropped hair, paint splattered boiler suits, and shoes with Situationist style (Rhodes's influenced) stencilled slogans on them such as *'HEAVY DUTY DISCIPLINE'*, *'REBEL TRUCE'*, *'STENGUNS IN KNIGHTSBRIDGE'* and *'HATE AND WAR'*, giving the Clash the appearance of an urban guerrilla outfit that had exchanged their bombs and shooters for guitars and a drum kit. Weapons which Joe looked upon as being every bit as effective in their war against apathy as instruments of death were for the killing revolutionaries such as the Brigade Rosse - an organisation Strummer openly supported by occasionally wearing a machine gun and red star motif T-shirt with their name emblazoned on it.

They unleashed this potent combination of radical 'chic' and radical sound to a live audience for the first time at their maiden gig in the industrial northern English city of Sheffield in June, 1976. Rhodes then officially unveiled them to an impressed crowd of journalists and A & R sorts at their rehearsal studio, suitably paint splattered for the occasion Jackson Pollock style to match their outfits, some two months later.

With the Pistols winning more and more publicity that summer, punk rock started to gain acceptance. Influential people started to talk of this new musical/artistic movement as the next big thing, and the Clash city combo found themselves with increased gigging opportunities.

Despite the growing rivalry between Rhodes and McLaren, the band were invited to appear with the Pistols at their Screen On The Green extravaganza, McLaren's 100 Club punk festival, and secured a spot for themselves on the 'Anarchy In The UK' tour. But, far from enjoying their first experience of a package tour, they were revolted by the blatant bigotry, censorship, and the distorted coverage from the Grub Street Press that surrounded the lumbering Pistols bandwagon from day one. Utterly disenchanted by the whole experience, drummer Terry Chimes left the band believing these events heralded the advent of a British police state.

JOE STRUMMER: *"All that business on the Pistols tour! I hated it. I HATED it. It was the Pistols' time. We were in the background. The first few nights were terrible. We were just locked up in a hotel room with the Pistols doing nothing. When I got back to London on Christmas Eve I felt awful. I was really destroyed, because after a few days you get used to eating. We were eating Holiday Inn rubbish but it was two meals a day and that. And when I got off the coach we had no money and it was just awful. I felt twice as hungry as before."*

Despite the 'Anarchy' tour disaster, it wasn't all bad news for the Clash. Major record company CBS had been tracking the progress of the band for some time, and with 1976 coming to a close, a firm bid was made to Rhodes for the long term services of the band. The deal was worth £100,000, enough to ensure that Strummer and Co. needn't go hungry again for quite a while.

However, not everyone in the new wave fraternity was impressed by this marriage of radical punk to corporate capitalism.

Believing they should have signed to an independent label (preferably his own), Mark Perry wrote in the next edition of 'Sniffin' Glue' that *"Punk died the day the Clash signed to CBS"*, echoing John Lennon's assertion made a decade before, that *"Rock 'n' roll died the day Elvis Presley joined the army"*.

Dismissing this talk of sell out and betrayal, the group set about capturing their raw and rebellious sound on tape, in a studio. The Clash's first, self-titled LP was recorded at the CBS studios in London's Whitfield Street, over three weekend sessions at the beginning of 1977. Duplicating the same argument the Sex Pistols had used to EMI for their own record company, the band insisted that their live sound engineer Micky Foote should be the producer as A) Having been on the road with them he was the best qualified to successfully capture their sound, and B) The producers that CBS had suggested were all a bunch of drunks.

Those observations did not exactly impress the powers that be at the company, but having made it clear that they would not budge on this issue CBS had no choice but to eventually agree. Foote took the controls and despite the flat sound quality present throughout the record, the result was a blistering blend of distilled anger, explosive energy and speed (both drug and tempo) - strong sloganeering fused with rough and ready pop hooks played with much passion. It was punk rock at its finest.

Kicking off with a double-time guitar/drum intro, the band introduced themselves with a song about the 1960's vice queen 'Janie Jones', with live favourites 'Romote Control', 'I'm So Bored With The USA', 'White Riot' and 'Hate And War' hot on her (stiletto) heels. 'What's My Name', 'Deny' - a Strummer song about a girl he knew who was fucked up on junk - and the band's anthem 'London's Burning' completed side one. Side two of the album began with a protest about the lack of gainful employment in the UK in the shape of 'Career Opportunities', and continued to point accusing fingers with 'Cheat' and 'Protex Blue'. Things slowed down a touch with the Junior Murvin, reggae cover 'Police And Thieves', before ending proceedings with '48 Hours' and 'Garageland', where Strummer proudly announced to the world: *"We're a garage band, we come from garage land"*.

On its release in the spring of 1977 the album scored a direct hit with both punks and press alike. It entered the British album charts at number twelve selling 100,000 copies in that territory alone. America's 'Rolling Stone' magazine called it *"The definitive punk album"* and even 'Sniffin' Glue''s Mark Perry had to admit that his Juda's tag was premature and Strummer and Co. had done good...

"The Clash album is like a mirror. It reflects all the shit. It shows us the truth. To me, it is the most important album ever released. It's as if I'm looking at my life in a film. A story of life in London. Playing in and out of the flats. A school that didn't even know what an O-Level was. A job that sat me behind a desk and nicked my brain. All that shit is no longer in the dark. THE CLASH TELLS THE TRUTH!"

'White Riot' was chosen as a single release and jumped into the UK top forty, competing with the likes of Abba and Rod Stewart.

As the group prepared to go out to promote their well received LP and 45 rpm, a small problem still needed to be resolved. Terry Chimes had been brought back to play on the record - credited on the back cover as Tory Crimes - but a permanent drummer was now needed to fill his shoes.

Left: Clash City Rockers - Mick Jones & Joe Strummer (1978) / Photograph © B. Plummer

Two hundred and six skin beaters were auditioned for the job, the two hundred and seventh and yet another London SS alumni, Nicky 'Topper' Headon, became the new member of the Clash. Rehearsed, determined and ready, the outfit took their sound and vision to the cities and citizens of the UK yet again... though this time it would be on their terms.

THE DAMNED are a band responsible for an impressive series of punk firsts. First British punk rock single, 'New Rose', first British punk rock album, 'Damned, Damned, Damned', and first British punk rock outfit to take the UK's translation of the predominantly American inspired sound, to the cities of the USA.

Their story begins with guitarist Brian James and drummer Chris Miller's departure from London SS in the January of 1976, and continues to unfold to this day. James had cut his guitarist teeth in various small time, southern English, R & B combos in the early 1970's, while Miller had kept time for a little outfit called Tor (Rot spelled backwards) which contented itself with playing the youth clubs, pubs, parties and dives of my home town, Croydon.

I know this all too well 'cause I saw this band perform on a number of occasions during 1975 and they were pretty dreadful. Never ending progressive rock jams over which the singer, doing a third rate impersonation of Jim Morrison, would howl and recite bad poetry while their predominantly skinhead following (never could work that one out!) took lumps of flesh out of each other, and any one else in striking distance - a foul evening all round. It seems Miller wasn't exactly happy with this combination either...

RAT SCABIES: *"Tor played nothing except well over the top arty-farty stuff... a lot more complicated and musical than Television were ever capable of. I hated every minute of it; they made me put towels over my drums because I was too loud."*

Though not much cop, Tor at least produced for the movement both the future Damned drummer Scabies, and Croydon guitarist Slimy Toad, who would also go on to (slightly) bigger and better things - an album titled 'Cycledelic', plus three singles for Chiswick Records - with legendary loony-punk outfit Johnny Moped.

After meeting James as a member of London SS, Miller and the Stones/Stooges loving guitarist hooked up with journalist turned attempted vocalist Nick Kent, and Croydon bassist Ray Burns, to play

Right: Vanian & James (The Damned) / (1977) / Photograph © Sheila Rock / Rex Features

two unremarkable gigs as the Subterraneans before promptly disbanding. Taking Burns with them, James and Miller found a ghoulish, Alice Cooper style front man/vocalist in grave digger Dave Letts, and deciding this combination was destined for lasting failure called their band the Damned.

Following a bout of the nasty disease, Miller changed his stage name to Scabies with Letts giving his surname the heave-ho in favour of the more suitable - considering his gothic, Bela Lugosi/Nosferatu image - Vanian. When the band visited a military surplus store to pick stage clothes, Burns chose a naval outfit and was given the name Captain Sensible by the rest.

BRIAN JAMES: *"We called him Captain Sensible 'cause that's what he was at that time... very sensible. The first time I met Ray was when he turned up at my flat to work on some songs with his bass and a bunch of Yes records under his arm. He had long, greasy hair and was very introverted, hardly spoke a word. I kept telling him to work on his look and eventually he cut his hair and lost the flared jeans, but on stage he was so shy he would turn his back to the audience to play. Eventually I'd had enough of this and at a pub gig somewhere in London, I picked up my pint of beer from the top of my amp and poured it over his head. From that moment on he became the extroverted, tutu wearing Captain Sensible we all know and love."*

James, with his macho Keith Richards looks and guitar style, was the only member to resist a name change at this point having already replaced his real surname, Robertson, some years before though he occasionally would change the spelling of his first name from Brian to Bryan as the mood took him.

Images and stage names in place, this unlikely foursome worked up a set of riffing, ramming-speed tunes with sing-a-long choruses such as 'Neat, Neat, Neat', 'Stretcher Case Baby' and 'New Rose'. Songs that sounded like the fastest MC5 and Stooges 33 rpm tracks played at 45 rpm, with Scabies kicking the band along at a breakneck tempo playing Keith Moon style - very little high hat, lots of splash cymbals and floor drum.

They were soon head-hunted by Vivienne Westwood's friend and accountant Andy Czezowski who was determined to find a rock group of his own, and as their new manager, got them their first 'official' gig at the 100 Club in July, 1976.

Quickly becoming associated with the Pistols and the punk movement, the band were offered a spot on the Mont de Marsan 'First European Punk Rock Festival' a month later, along with McLaren's proteges and the Clash. After the infamous Nick Kent chaining at the

100 Club, the Pistols were dropped from the bill and the Clash pulled out in solidarity with their punk rock brethren.

The Damned had no such principles, happily playing the festival and carrying on in the traditional rock 'n' roll manner. This entailed consuming plenty of drugs and booze, hotel high jinx, a hysterical manager trying to impose order on a band hellbent on chaos, and a disastrous noon appearance in front of a handful of equally chemically and liquor deranged French punters. The nerve ripped Czezowski withdrew his services from the band immediately on returning to London and 100 Club's booker Ron Watts stepped into his managerial shoes for a brief time.

Whereas the Pistols combined their talent for mayhem with McLaren's serious Situationist philosophy and anarchic, political views, and the Clash played their guitars with venom to change the world, the Damned had no such lofty intentions nor political/philosophical axes to grind. They were simply out to play fast and loud music to their taste while pursuing as hedonistic a lifestyle as was humanly possible.

CAPTAIN SENSIBLE: *"The Damned were just hell-for-leather destruction merchants. They were the Bash Street Kids of punk!"*

In September 1976 these Croydon rakes headlined the second night of the 100 Club Punk Rock Festival, where Scabies inadvertently started a new punk convention to add to Sid Vicious' 'pogo' dance invention of the previous festival night. None too happy with the reaction from the crowd at the front of the stage, the irritated drummer decided to register his protest by taking great mouthfuls of beer and showering selected members of the audience with the stuff. This produced a counter attack of spit and mouth-warmed lager from the crowd that grew in intensity as the evening progressed. At their next show the Damned found themselves being greeted by their audience, most of whom had witnessed the 100 Club spit battle, with a hail of gob and saliva. New converts took this to be the thing to do at punk rock shows and soon it was a feature of all new wave performances, eventually becoming a very foul and twisted compliment; if you weren't being spat at, they didn't like ya!

Beating Chiswick Records to sign the band, Stiff Records put out the Damned's and British punk's first ever piece of vinyl, the audio amphetamine rush that was the single 'New Rose', in October 1976.

'New Rose' was a worthy first example of the new UK genre. Starting with a four chord guitar intro with pounding floor tom-tom backing, the song explodes into hyperactive life with a glorious snare drum roll from Scabies and a simple but catchy three note riff coming off James' Gibson SG axe - which Brian told me when I played the song on numerous occasions with him a couple of years later, was based on the famous intro motif to Beethoven's fifth symphony. The B-side was a frantic version of the Beatles mid-sixties hit 'Help' - a choice calculated to enrage the majority of the mainstream, popular music enthusiasts who looked upon these new punky outfits as vermin and considered the fab four's songs sacrosanct.

The record charted and a follow-up forty five 'Neat, Neat, Neat' was released on its tail.

At this point Stiff Records executive Jake Riviera took over management of the group, and it was partly as a result of his strained relationship with McLaren that the Dammed found themselves dismissed from the ill fated 'Anarchy In The UK' tour after just a couple of shows. More determined than ever to beat the Sex Pistols to the release of the first UK punk long-player, the band hired the production talents of Nick Lowe and recorded a suitably MC5-esque selection of songs for 'Damned, Damned, Damned' which found its way to the stores ahead of the pack in early 1977.

Not taking itself nearly as seriously as the Clash debut album, 'Damned, Damned, Damned' was a predominantly speedo-punk record interspersed with the occasional, restrained retro sounding track like the twanging, heavy reverb guitar led 'Fan Club'. 'Stab Your Back' was a swipe at inter-band jealousies and politics, and the singles were duly added, being a tried and tested way of increasing sales .

The album generally got good reviews and chart positions, and in the spring of '77 buoyed-up by their success, the Damned took a flight to New York City to play at that home of the genre, CBGB's on the Bowery.

To some this was like taking coal to Newcastle, but to others present at that Damned's CBGB's performance, a schism between the cool, New York intellectual style as exhibited by the likes of Television, Patti Smith and Talking Heads, and the wild approach of the English variation had became apparent. This was even more obvious to the West Coast audiences who had always found it hard to relate to East Coast punk and proto-punks like the Velvet Underground. This theatrical London interpretation of the NY style suited their extrovert chemistry all the better.

American writer, and West Coast punk connoisseur Craig Lee tells of the effect the Damned had on the crowd at their first Los Angeles show in the book 'Hard-core California'...

"As the Damned charged through the sloppy, intense, shambles of a set at the Starwood, the LA kids immediately picked up on the energy and the theatricality of the band. It was making them FEEL SOMETHING. By the end of the Damned set, people looked around, some with a shock of recognition on their faces. Bonds were forming. The poseurs were being separated from the possessed."

The Damned had opened up another front in the war against the lethargy and predictability prevalent in mid-seventies contemporary music by taking the London sound to America for the first time. They had blazed a trail that would be continually used to greater and lesser effect by other outfits of the British chapter of the movement for many years to come.

* * * * *

Both the Clash and the Damned had secured their rapidly building profiles by appearing at McLaren's British punk festival at London's 100 Club. That same two day event had unveiled a selection of punk rock wanna-be's, some of whom had never played an instrument or attempted a song before setting foot on its stage. Others had hastily made the transition from pub to punk after spotting the window of opportunity. Together, they formed the backbone of an expanding British movement, together, they would become missionaries for the new music doctrine.

NO EXPERIENCE NECESSARY
THE BIRTH OF THE BANSHEES
AND OTHER 100 CLUB PUNK FESTIVAL STORIES.

The first night of the McLaren/Watts punk showcase saw the transition of SIOUXSIE SIOUX from fan to star. Coming on like a hundred pounds of bad juju, she'd taken the room by the sheer force of her personality while her appropriately inept backing band the BANSHEES, comprising of fellow Bromley contingent companion Steve Severin - bass, Pistols follower and thug Sid Vicious - drums and Marco Pirroni (later to emerge in Adam and the Ants) - guitar, struck up a discordant, vaguely musical, dirge.

Together they performed a twenty minute set consisting of an almost unrecognisable version of the Velvets 'Sister Ray', Bob Dylan's

Siouxsie Sioux

'Knocking On Heavens Door', a nasty and quickly disintegrating Beatles 'She Loves You' and a beautifully malicious rendition of 'The Lord's Prayer'. This was the pure punk ethic in action - Just get up and *do* it: fuck lack of musical ability, fuck the old rules and regulations. Shock tactics, expression, mutilation and destruction were the new rules.

An element of these shock tactics almost led to the performance being cancelled. Originally Siouxsie and her Banshees were due to play using the Clash backline. An outraged Bernie Rhodes though, refused to let them use the equipment after he had spotted Siouxsie's swastika armband and a hand drawn, felt-tip version on Sid Vicious' T-shirt. Rhodes, a man of the Jewish persuasion, considered confrontation and the ability to shock all well and good as long as the targets met his approval, but by wearing this symbol of the evil perpetrators of the holocaust, Siouxsie, her sidekicks, and the confrontational approach had, for him, gone too far.

McLaren, also a man of the Jewish persuasion, had no such qualms. Considering Rhodes' attitude *"censorial"* he gave Siouxsie his full blessing to use the Pistols' amplifiers and drum kit and the performance went ahead.

Excited by her first taste of fronting a band, Siouxsie put together a more permanent version of the Banshees with Kenny Morris - drums, and Pete Fenton - guitar (later replaced by John McKay), leaving Pirroni to return to his old band the Models, and Vicious to form the Flowers Of Romance with ex-Clash guitarist Keith Levine and future Slits guitarist & drummer Viv Albertine and Palm Olive.

This new and improved version of the Banshees took to the road supporting Johnny Thunders' Heartbreakers, building a devotional following for their dark and brooding sound, and giving Siouxsie with her heavy make-up and leather dominatrix imagery, a reputation as being the Cruella de Vil of punk. A strong and vampish breed of new womanhood.

SIOUXSIE SIOUX: *"I always liked the shiny black SM gear and dark-haired women like Louise Brooks. So much went into why I looked the way I did. Part of it was to be threatening looking, part of it was to be confrontational."*

This uncompromising sound and image led to Siouxsie and the Banshees being passed up time and again for bands with a less powerful and threatening look, and noise, by the record companies who were desperate to sign new wave talent in 1977. The Banshees leader though, was adamant...

Left: Siouxsie Sioux (of the Banshees) / Illustration © Adam Cansino

---

SIOUXSIE SIOUX: *"We'll do it on our own terms; we're not going to water our music down to make it acceptable to the people who sit behind desks."*

It took a concerted effort by media Banshees supporters such as Caroline Coon and John Peel - the group did numerous sessions for his BBC punk talent showcase of a radio show - before Polydor finally signed the group up in 1978.

Their first record was the captivating forty five 'Hong Kong Garden' which reached the UK Top Ten and drew the admiration of other DJ's and journalists who had previously been unsympathetic to punk recordings. The debut album 'The Scream', solidified their growing reputation.

The departure of both Morris and McKay - due to musical and personal differences during their 1979 UK tour to promote their second LP 'Join Hands' - didn't stop the band's momentum any, with the addition of ex-Big In Japan drummer Budgie and ex-Magazine guitar man John McGeoch adding a new depth and polish to the Banshees beguiling sound. This line-up would go from strength to strength with critically acclaimed and chart topping albums such as 'Kaleidoscope', 'Juju', 'A Kiss In The Dreamhouse' and 'Nocturne' taking them into the 1980's, with Siouxsie Sioux, her exotic look copied by thousands of women worldwide, firmly established as a punk icon.

On the same night that Siouxsie Sioux and her howling Banshees had turned in their debut, another outfit of minimal experience had presented themselves for inspection before the 100 Club punk fest' audience.

SUBWAY SECT, formed by Londoners Vic Godard - vocals, and Rob Symmons - guitar, had a brief incarnation as a shabby R & B group before the witnessing of a Sex Pistols performance had changed their direction for good. Adding Paul Myers - bass, and Mark Laff (later with Generation X) - drums, to their line-up, they approached Malcolm McLaren with the intention of getting themselves added to his festival bill.

McLaren checked them out at a rehearsal, and thought they were dreadful. Never the less, he paid out for a rehearsal studio for a week so that they could get into some kind of musical shape for their appearance.

Whereas the Pistols had been poured from the speedo/metallic cauldron of the Stooges and the Dolls, the Sect were firmly in the darker, monotone, Velvet Underground camp. This was reflected in their stage clothing which consisted of baggy, second-hand garments that had been dyed several shades of grey.

The band had only four songs written for their debut, but their Spartan, droning, wall of sound provided a welcome contrast to the super-fast attack of fellow festival players the Clash and the Pistols, and opened up with the Banshees a move into musical territory previously inhabited by American new wavers such as Television and Suicide. Here's what 'Sniffin' Glue' had to say about them in their special 100 Club punk fest' issue...

"The Subway Sect hit the stage and had all the intellectual wimpys cringing in horror and yapping about how the band couldn't play etc. It was their first gig and I loved 'em. They chew gum on stage and look vacant. The four songs they did were great."

Joining the Clash for their 'White Riot' tour in 1977 gave Godard and his band the opportunity to tighten their playing and exposed them to an army of record company A & R men who at the time were frantically signing up punk rock outfits by the bucket load. As was the case with the Banshees though, Subway Sect's non-commercial brand of noise led to a long wait for a label willing to take a chance on them. Their first record, the single 'Nobody's Scared', was released in 1978 on an obscure indie label called Braik, with their follow up forty-five 'Ambition' appearing on the respected Rough Trade label at the end of that same year.

Nothing much came of these releases and the Sect, with a change of personnel, slowly mutated into a new romantic outfit in time for the early 1980's.

Both the Banshees and the Sect had been bands of little or no experience. The second night of the festival featured, in contrast, a band that had been playing the pubs and clubs for some years previously and hoped to make the transition from pub to punk rock. THE VIBRATORS, though not bothering to cut their hair, never the less swopped their flared jeans for drainpipes, and having sensed a career opportunity at the onset of the Pistols led revolution, waded into the new wave and found themselves included in McLaren's showcase of talent.

Formed in the early 1970's by singer/songwriter/guitarist Knox (real name Ian Carnochan), the Vibrators line up that graced the 100 Club stage also consisted of Pat Collier - bass, John Ellis - lead guitar,

and sticksman Eddie. Playing both their own set and acting as a backup band for sometime Bryan Ferry sidekick and session guitarist with a freak hit single 'Motorbikin'', Chris Spedding, it has to be said that on that punk and sweaty night of the September 21st 1976 they were not to everybody's taste...

"The worst band of the whole two days, the Vibrators played a rather predictable set. Old rockers mixed with a couple of self-penned newies. You know, the Vibrators are just out of place, they give themselves a 'tee, hee' name and make out they're punks. I don't reckon they should have been on the bill." MARK P. 'Sniffin' Glue' # 4.

This perception of the Vibrators as fake outfit, a bunch of old pub rockers on the make, became the general view. It was one that I personally didn't subscribe to. It seemed to me that most of the participating punk musicians had checkered past of some description: the Clash had ex-pub and glam rockers Strummer and Jones in their line up, the Pistols had their secret lovers of Rod Stewart and the Faces in Jones and Matlock, and the Damned's drummer and bass guitarist had learned to play their instruments from listening to Led Zeppelin and Yes records - what was so wrong with the Vibrators' transition from old to new?

Despite having their detractors, the Vibes were among the first handful of NW outfits to secure a record deal, having their first single 'We Vibrate', and the second 'Bad Time' released in late 1976 and early 1977 on the RAK Record Label. Knox's wonderful neo-pop punk tunes eventually brought them to the attention of the mighty major CBS.

Signing to CBS in 1977, they produced one of the most enjoyable albums of the period in 'Pure Mania' off which the overtly commercial, Stones-with-attitude sounding single 'Baby, Baby, Baby', was taken. 'Baby, Baby, Baby' was an instant hit with plays aplenty on even the mainstream radio shows that usually passed up on playing the recordings of the new genre.

Replacing bass player Collier who had left to form his own band the Boyfriends with Garry Tibbs (destined to become a future member of Roxy Music), the Vibes toured to promote their new product across the UK and Europe, where, despite the press jibes, the band built a healthy fan base.

The follow up album 'V2' (1978) had few of the thrills of their debut, though the single releases 'London Girls' and 'Automatic Lover' were worthy slices of up-tempo spiky-pop, with the B-side to the 'London Girls' forty-five 'Stiff Little Fingers' providing the name for a future second-wave outfit from Northern Ireland.

Left: The Vibrators / Illustration © Adam Cansino
Insert: Knox and the boys (The Vibrators) striking a pose / Photograph © Ray Stevenson

SNIFFIN' GLUE...
AND OTHER ROCK'N' ROLL HABITS FOR... ~~YOU~~ WHO CARES !

28th Sept '76.

THIS ISSUE IS RARE.....RIP IT UP AND IT'LL BE RARER! Price: EMPTY YER WALLET, YOU BASTARD!

3½

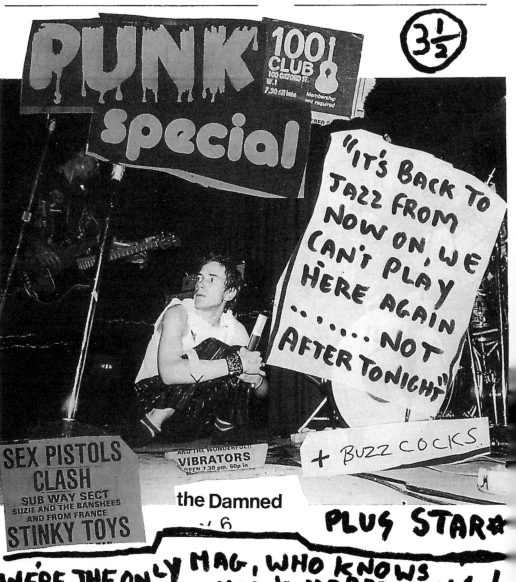

PUNK special

100 CLUB
100 OXFORD ST.
W.1
7.30 till late
Membership not required

"IT'S BACK TO JAZZ FROM NOW ON, WE CAN'T PLAY HERE AGAIN ...... NOT AFTER TONIGHT"

SEX PISTOLS
CLASH
SUB WAY SECT
SUZIE AND THE BANSHEES
AND FROM FRANCE
STINKY TOYS

AND THE WONDERFUL!
VIBRATORS
OPEN 7.30 pm. 60p in

+ BUZZ COCKS.

the Damned

PLUS STARS

WE'RE THE ONLY MAG, WHO KNOWS WHAT'S HAPPENING !

All of the festival bands mentioned so far in this chapter were London based outfits. However, by that summer of 1976 the Pistols earlier gigs in the wider UK were starting to pay punk rock dividends elsewhere in the country.

Present for the Pistols first ever show in the northern English city of Manchester had been Howard Trafford, and his friend Peter McNeish. Astounded by the sheer audacity of the Pistols performance, Trafford, following the established new wave name-change tradition became Devoto, with McNeish dropping his surname for the more poetic Shelley. Together they formed the BUZZCOCKS.

Recruiting fellow Manchester musicians Steve Diggle - bass, John Maher - drums, with Shelley on guitar and Devoto taking the vocal duties, the foursome wrote and rehearsed a set of songs and performed them for the first time in front of a live audience as support act to the Pistols at their second Mancunian gig. Establishing themselves nationally with their Screen On The Green and 100 Club punk festival appearances, the Buzzcocks became the first to put out a record on their own label - the 'Spiral Scratch' EP on New Hormones.

Despite this promising start to the band's career, Devoto quit the Buzzcocks in March 1977 and formed his own outfit Magazine, leaving Shelley to take the lead vocals. Diggle moved from bass to lead guitar and a replacement bassist was recruited in Garth Smith, a school friend of Shelley's. This new line up of the Buzzcocks was added to the bill for the Clash 'White Riot' tour the same year of the Devoto split, and became the focus of a record company bidding war that resulted in the band signing to major label United Artists in the summer of 1977.

Their first record for UA, the single 'Orgasm Addict', was the first of a string of classic forty fives that the band would provide for the label. Songs with a perfect blend of catchy choruses, insightful lyrics, and finger on the pulse subject matter; a new wave version of the quintessential UK singles bands of the 1960's such as the Kinks, the Stones, the Who and the Beatles. 'What Do I Get', 'Love You More', 'Ever Fallen In Love' and 'Everybody's Happy Nowadays' were some of the finest vinyl moments of the 1970's. Very English, very skilful.

Before their first LP 'Another Music In A Different Kitchen' could be released though, bassist Smith was sacked for erratic behaviour and a permanent bassman was found in ex-Fall member Steve Garvey. This Buzzcocks line-up went on to make three albums for UA and earned them the deserved reputation of being one of the best outfits to emerge from the era.

As well as Scabies' second night spitting ritual, another lasting punk

Left: Sniffin' Glue's 100 Club Punk Festival special issue No. 3 1/2 (1976)

tradition was established on the opening night of the 100 Club festival by none other than that Pistols pugilistic protege, Sid Vicious.

High on Amphetamine Sulphate, and squeezed in with the punk hordes at the front of the 100 Club stage, Vicious decided the only way to move to the Pistols emphatic sound at the super-crowded event was to head upwards. Putting his arms flat against his sides, Vicious started to leap towards the ceiling like some demented Masai warrior which in turn brought about a number of copyists. By the later stages of the Pistols set, he had managed to inspire a large section of the audience to emulate the new dance and the whole front portion of the crowd leaped and landed in a heaving mass following, in unison, the Vicious prototype.

Punk's own unique dance the 'Pogo', had been successfully invented, created and accepted.

Those that had copied its basic moves...

ONE: Put your arms flat against the side of your body.

TWO: Leap for the roof as high as possible.

THREE: While in mid-flight aim a large portion of gob at the band playing on the stage (only to be attempted by experienced pogo-ers!).

FOUR: On your return to Earth land on your annoyed neighbour(s) in the hope of getting into a fight.

FIVE: Repeat the process till exhausted, badly injured or removed from the venue by an enraged bouncer who thinks you're taking the piss.

... passed on the knowledge to others at future gigs in provincial towns, where the Pogo flourished, spreading like wildfire throughout the whole UK punk rock community. It was also exported with great success to Europe and the USA where the West Coast hardcore enthusiasts adapted it for their more aggressive variation, the 'Slam Dance'.

Sid Vicious has the distinction of being one of the few musicians to have started a popular dance craze - the Chubby Checker of the new wave!

One more combo had appeared at McLaren's new sounds showcase who unlike all the other participating parties, were neither from London or the north of the country. They were from France, and as such became the first non-UK/USA, new wave outfit to get hooked onto the movement...

STINKY TOYS were an early Euro attempt at a British style, punk rock band. McLaren thought it would look good to have a French outfit on the bill and invited them over to play sight unseen, their appearance he reasoned, confirming that the movement had already spread to other shores and had the potential for worldwide expansion.

Stinky Toys played on the second night of the festival as support to both the Vibrators and the Damned. I'll leave the summation of their performance to the acidic pen of Mark Perry...

"Stinky Toys would have been great if they had done a few songs and then left but they played on and on and on and they sounded the same all the way through their set. The girl singer was a real screamer, who looked like one of those SS birds in her drab shirt and black tie. She squealed and croaked and jerked and jostled. No one could tell the words she was singing but all through those wincing screams she sounded as if she was saying something. The songs I did know were, 'Under My Thumb', 'Substitute' and a pretty good version of Bowie's 'Hang On To Yourself'. Back to France though please, Toys."

Their 100 Club appearance was to be the French band's biggest claim to fame. They were proof positive that the country that had given the world Johnny Hallyday was just not capable of producing a good rock 'n' roll band of any description. I'm afraid Stinky Toys didn't even come close to getting their fifteen minutes. Back to France indeed!

* * * * *

The fact that the Sex Pistols first single 'Anarchy In The UK' had sold over 50,000 units, despite having received just five radio plays plus the adverse post Grundy fallout and the virtual cancellation of a nationwide tour to promote it, had sent the once cautious and sceptical record industry into a punk feeding frenzy. Every label in the land now wanted their own Sex Pistols.

A & R men searched the length and breadth of the UK to find suitable outfits to sign up. Record contracts were handed out to groups of exceptional and dubious ability alike, with many being scooped up only to be dropped again when all the fuss had died down, while a talented few would go on to have long term careers.

The naked energy of punk had proved infectious, and across Britain in 1977 a proliferation of raw combinations were ready and waiting to secure their record deals by hanging on to the Clash, the Damned and the Sex Pistols coat-tails.

FROM LONDON WITH HATE
THE CAPITAL CONTINGENT

With the London punk trinity of the Pistols, the Damned, and the Clash leading the way, the capital city of the UK had indisputably become the Mecca of its new wave. The first British punk rock festival had been successfully staged there, and the uniforms and doctrine of the movement continued to be manufactured at Westwood's and McLaren's Kings Road 'SEX' shop and at the Glitterbest office in Oxford Street. Realising along with the record companies that there was a pretty penny to be made out of this *"punk thing"*, a significant handful of London clothes designers, manufactures and stores, started to produce and stock lines based on Westwood's 'SEX' originals.

'BOY', opened for business as a direct challenger to 'SEX' at the Sloane Square end of the Kings Road and served up T-shirts stained with dry animal blood plus other variations of the uniform for poseurs, fashion hounds and Sloanies. 'SMUTZ' and 'ROBOT' followed suite on the same stretch of street, along with the various stalls that provided cheap imitation Westwood bondage trousers, zipped and ripped shirts, punk badges and paint splattered ties and jackets in the Beaufort Market.

That same year of 1977, mainstream London based designer, Zandra Rhodes, unveiled her 'Conceptual Chic' collection which utilised punk cliches aplenty - ripped and torn garments, safety pins, razor blades and lots of straps and zips.

ZANDRA RHODES: *"Punk was the first truly original movement to enter the fashion scene since flower power. The clothes I created with the beaded holes and beaded safety pins I will always believe in. Unfortunately for me, I could not produce them for a low enough price to make the concept sell commercially."*

By the summer, ex-Dammed manager Andy Czezowski had opened the country's first punk club in Covent Garden's Neal Street, where seasoned and untried talents alike would perform nightly, providing a CBGB's style home for the movement and a launching pad for a number of careers.

'Sounds' got its very own young, firebrand punk journalist in Jane Suck, and posters promoting tours by the Clash, the Vibrators and advertising record releases from the Damned or Pistols along with chunks of punk graffiti started to appear on walls around the city.

Right: 'BOY' fashion - 'SEX' and 'Seditionaries' rival (1977)
Photograph © Sheila Rock / Rex Features.

London was a metropolis filled with a sense of expectation and excitement again. A feeling that must have been tangible in the capital in the 1960's during the Stones/Beatles music, youth culture and fashion explosion; the feeling that this city was at the very centre of things, the place to be, the generator for a movement that was going to change the world.

In the summer of 1977 in London, at that moment in history, it really was *that* exciting.

With the growing buzz on its streets, and the heightened sense it gave us of being in the right place at the right time, it is no small wonder that London and the south-east of England gave birth to more 'first wave' punk outfits than all the other cities in the country put together. Here's some of their stories...

STRANGLERS: First formed in 1974, this Doors tinged, psychedelic-punk combo found a winning line-up in Hugh Cornwell - vocals/ guitar, Jean-Jacques Burnel - bass, Jet Black - drums and Dave Greenfield - keyboards.

Receiving positive press attention after a support tour with Patti Smith in 1976 the band were signed to United Artists at the close of that year. Their debut record, the catchy, psychedelic keyboard bathed single 'Grip' jumped into the UK top fifty before jumping straight back out again, though their first LP 'Rattus Norvegicus' received both good reviews and a much longer stay in the album charts. Despite this taste of commercial success, the Stranglers seemed determined to court controversy as a way of life.

Cornwell got the group banned by the Greater London Council in 1977 for wearing a T-shirt emblazoned with the word 'FUCK' (parodying the Ford logo) at a gig in the capital and memorably explained, at a university show that was being broadcast live on TV, that the Stranglers hated playing for *"elitist audiences"* before finishing with a *"so fuck off!"* and storming from the stage. Later on, his rebel credentials were hugely enhanced by doing prison time for a drug bust. Drummer Black did his bit by getting arrested for being drunk and disorderly, and Burnel, a Karate black belt, made a point of jumping into the audience to punch out hecklers at every given opportunity. The release of their second 1977 single, 'Peaches', brought accusations of misogyny and sexism. The Stranglers reply to this was to hire a bunch of busty, gyrating strippers to dance on stage with them at an outdoor show in London's Battersea Park while Burnel alienated the press still further by practising his proficient Karate on all critics. Their records just kept on getting better though.

'Something Better Change', 'No More Heroes', 'Five Minutes' and the growling, 'Nice And Sleazy', were all killer forty-fives that made it into the UK Top Twenty. The albums, 'No More Heroes' (1977), 'Black And White' (1978), 'Live - X Cert' (1979), 'The Raven' (1979) and 'Meninblack' (1981) all sold extremely well with the band's outlaw image also being secured for good in 1980 after the whole group were arrested, imprisoned and fined for (allegedly) starting a riot at a French concert. 1981 though, saw their finest musical and commercial moment.

The brilliant single, 'Golden Brown', taken from the LP, 'La Folie' released that same year, reached #2 in the British charts and received deserved acclaim for being a near perfect, post-punk composition. Despite its obvious (to some) drugy theme, it brought them praise from a host of journalists and media commentators that had never before shown a liking for their music.

A gem of a band, a British punk rock institution.

HAMMERSMITH GORILLAS: A three piece consisting of long side-burned singer, guitarist and bandleader Jessie Hector, bassist Alan Butler, and Drummer Gary Anderson, who were all collectively brought to our attention in issue #2 of 'Sniffin' Glue'.

Enthusiastic and enterprising, Hector became a one man publicity campaign, releasing his own singles - a high energy version of the Kinks 'You Really Got Me' was one of the first - and convincing Mark Perry, among others, that he was the possible future of rock 'n' roll. Perry signed them for his Deptford Fun City indie-label, and a series of singles, 'Gatecrasher', 'It's My Life' and 'She's My Girl', followed along with a solitary album, 'Message To The World', which was released in 1978.

The problem for the Gorillas though was that the world wasn't listening. All these records did poorly and by the late 1970's the band had been commercially eclipsed by a host of other more generic punk outfits and were forced to the fringes of the scene where they eventually dismantled.

EATER: Formed in 1976 and featuring Andy Blade - vocals, Dee Generate - drums, Brian Chevette - guitar and Ian Woodcock - bass, Eater's main claim to fame was that they were the youngest outfit on the scene with no member of the band over the age of sixteen.

Playing bad punk with a hollow beat they were positive proof that although the energy of the new wave was essentially adolescent, it took more mature heads to harness and transmute it into good music. A support band favourite at the Roxy Club they were eventually picked up by The Label for which they released five consecutive singles - 'Outside View', the first, 'What She Wants (She Needs)', the last, and an LP, 'The Album' (1977).

Eater's bastardized version of Alice Cooper's 'Eighteen', retitled '15', appears on the 'Live At The Roxy' compilation record and stands as a lasting testament to the band's lack of ingenuity and limited ability. Let's face it, they weren't even funny!

THE JAM: Not technically a London band this (formed in Woking, Surrey), but close enough to the capital for our purposes, Paul Weller - guitar/vocals, Bruce Foxton, bass and Rick Butler, drums, set out from their suburban rehearsal room in 1974 in search of fame and fortune.

They did not get off to an easy start. I saw them the year of their formation supporting long haired, hard rockers Thin Lizzy at the Croydon Greyhound, where sporting their Beatles haircuts, suits and ties, they were treated as a complete joke by the denim clad, hip and hairy audience.

Unruffled by these negative reactions, Weller and Co. stayed true to their purpose and at the onset of the new wave revolution made their decisive move. Taking on a series of punk band support slots they discovered a new and accepting audience for their 1960's, mod-driven, power pop sound and look. 'Sniffin' Glue' liked them and so did Coon, Parsons, Ingham and other music press NW enthusiasts.

Polydor Records snapped them up in early 1977, and their first record, 'In The City', received single of the week status in 'Melody Maker' and 'Sounds'. Opening with a classic R & B guitar/bass riff, 'City' delivered the memorable lines...

"In the city there's a thousand
things I want to say to you...
But whenever I approach you,
you make me look a fool"

...showing much promise in Weller's lyrical ability. Rickenbacker guitars to the fore, the Jam released a string of quality singles in '77 - 'All Around The World', 'News Of The World', 'David Watts' (originally by the Kinks), and two LP's, 'In The City' and 'This Is The Modern World'. All these records did commercially well, but it was the tough and taunt, anti-racist forty-five, 'Down At The Tube Station At Midnight', that provided the breakthrough.

This release gave the group their first UK Number One record in

1978, with its companion album 'All Mod Cons' receiving lavish journalistic praise and chart success. For the rest of the decade and into the 1980's the group's star rose. LP's, 'The Eton Rifles' (1979), 'Sound Affects' (1980), and 'The Gift' (1982), sold units in impressive numbers, and the Jam travelled from being a support act to the Damned at the cramped Roxy Club to headlining their own show at the 10,000 seater Earls Court Arena.

Singles 'Start' and 'A Town Called Malice' both reached the No. 1 spots in the UK Top Ten, but no matter how successful the band had become in Britain and the rest of Europe, they just couldn't make a dent in the all important American market. They were just *too* English to translate. In 1983, at the peak of their celebrity and prosperity, Weller made the shock decision to split up the band. Their final single 'Beat Surrender' entered the British charts at Number One.

The Jam, like the Stranglers, were always somehow on the outside of the movement. They rode in on the back of the new wave but in style and attitude were detached. Weller, Foxton and Buckler were never punks, they were too conservative, both politically and stylistically, with no time for anarchist posturing or ripped and torn fashions. They were authentic modern mods with french cropped hair, double-vent suits, skinny 1960's ties and two-tone shoes.

The group's style and music inspired the short-lived mod revival of 1978-79 with Weller playing for a time the 'Capo di tutti capi' of that ill fated and anaemic movement. Still, they were truly great.

When I saw them for the second time in 1977, I remember Foxton had a Union Jack flag draped over his bass amplifier, and on the other side of the Buckler's drum kit, Weller had the words 'FIRE AND SKILL' painted on his. Unlike their Croydon debut, nobody was laughing. Fire And Skill - I can't think of a better epitaph for the Jam.

ONLY ONES: Pretty boy lead singer/guitarist Peter Perrett teamed up with John Perry - lead guitar, Alan Mair - bass and ex-Peter Frampton and Spooky Tooth drummer Mike Kelly in that explosive year of 1976.

Releasing their own single, 'Lovers Of Today', and taking to the clubs to show their wears, they made enough live waves to receive a contract from CBS in 1977. Their first record for the company, the single, 'Another Girl Another Planet', is a rock 'n' roll classic. Wonderful, Lou Reed-esque vocals from Perrett over a driving, guitar-led, pop-punk backing makes this song required listening for those interested in the quality music of this era.

Their self-titled debut album received rave reviews but sales proved sluggish. In the hope of cracking the American market, the Only Ones were dispatched by their label to the USA in 1979, to support the Who on a major North American tour. This was a perfect opportunity for the group to play before vast audiences and to take a giant leap towards supergroup status in the country that had the most important market in the world. They blew it.

On 'Another Girl Another Planet', Perrett sang *"space travel is in my blood"*. Unfortunately, it seems planetary wanderlust wasn't the only thing running around his veins. An insider from CBS at that time told me that they only lasted two gigs on the tour *"'cause they were too messed up to make it to soundchecks and even shows... drugs had become a big problem to them"*.

Yes indeed, drugs had become a problem and despite being given a couple of chances to get it together in the shape of two more LP's, 'Even Serpents Shine' and 'Baby's Got A Gun', both the company's patients and the record sales finally dried up leaving the group label-less.

The self-destruct button was finally pushed by all concerned in 1981. Perry's continuing drug addiction made sure no comeback would be possible. This is a pity though, the Only Ones, with a bit of self discipline and the aid of some common sense could have been real contenders.

THE BOYS: Ex-London SS men, Matt Dangerfield - guitar/vocals and Casino Steel - keyboards/vocals, added Jack Black - drums, Kid Reid - lead vocals/bass and John Plain - lead guitar, to their new musical endeavour in the summer of 1976 and called it The Boys.

Quickly making a name for themselves as a no-nonsense, new wave, rock 'n' roll act while supporting John Cale on a European tour in 1977, they signed to NEMS Records that same year and cut a single with the deliciously cliché punk title of 'I Dont Care'. A self-titled debut album followed, but as with their debut forty-five, nobody was too impressed and journalistic praise was hard to find for these Boys and their records.

Two more LP's were recorded for NEMS, 'Alternative Chartbusters', and 'To Hell With The Boys', before they were dropped by the label to re-emerge with two records, 'The Christmas Album' and 'Boys Only', for indie company Safari. Though making no headway whatsoever in the UK and USA, the Boys never the less built up a considerable following in Scandinavia and a number of European countries where they are able to tour and make a living to this present day.

Entertaining to watch, the Boys were a good-time, club band with limited ambitions. Their sound never made a successful transition from live to record, though I will always be personally grateful to them for writing the song that my own early 1990's rock 'n' roll outfit, Cheap And Nasty, would play as a regular encore track, 'T.C.P'.

THROBBING GRISTLE: Having already caused a scandal with an art exhibition that had included a used sanitary towel, condoms and a selection of vibrators and rubber penises at London's ICA in the mid-1970's, the perpetrators, Genesis P-Orridge - vocals, Cosey Fanni Tutti - guitar, Chris Carter - synthesizer and Peter Christopherson - electronics, turned their beautifully twisted minds to putting a group together.

Calling themselves Throbbing Gristle they mixed performance art with an avant garde noise and controversial subject matter - genitalia, oral sex and masturbation, one song was titled 'Five Knuckle Shuffle' - to shock and entertain. Realising that no record company would release such material, they formed their own label and put out a string of albums that would best be described as difficult listening, some musically challenging, others merely tasteless. The first, 'Second Annual Report', came out in 1977 with 'D.O.A. - The Third And Final Report' (1978), '20 Jazz Funk Greats' (1979), 'Heathen Earth' (1980), 'Funeral In Berlin' (1981), and 'Music From The Death Factory', 'Journey Through The Body' , 'Assume Power Focus', and their final LP, 'Live At The Death Factory' all being released in 1982.

In 1983 Fanni-Tutti and Carter split to sign to Rough Trade Records with whom they released their techno-dance beat compositions under the brand name Chris and Cosey. P-Orrige and Christopherson re-emerged as the slightly more commercial Psychic TV who had a minor hit with the excellent single 'Godstar' in the late-1980's.

Gristle had the hundred percent, shock and confront punk attitude minus the stereotype music. They were not for the squeamish.

CHELSEA and GENERATION X: On dispensing with London SS, bassist Tony James hooked up with Bromley contingent member Billy Idol, then playing guitar, in the summer of 1976.

Responding to a Melody Maker, 'BASS PLAYER AND GUITARIST WANTED', advert together, that same year, they teamed up with vocalist Gene October and drummer John Towe to form Chelsea. Playing identikit punk at a handful of gigs about the capital, the band were well liked by Perry's 'Sniffin' Glue' and were signed to his / Miles Copeland's indie-label, Step Forward, in 1977.

Unhappy with October's dictatorial style, James, Idol and Towe left before the deal was made, and lifting the title from a 1960's paperback book, called themselves Generation X. October recruited London

musicians Carey Fortune - drums, Henry Daze - bass and James Stevenson - guitar, and cut his first record - the sanctimonious and feeble, full employment tirade, 'Right To Work'. This forty-five with its smug, not to mention hypocritical declaration from October that "*I dont take drugs* (oh yeah!) *and I dont drink beer*" - I've spent many an hour propping up a bar with Gene - complete with its punk-by-numbers backing, which annoyed me then, and having just played it again - in the hope it may have improved for nostalgic reasons - annoys me still. The second single 'High Rise Living', and self titled, debut LP weren't much better.

Meanwhile, Generation X had found themselves an ace guitarist in Bob Andrews and had played their first batch of shows which included a headliner at the Central College Of Art And Design, and the opening night of the Roxy Club. Deciding that Towe didn't have the right face to match their pretty boy, glam-punk image, James and Idol sacked the drummer and replaced him with Mark Laff in 1977.

Roxy owner Andy Czezowski picked up the management and with their cool pop-art T-shirts - made for the band by James - dyed spiky hair and wasted good-looks, gained for themselves the negative reputation of being a bunch of posers in some quarters. Still, they had the commercial crossover potential that Chrysalis Records had been looking for, and they were soon in the lower reaches of the UK charts with their debut single 'Ready Steady Go'. Another forty-five 'Your Generation' and a promising self-titled LP followed, full of musical references to glam rockers like T. Rex, Bowie and Sweet - to many it seemed that Gen X were just a traditional rock band in punk clothing.

Chelsea too had realigned their sound from thrash punk to a more familiar rock 'n' roll style. October started to come on like a short haired Mick Jagger, wiggling his arse at shows and releasing rockist records like the 1982 album, 'Evacuate', and the Stones-esque single, 'Rocking Horse'.

Generation X came out of the trad-rock closet earlier than October's Chelsea with their 1979, 'Valley Of The Dolls' LP, and their own up single 'King Rocker' which charted at number eleven in the UK. 1980 saw Andrews and Laff departing to form their own band, Empire, with Idol and James bringing in ex-Clash drummer Terry Chimes and Chelsea guitarist James Stevenson to take their places. Gen X #2 got off to a healthy start in 1981 with a hit single 'Dancing With Myself' and an album that established their new commercial rock credentials. But Idol had been in secret talks with American management interested in acquiring his famed sneer and bleach-blonde barnet for a solo deal

Left: Gene October's Chelsea (1977) / Photograph © Rex Features

and despite the promising start to the new Gen X career he finally decided his future lay in the big country, splitting for New York and leaving behind a bitter James, Chimes and Stevenson. Generation X were dead.

October kept on trying his hand at attaining stardom with an ever changing line-up of Chelsea throughout the 1980's and into the 1990's. His list of LP's include, 'Just For The Record' (1985), 'Rocks Off' (1986), 'Backtrax' (1988), 'Underwraps' and 'Ultra Prophets' (both 1989). You have to admire that kind of resilience.

I was once in a club having a drink with October and a few others when David Bowie walked up to us, looked at Gene and said *"You've got a pretty face October, but a brain like a peanut"*. Gene just smiled then shouted after him *"Bollocks Bowie, I'm gonna be bigger than you"*. Well it seems that it's unfortunately not going to be the case now, though it won't be for the lack of trying on Gene October's part.

ADVERTS: Tim 'TV' Smith - vocals, Gaye Advert - bass, Howard Pickup - guitar and Laurie Driver - drums, came to prominence in 1976 as one of the Roxy Club house bands.

Impressed with Smith's acidic compositions, the Damned invited them to be the support band for their first UK tour, where on viewing the entertaining live show - Gaye, panda eyed, pretty and statue still while TV, covered in badges, cut-out newspaper headlines, and safety pins , twists and cavorts and dances on one leg - Stiff Records took a shine to them and signed them up in time to release a debut forty-five 'One Chord Wonders' in 1977. Their second single outing, the controversial, macabre 'Gary Gilmore's Eyes' brought them both notoriety and a Top Twenty chart position. The media loved them. Gaye was portrayed as a glamourous, punk-sex-kitten, England's answer to America's new wave babe Debbie Harry, and tabloids used her photo whenever possible.

By contrast, Smith earned himself the reputation of being one of the most intelligent lyricist in the British movement. This was fully justified and shown to good effect on their next chart hit, the searing 'No Time To Be 21'. *"The plot sickens!"* sneers TV at the end of the last verse before delivering that 'No Time' passionate, lament of a chorus. Their debut album, 'Crossing The Red Sea With The Adverts' (1978), also contained plenty of cool and clever wordplay though the music was never quite up to the sharpness of the lyrical content.

After the release of the LP, drummer Laurie Driver was replaced by ex-Gen X kit hitter John Towe, but none too happy with his new

Right: The Adverts / Illustration © Adam Cansino

situation, Towe left for pastures new after just a couple of months allowing Rod Later to take up the position on the Adverts' drum-stool. Another album was duly recorded and released, 'Cast Of Thousands' (1979), but there were no takers. Sales had dried up, audiences had dwindled. Smith split to form his own outfit, the TV Smith Explorers, which included my ex-Marionette keyboard playing friend and new wave enthusiast, Mel Wesson.

LONDON: Here today, gone tomorrow bandwagon jumpers of the worst kind, London released two (bad) singles 'Everyone's A Winner' and 'No Time' (both 1977,) before releasing a (badder still) album titled 'Animal Games' in 1978.

All the right gear and poses with none of the passion or ability - you get the picture? Still, drummer Jon Moss would go on to do good in the 1980's with a group called Culture Club featuring Boy George on vocals.

THE MEMBERS: Out of the London suburbs came the Members in the summer of 1977. Consisting of Nicky Tesco - vocals, Jean-Marie Carroll - guitar, Gary Baker - 2nd guitar, Adrian Lillywhite - drums and Chris Payne - bass, this combo had their first recorded composition, 'Fear On The Streets', put on a punk compilation LP, 'Streets', the year of their formation.

This in turn got them a debut single release, 'Solitary Confinement' with Stiff Records, before Virgin grabbed them and provided the where with all for an album - 'At The Chelsea Nightclub' (1979). The LP spawned a hit single, 'Sounds Of The Suburbs' and was quickly followed up by the wisecracking, punk-meets-reggae' forty-five, 'Offshore Banking Business'. Another Virgin LP, 'The Choice Is Yours' was forthcoming before the label dropped them in 1980 whereupon the Members moved to Albion Records, released one more LP, 'Going West' (1983), before heading back to the suburbs for good.

999: Rejecting a series of band names such as the Clash inspired 48 Hours, the Fanatics and the Dials, Nick Cash - vocals, Guy Days - guitar, Jon Watson - bass and Pablo LaBrittain - drums, eventually settled on the UK emergency services telephone number for their collective title.

A single, 'I'm Alive' (1977), on their own label, was their first offering to the movement which brought them to the attention of United Artists. UA released two singles that combined energy with melody, 'Nasty Nasty' and 'Emergency' (both 1978), and a quality record in their first LP, '999'. Their second, 'Separates' (1978), was even better, and the chosen single from the album, 'Homicide' - a wonderfully crafted mid-paced piece of new wave pop with a memorable hook - became a hit for the band in the USA, and a live anthem.

Taking full advantage of this turn of events, the group concentrated their energy on touring America throughout the early 1980's, boosting sales on that side of the Atlantic but also earning them the resentment of their domestic fans. A change of record companies, from UA to Polydor, occurred in 1980 with their third LP, 'The Biggest Prize In Sport', being released on their new label that same year. Despite the two accomplished albums that followed, 'Concrete' (1981) and '13th Floor Madness' (1983), the arrival of a new breed of UK and Irish rock in the form of Simple Minds, the Pretenders and U2, soon eclipsed the American popularity of the 999 boys and saw them rapidly squeezed out of the states-side market. Left at the (American) altar they returned to UK where they took once more to the clubs and pubs in relative obscurity.

LURKERS: Pete Stride, a London (Uxbridge) guitarist with a Ronnie Wood hairstyle and a taste for the new punk rock music on the radio, formed a group in 1977 with fellow Londoners Howard Wall - vocals, Nigel Moore - bass and Esso - drums, in the desire of becoming the English Ramones.

It was a good try. Like that New York foursome, the Lurkers played two minute numbers at breakneck speed and built a decent following in the clubs and pubs for it. Signed to Beggars Banquet, in 1978 they released a string of charmingly naive and basic singles which included two very minor hits in 'Ain't Got A Clue' and 'I Dont Need To Tell Her'.

'Fulham Fallout' (1978) and 'God's Lonely Men' (1979), are their two best known album efforts though Stride did record a well liked solo LP in 1980 featuring John Plain of the Boys, titled 'New Guitars In Town'. When all is said and done, the Lurkers were a straight ahead, unsophisticated and accessible punk rock unit. File under U for Under-rated.

ELVIS COSTELLO: Declan McManus gave up his computer programming day job in 1977, changed his name to Elvis Costello, and took up a life as a singer/songwriter.

A series of major record company rejections saw him eventually finding a home for his compositions with indie-label Stiff. New wave, but never really punk, Costello looked more like an un-reconstructed Buddy Holly than a Johnny Rotten figure, and the sophistication and

depth of his songs on his debut album 'My Aim Is True' (1977), were as far removed from the type of aggressive, speedo-punk material being produced by the likes of the Pistols, the Clash and his label mates the Damned, as could be.

Still, the movement has every right to call him one of their own. His vitriolic, lyrical attacks on racism 'Less Than Zero', hate and war 'Oliver's Army' and specifically the 1982 Falklands war 'Shipbuilding' were easily as effective in hitting their targets couched in his sublime music, as hard punk outfits were in hammering theirs with aggressive noise. Costello's personal attitude was also true to the spirit of 1976. During his first interview for 'NME', he showed the journalist a rusty nail he kept in his pocket and told him he had every intension of using it as a weapon on those *"who are asking for it"*.

'My Aim Is True', produced three superb singles in 'Red Shoes', 'Alison' and the big chart hit, 'Watching The Detectives'. For his second album, 'This Year's Model' (1978), Elvis dispensed with the session musicians and put together his own group, the Attractions. Consisting of Bruce Thomas - bass, Pete Thomas - drums and Steve Nieve - keyboards, the Attractions were to become an essential part of the Costello sound.

Elvis Costello and the Attractions released a host of excellent, big selling singles and LP's throughout the rest of the late 1970's and into the early 1980's: 'Armed Forces' (1979), 'Get Happy' (1980) and 'Trust' (1981), constituted the albums, with the forty-fives including Costello's rage against the new Kings Road fashion victims '(I Dont Want To Go To) Chelsea', the 'Subterranean Homesick Blues' inspired 'Pump It Up' (both 1978), along with 'Accidents Will Happen', 'Oliver's Army' (both 1979) and 'I Can't Stand Up For Falling Down' (1980).

These fine records not only established Costello as one of the best songsmiths in the UK, but also made him a star in the USA where his more traditionally melodic form of new music found a home on American radio far more readily than the radical sounds of other British outfits like the Fall, the Slits and the early Clash.

In 1981 Costello divorced himself from both the Attractions and the new wave, recording a country style LP, 'Almost Blue', in Nashville, Tennessee. The single chosen from the album 'Good Year For The Roses' was a major hit. Back to familiar ground with 'Imperial Bedroom' (1982) and 'Punch The Clock' (1983), Elvis has continued as a solo artist to deliver a series of high quality records throughout the 1980's and into the present decade.

Cynical but always realistic, political but never preachy, Costello

---

Left: His aim was true - Elvis Costello (1979) / Photograph © Rex features

was one of the greatest treasures to be washed ashore by the seminal wave.

BETHNAL: From the sublime to the substandard. George Csapo vocals /keyboards/violin, Nick Michaels - guitar, Everton Williams - bass and Pete Dowling - drums, had been operating for some years as a rock outfit when punk struck in 1976 and they decided it was commercially expedient to pin new colours to their mast.

Signed to Vertigo records in 1977, they released a lukewarm single 'The Fiddler' that same year. A cover of the Animals' 'We Gotta Get Out Of This Place' followed, and an artificial, punky sounding LP 'Dangerous Times' escaped in 1978.

So far, so ordinary. Things really dont get much better with a lacklustre album effort, notable only for the fact that the Who's Pete Townsend was its musical director, titled 'Crash Landing' getting them nowhere in late 1978 with the inevitable heave-ho from the record label occurring the following year. Bethnal finally realised it just wasn't worth the effort any more, picked up their instruments and went home for good in 1980.

LEYTON BUZZARDS: Regulars at the Roxy club from its opening, Geoffrey Deanne - vocals, Dave Monk - guitar, David Jaymes - bass and Kevin Steptoe - drums, abandoned their previous R & B set and replaced it with a new batch of spiky, pop-punk tunes in 1976.

Small Wonder Records released their first single, the entertaining '19 And Mad' in 1977 and the band entered the BBC's Radio One 'Band Of Hope And Glory' talent contest the following year and won the first prize of a contract with major label Chrysalis Records. The first single for their new company 'Saturday Night (Beneath The Plastic Palm Trees)' was a UK hit and got them onto nationwide TV. It proved to be their finest moment.

The Buzzards album, 'Jellied Eels To Record Deals' (1979) didn't capitalise on the success of the single, and by 1980 it was all over for the band, bar the shouting.

ALTERNATIVE TV. Sniffin' Glue's Mark Perry decided not only to promote the movement in the pages of his own fanzine and through the records on his own co-owned labels - Step Forward and Deptford Fun City - but also to take the musical plunge and front his very own combo. Formed in 1977, the first ATV line-up comprised of Perry on vocals, Alex Fergusson - guitar, Mick Smith - bass and John Towe (again!) - drums.

Their debut, a single titled 'Love Lies Limp' was provided free with each copy purchased of a particular edition of 'Glue', and an album, 'The Image Has Cracked', appeared on Perry's 'DFC' label in 1978. Considered somewhat too experimental for most mainstream punk tastes, ATV never the less received substantial critical acclaim, and with an ever changing line-up, released several LP's, taking them into the late 1980's. Worth a listen.

SLITS: Palm Olive - drums, and Viv Albertine - guitar, walked from Sid Vicious' monotonous outfit, the Flowers Of Romance, and with the aid of Ari Up - vocals, and Tessa - bass, put together one of the most confrontational and uncompromising, in-your-face groups to emerge from the scene. Despite having next to no musical ability, the Slits easily made up for this shortcoming with their enthusiasm and the sheer energy of their performances. Unleashed on an unsuspecting world in 1977 as support act to the Clash, they were invited to join the bill for the 'White Riot' UK tour and became an instant hit.

Loved by the punks they may have been, but the record companies that caught their gigs shied away from offering deals, most convinced that there was not an ounce of commercial appeal in this feminist foursome. The departure of Palm Olive and the recruitment of ex-Big In Japan and future Banshee drummer, Budgie, added the solid musical muscle that had been missing from their previous sound, and in 1979 Island Records took a chance on the Slits.

Going for a Jamaican dub influenced first album, to counteract the aggression of the majority of their compositions, they hired Reggae producer Dennis Bovell; the end result was the excellent 'Cut'. Touring and promoting the record filled in the rest of the year. 1980 saw them back in the studio for the laying down of tracks for their second LP, 'Bootleg Retrospective'.

'Return Of The Giant Slits', proved to be the group's swan song with Ari, Viv, Tessa and Budgie going their separate ways in 1981. Always entertaining both live (I saw them perform on several occasions myself and loved them) and on record, the Slits were as fine a punk band as you could wish to spend time with. First class.

IAN DURY AND THE BLOCKHEADS: Starting his musical career as lead singer for pub rock favourites Kilburn and the High Roads in 1970, Ian Dury signed to Stiff Records five years later and found himself caught up in the slipstream of the movement in 1976 with his new band the Blockheads. He was to become a very unlikely British new wave hero.

At the time of the release of the Blockheads critically acclaimed debut album 'New Boots And Panties' (1977) , Dury was in his mid-thirties with greying hair and had a pronounced limp in one leg as a result of a bad bout of polio when he was young. His musicians, Chaz Jankel - guitar, Norman Watt-Roy - bass, Charley Charles - drums, John Turnbull - rhythm guitar and Mick Gallagher - keyboards, had been around the block a few times themselves and their collective knowledge and experience resulted in some superlative music.

'Panties' spent over a year in the UK album charts and as part of a Stiff Records package tour 'Stiffs Live Stiffs', with Elvis Costello, Wreckless Eric, Nick Lowe and Larry Wallis, they ended up stealing the show and earned themselves a UK wide reputation as a class live act. A brilliant Hogarthian lyricist with a fondness for caricatures and a dry delivery, Dury and his Blockheads released the quintessential forty-five of the hedonistic 1970's in 'Sex And Drugs And Rock 'N' Roll' and followed that up with a UK Number One, 'Hit Me With Your Rhythm Stick' (1979).

The follow-on albums, 'Do It Yourself' (1979) and 'Laughter' (1980), were both musically inspired and enjoyable records, but by the start of the 1980's Dury and the Blockheads had got lost in the media coverage for the new romantic movement and the outfits that had successfully captured both the UK and American markets: the Police, Duran Duran, Eurythmics, etc. Dury released two more LP's, 'Lord Upminister' and 'Juke Box Dury' (both 1981), before turning to acting and appearing in numerous plays and films in the late 1980's. He could be seen hosting his own late night talk show ('Metro') on British TV just a year or two ago. Diamond Geezer!

WRECKLESS ERIC: Hard drinking, chaotic, pub rocker Eric Goulden changed his name to Wreckless Eric during the advent of punk and joined the roster of talent at Stiff Records in 1977. Soon overshadowed by his more commercially successful and musically gifted label mates, Elvis Costello and Ian Dury, he never the less released a wonderfully eccentric single, 'Whole Wide World', and gained respect on the 'Stiffs Live Stiffs' tour as a committed performer and a heroic drinker. His self-titled debut album and its follow up, 'The Wonderful World Of Wreckless Eric' (1979), did nothing to change his poor commercial standing, nor to fire the imaginations of the music press and a dwindling cult following. Two more records were released to no avail and Wreckless reverted back to his surname and formed Le Beat Group Electrique in the mid-1980's, with whom he continues to release records to this present day.

Like Costello, and Dury, Wreckless was never punk in the strict definition of the word, but he did emerge from the 1976-77 new wave maelstrom, and he most certainly had his punk moments. Eccentric, shambolic and good fun.

SQUEEZE: As with Wreckless so with Squeeze. Another non-punk outfit that hitched itself to the movement; Squeeze were formed in 1974 by south-east Londoners Chris Difford - guitar/lead vocals, Glenn Tilbrook - guitar/vocal and Jools Holland - keyboards.

First release for the band was an EP on Mark Perry's Deptford Fun City label, 'Packet Of Three' (1977), produced by ex-Velvet Underground bassist John Cale. This led in turn to management from Miles Copeland, a major contract with A & M Records, and two UK Top Twenty hits in 1978 - the infectious 'Take Me I'm Yours' and the ultra melodic 'Goodbye Girl'.

The debut 'Squeeze' LP did OK, but it was their second album that really got them noticed. 'Cool For Cats' (1979) delivered two big forty-five hits, with the title track off the LP and the very English, very poignant, 'Up The Junction', both reaching No. 2 in the UK charts. Cutting their ties to the movement as soon as was expedient (early 1980's), Squeeze took to the USA where they sold records in large quantities and became the first new wave related group to headline and sell out a show at New York's famed Madison Square Garden.

JOE JACKSON: Also fits snugly into this new wave, not punk categorisation. Releasing a string of hit singles with A & M Records starting with 1978's 'Is She Really Going Out With Him', Jackson was also to score chart success with his debut and second LP's 'Look Sharp' and 'I'm The Man' (both 1979). A change of style to a big band swing sound on the 1981 album 'Jumping Jive', saw him spend more and more time in the USA where he continues to reside and release records to varying degrees of success.

X-RAY SPEX: Day-glo, plastic punk group, featuring a female lead singer with braces on her teeth and a voice that could crack a tough lobster wide open at fifty paces, Poly Styrene. The rest of the Spex comprised of Lora Logic - saxophone (a short stay before going on to form her own quirky band, Essential Logic, replaced by Glyn Johns), Paul Dean - bass, Jak Stafford - guitar, and B.P. Hurding - drums.

Their second gig was recorded at the Roxy Club for that establishment's live compilation album with their true debut, the single, 'Oh Bondage Up Yours!' being released on the Virgin label in 1977.

'Identity' and 'Germ Free Adolescence' (both 1978), were mildly entertaining 45 rpm's, most notable for the first extended use of saxophone on punk records, with the LP of that same year, 'Germ Free Adolescence' getting them good media attention with appearances aplenty on UK TV and a generally enthusiastic music press.

Personally I couldn't see what all the fuss was about. Too premeditated and manufactured for my taste, I was not exactly suicidal when Ms. Styrene folded the group in 1979, went back to being called Marion Elliot and swopped her spiritually redundant life as a punk rock songstress for one as a Krishna devotee looking to obtain a higher conscious by chanting and playing finger-cymbals on the Charing Cross Road. The movement's loss was Brahman's gain!

ADAM AND THE ANTS: Stuart Goddard, as bassist for Bazooka Joe, had watched with fascination his support act the Sex Pistols, play their first ever, hate provoking, show at St. Martin's School Of Art and with blinding clarity saw the punk light. Like a new wave St. Paul, he renounced his traditional rock ways, embraced the McLaren/Pistols faith, and changed his name in search of fame.

As Adam Ant, he recruited like minded musicians - constant line up changes were a hallmark of the Ants until he hit the right combination in 1980 with the addition of Marco Pirroni - and with the rubber bound 'SEX' shop assistant Jordan as manager, set about gaining a cult following in the capital city and the south east. A less than satisfying album, 'Dirk Wears White Socks', was released in 1979 and Adam looked set for a short term career as a lower division punk artist.

With the arrival of the 1980's though, a change of musical approach, a restyle and a major label, ensured that the Ants would become one of the most commercially successful acts of the early part of that decade, and Adam an international superstar.

* * * * *

For sure, there are many other first wave, punk and punk-influenced outfits left out of this London List. Some will be dealt with in future chapters, others, I apologise now for their omission. What strikes one the most though with this Capital City Collection, is the great diversity of sound and style of the artists and groups, even though each one was a product of the same mid-1970's, music revolution.

But even at this early stage, two specific categories of musical approach could be detected among those London names:

Category A) comprised those outfits that took their sound directly from the Proto-Punk/Ramones/Sex Pistols school of speedo, hard-edged punk rock - bands like the Clash, Damned, Lurkers, Adverts and the Boys.

Category B) were those with a more distinctly commercial and less abrasive musical formula - Elvis Costello, Ian Dury, Joe Jackson and Squeeze.

At first, the titles 'punk' and 'new wave' were used ad-hock for all who had emerged from the movement. Within a couple of years though, the music industry had imposed the term 'punk' on those they considered too radical and therefore unmarketable (category A), while reserving the 'new wave' tag for those they perceived had that all important commercial, crossover potential (category B).

This distinction was also readily used by the record biz in the USA. For instance, the Ramones, Voidoids and the Heartbreakers were looked upon as having, just 'punk' potential by the American industry, whereas the likes of Blondie, Talking Heads and Patti Smith were awarded the coveted 'new wave' designation.

From the early years onwards, the corporate powers-that-be were determined to separate the commercial cream of the movement from the milk.

Though London initially produced the highest numbers of bands and artists, by 1977 a Northern English metropolis had firmly established itself as the second UK new wave city ...

THE MANCUNIAN CANDIDATES
MANCHESTER'S FIRST WAVE.

By 1977, with the Buzzcocks up and running, Manchester had already contributed one of first and finest punk rock groups to the UK movement. Their success, combined with the early visits of the Sex Pistols and the legendary 'Anarchy In The UK' tour show at the Electric Circus, featuring the Pistols, Clash and Heartbreakers, had motivated a significant portion of the city's musicians and non-musicians alike to put together outfits emulating the new style. As the Manchester scene started to thrive, so more of its bored, restless and thrill-seeking teenage populous became infected by the glorious disease, and before long it had spread through its clubs and pubs to all four corners of the city. Here are some of its first victims.

SLAUGHTER AND THE DOGS: Formed in 1976 and signing to

Manchester's very own indie label, Rabid, that same year, the original Dogs line-up was as follows: Wayne Barrett - vocals, Howard Bates - bass, Mike Rossi - guitar, and Mad Muffet - drums.

As four working-class louts from south Manchester's rough Wythenshawe council estate, the Dogs first incarnation was as a hooligan, three chord, three hundred miles per second outfit in the classic Pistols/Damned mould. By the time they had made the switch to Decca Records in 1977 though, Rossi's love of Mick Ronson (Bowie's guitarist), T. Rex and the Rolling Stones had won out and the group had metamorphosed into a Gen X style, glam-punk combo.

Their debut album, 'Do It Dog Style' (1978), was a classic example of the merging of early 1970's glitter with late 1970's guts. Going down to London to make their presence known to the new wave aristocracy, they became firm favourites at both the Roxy Club and its successor, the Vortex. Problems were afoot though; in 1979 Barrett left the band and took off for France.

Rossi auditioned a number of vocalists - including future Smiths front man Morrissey - rejected them all and took on the singing role himself adding a second guitarist, Billy Duffy, for good measure. Barrett returned to the fold briefly, and a second studio long player surfaced in 1980, 'Bite Back'. However, the reunion soon turned sour, with Barrett once again splitting for pastures new. Rossi devised his own Stones sound-alike outfit, the Monsters, followed by the even more glam tinged Duellists. Billy Duffy founded the neo-punk band Theatre of Hate before finding multi-platinum, hard rock stardom with the Cult.

THE DRONES: Third division band with a short lived career, the Drones consisted of M. J. Drone - vocals/guitar, Steve Cundall - bass, Gus 'Gangrene' Callender - lead guitar, and Pete Perfect - drums.

Formed in 1976, they released their first piece of vinyl, an EP entitled 'Temptations Of A White Collar Worker', the following year on the Ohm indie label. 'Further Temptations' (1977), their debut album released on their own Valer label followed, failed miserably to make an impression and proved to be their last studio LP. They did emerge with some tracks though on that essential document of the Manchester punk scene, 'Short Circuit - Live At The Electric Circus' (1978).

MAGAZINE: After leaving the Buzzcocks in 1977, Howard Devoto put together his own more experimental, angular outfit, Magazine. Backing up Devoto on vocals were John McGeoch - guitar, Martin Jackson - drums, Barry Adamson - bass and Bob Dickinson (later replaced by Dave Formular) - keyboards.

Their first gig together came as surprise guests of the Buzzcocks on the closing night of what had been *the* Mancunian premier punk venue of the 1976-1977 period, the Electric Circus. Three songs were offered up for consumption that night with a more substantial set being presented at their 'official' debut some months later at the city's Rafters Club (late 1977).

Virgin Records snapped them up shortly afterwards and by the new year they had cut and released their first record, the single 'Shot By Both Sides'. The accolades for this superb forty-five came thick and fast with America's 'Rolling Stone' summing up the music press consensus: *"The best rock 'n' roll record of 1978, punk or otherwise"*. The debut album 'Real Life' (1978) also received rave notices, and looking seriously like candidates for greatness, Magazine took to the road to promote their first LP in the UK, Europe and the USA. It burned them out.

Jackson quit the band to be replaced on drums by Paul Spencer, for a tour, and John Doyle on a more permanent basis thereafter. McGeogh split for membership of Siouxsie's Banshees and valuable momentum was lost, Magazine's early promise never to be fulfilled. A replacement guitarist, Robin Simon, was added, but despite the release of four more LP's, 'Secondhand Daylight' (1979), 'The Correct Use Of Soap', 'Play' (both 1980) and 'Magic, Murder And The Weather' (1981), these records and the subsequent tours produced nothing more than diminishing returns.

In 1981 Devoto folded his magazine and began a solo career of little consequence.

THE FALL: Mark E. Smith's lyrical cynicism and deadpan vocal delivery found expression throughout the late 1970's, the 1980's and into the present decade with an ever changing line up in his backing band the Fall. Together they produced a series of surreal, bizarre and vital records and performances starting, vinyl wise, in 1978 with the seven inch, 'Bingo Master's Break-out' and the follow on twelve inch, 'Live At The Witch Trails' (1979) on the Step Forward label.

Signing to Rough Trade in 1980, more discordant and dark music was duly recorded and released for the albums, 'Grotesque' (1980), 'Slates' (1981), 'Hex Enduction Hour' and 'Room To Live' (both 1982), with their live appearances bringing either abject adoration - long mac wearing students loved them - or hatred; I watched them get bottled off stage by leather-clad punk traditionalists when they supported Generation X at London's Lyceum in 1978.

It wasn't just the Fall's uncompromising sound - a sound that owed more to the likes of the Velvets and Suicide than to the Pistols, Clash or Damned - that failed to endear them to mainstream punkdom. Other aspects of their stance also caused offence to the new establishment. Smith's interview technique for instance, seemed to consist of slagging off every other band in the land - he once told the 'NME' that my future band the UK Subs was a moronic version of Black Sabbath! - with the result that there was many a punk rocker looking to lay a set of knuckles into his big mouth.

Still, you couldn't help but secretly admire this skinny, dour looking Mancunian in his dodgy grandad sweater and baggy trousers, berating the punks for their lack of imagination and uniformity - all of which, with hindsight, was perfectly true.

The Fall were never part of the movement. They were, if anything, the radical wing of an anti-movement. They never dressed in punk clichés, never paid homage to the Pistols or the new wave, nor gave a fuck for fashion or fame. Paradoxically, this makes them, for me, the only pure punk outfit that Britain has produced.

JOY DIVISION: Born under a Mancunian moon in 1977, Joy Division emerged from their city's new wave swamp to reach national prominence with a forty-five, the hypnotic 'Transmission', and album, 'Unknown Pleasures' (1979). Comprising of Ian Curtis - vocals, Bernard Albrecht - guitar, Peter Hook - bass and Steve Morris - drums, the band also proved a riveting live phenomena thanks to Curtis' robotic/neurotic dancing and intense stage presence, and achieved a cult following across the UK come the advent of the 1980's.

As with the Fall, university students especially seemed to have an affinity for their cerebral approach and loved them. Tragically, the new decade didn't last long for the sensitive and suffering Ian Curtis. Prone to ill health - he had experienced a number of epileptic fits while on tour and dreaded them - he left a note for his wife: "At this moment I wish I was dead. I just can't cope any more", and hung himself. The posthumous single release, 'Love Will Tear Us Apart' (1980), was a haunting tribute to Curtis' sublime vocal talents and the finest of a series of fine Division musical moments.

Two albums of material featuring Curtis were released by Factory Records, 'Closer' (1980) and 'Still' (1981), the remaining members going on to find considerable artistic and commercial success with the group New Order.

Though London and Manchester were without doubt the two leading punk cities, a number of other British towns and municipalities had thrown up their own contenders during those early movement years.

Liverpool had first wavers BIG IN JAPAN, a band of dismal vinyl output - one self titled single released in 1977 - but with a big reputation due to the success of the follow-on projects of its original line up. Drummer Budgie left B.I.J. to play with both the Slits and Siouxsie and the Banshees, while guitarist Bill Drumond founded Zoo Records and now comprises one half of dance music giants KLF. B.I.J's other guitarist, Ian Broudie, formed the excellent Lightning Seeds, bassist Dave Balfe went on to play with Teardrop Explodes, and singer Holly Johnson found both fame and infamy as front man for Frankie Goes To Hollywood. Other Mersey-punk favourites of the same period include DALEK I LOVE YOU and PINK MILITARY.

Further north, in Newcastle, Pauline Murray had constructed a band in 1977 with the same general approach and sound of the groups she had seen in Manchester that year, and named it after an Iggy Pop album cut, PENETRATION. Further north still, in Edinburgh, Scottish vocalists Fay Fife and Eugene Reynolds put together an overtly plastic pop-cum-punk group in the mould of Blondie, called it the REZILLOS and had a UK Top Twenty hit with their satirical single 'Top Of The Pops'.

One of the most underrated outfits of the British early wave, WIRE, emerged from the west of England to play for, and impress, the Roxy Club crowd, and won a track on that punk institutions live LP, 'The Roxy, London WC2'. Their debut album, 'Pink Flag' (1977) was magnificent, as were their weirdly melodic forty-fives, 'Map Reference' and 'Dot Dash'.

Also from that part of the nation, THE CORTINAS, swopped R & B for high energy punk in 1976 and became Bristol's first new wave band. Signing a contract with Step Forward the following year, they released a single that could be found in any self respecting punks record collection during that era - 'Fascist Dictator'.

Leeds gave us both the GANG OF FOUR - strident new wavers who introduced themselves in 1977 by way of an accomplished EP, 'Damaged Goods'- and THE MEKONS, a naive amateur-hour outfit who, despite their lack of musical ability, have successfully utilised their wry sense of humour and enthusiasm to forge a low key, long term career. Preston and Coventry cooked up THE MEMBRANES - a brash punk outfit, circa 1977, who got to make albums of varying quality in the early 1980's after John Peel put their 'Muscles' EP on his shows play-list - and incubated THE FLYS: 'Bunch Of Five' EP, got the ball rolling in 1977 with two studio albums, 'Waikiki Beach Refugees' (1978) and 'Fly's Own' (1979), to follow.

Swindon's sons, XTC, composed their own quirky, highly polished new wave tunes in 1977 and received blanket press approval for their accessible and enjoyable debut album, 'White Music' (1978). Excellent musicians all, the band have produced both LP's and singles that have consistently charted both in the UK and the USA, and continue to be much admired into the 1990's. Meanwhile, some miles east, that classical seat of learning, Cambridge, had sent (down) to the movement a classic punk rock act in THE USERS (formed in 1976), who would, in turn, spit out two fine Stooges/MC5 inspired forty-fives in 'Sick Of You' (1977) and 'Kicks In Style' (1978), and on relocating to London would recruit a bassist by the name of Alvin Gibbs.

It was not just musicians nationwide who were being influenced by the insistent beat of this new sound. During those formative years a collection of poets had also taken the opportunity to align themselves with the movement and could be found sharing their verse with the spiky set as a warm up act for the likes of the Clash and the Buzzcocks.

Punk poets such as JOHN COOPER-CLARKE, a Mancunian Bob Dylan look-alike who would recite his hilarious word pictures at top speed, imitating the tempo of a super-fast rock band. Fine pieces such as 'I Married A Monster From Outer Space', 'Gimmix', 'Beasley Street' and 'Psycle Sluts'... "... *those nubile nihilists of the North circular the lean leonine leatherette lovelies of the Leeds intersection Luffwaffe angels locked in a pagan paradise - no cash for passion trash...*"

... resulted in Cooper-Clarke netting himself a record deal in 1977. Albums 'Disguise In Love' (1978) and 'Snap Crackle And Bop' (1979) did well but by the time of his 1980 release 'Qu' est La Maison De Fromage', the bottom had started to drop out of the punk poet market and John found the live work drying up.

Track down his autobiographical book of poems 'Ten Years In An Open Necked Shirt' - it's well worth the effort.

Other new wave wordsmiths included ATTILA THE STOCKBROKER - album 'Ranting At The Nation' provided a punky selection of verse and spoken word - SEETHING WELLS, JOOLZ - ranting poets each - and LYDIA LUNCH - New York 'No Wave' beauty who collaborated with West Coast American songstress Exene Cervenka of the superb X, for a book of poems entitled 'Adulterers Anonymous'.

* * * * *

In 1976, the record industry had been caught 'in flagrante' with the punk rock movement. In spite of the Pistols/Grundy/EMI debacle, by 1977 it was proposing marriage. This new wave was proving itself attractive and viable.

The Pistols single, the Clash and Damned LP's, had all sold in surprising quantities. Bands like Blondie, the Buzzcocks, the Jam and Squeeze all had obvious commercial appeal, and even the less radio friendly acts such as Magazine, Patti Smith, Television and the Fall had demonstrated that though this new music hit below the intellect, it still had the capacity for elaborate thought.

For the bands that had neither the potential saleability of a category A outfit nor the desire or savvy to grab the populous by the short hair of their intellects, their power drill, two minute tunes had proved perfect for the limited attention spans of the late Twentieth Century Tee-Vee Generation.

Punk was becoming established and expansionist, confident and ambitious. The question was though, whether a movement forged on the anvil of teenage boredom, frustration and belligerent energy, could sustain its momentum and have a lasting impact on the contemporary music scene, on fashion, the arts and culture.

Back in 1977, that was as easy to predict as reading the wind.

6
NEW LONDON, NEW YORK
SEDITIONARIES AND PSYCHO KILLERS

"Here we come/ Walking down the street/
We get the funniest looks from/ Everyone we meet."
The Monkees 'Theme' (1966).

SEDITION: The inciting of hostility against the
government, likely to cause rebellion or insurrection, but
not amounting to treason.
'New Webster's Dictionary' (1995).

There was both immense enthusiasm and extreme loathing for the
punk movement the year that two sevens clashed. The Devoted and
the Disgusted. During the first part of 1977, enthusiasm and devotion
seemed to have the upper hand.

Punk had been transformed into a powerful, collective endeavour
and was at last being taken seriously by the record industry. Dozens
of new wave bands were signed up by labels in the first six months of
that new year - the encouraging sales figures for the first punk releases
had seen to that - and established promoters were no longer cagey
about giving gigs to the purveyors of the new sounds - there was money
to be made.

Fully confirmed as a devotee by this time, I made my first visit to
the London home of new wave, Andy Czezowski's Roxy Club. The
Roxy was a dump; smelly, cramped and dilapidated, but for me, and
other raw recruits, it was a Palace of possibilities, the pulse of the
movement.

Witnessing the Clash playing their blistering set of politico-anthems
is a vivid memory of my first visit, as is Mick Jones having to tune
Paul Simonon's instrument for him in-between songs as the bassist
hadn't a clue how to do it himself - Simonon would go on to be a very
fine bass players.

On my second trip to that glorious Covent Garden toilet to see the
rable rousing Damned, a rumour circulated the club that Robert Plant
and Jimmy Page, singer and guitarist of dinosaur heavy rock outfit

Led Zeppelin, had tried to get in but had been told to *"fuck off"* at the door. I have never been able to find out if this particular piece of Roxy gossip was true or just wishful thinking, but either way, that night, we were ecstatic at the thought of two of the rich, rock establishment being turned away so unceremoniously from our territory.

The new order was being established and the old guard were being ejected and put in their place - we were in charge now!

Another abiding memory of my visits to the Roxy is, despite the club being the UK's premier punk rock establishment, that very little new wave music was actually played by the DJ between band sets. It was mostly reggae music that boomed out of its shabby PA.

'Acme Attractions' store assistant Don Letts had been put in charge of the club turntables by Czezowski, and being a black Rasta with a love of Jamaican music, made sure most of the vinyl played was to his liking. As a consequence punks were exposed to reggae nightly and a kind of solidarity and affinity grew between the two genres. Letts gave his perspective at an interview conducted at the club in 1977...

DON LETTS: *"Like, to me, the reggae thing and the punk thing ... it's the same fucking thing. Just the black version and the white version. The kids are singing about change, they wanna do away with the establishment. Same thing the niggers are talkin' about, "Chant down Babylon", it's the same thing. Our Babylon is your establishment, same fucking thing. If we beat it, then you beat it."*

This unity of purpose gave rise to a new breed of British based Reggae outfits who profited by the association. Bands like Steel Pulse, Black Slate and Aswad found acceptance among the young and eager punk rockers and soon a punk act sharing the bill with a reggae group (and vice versa) became a regular feature of the scene. This alliance was eventually given the less than imaginative title of 'Jah Punk' by the UK music press.

The Clash drew praise from Jamaican musicians for their debut album version of Junior Murvin's 'Police And Thieves', and in return Mick Jones and Joe Strummer visited the Caribbean island to pay homage to the music of Rastafari and seek inspiration for a new record. This punk/reggae admiration scenario reached an impressive climax with the release of the single 'Jamming' in the summer of 1977.

Written and recorded by the legendary Bob Marley and the Wailers, the B-side was a dedication to the movement entitled 'Punky Reggae Party'. Opening with a *"New Wave, New Braves!"* exultation, the great reggae songsmith invited all punks to a joint celebration of mutual aims, reassuring us that *"The Wailers will be there, the Damned, the Jam,* the Clash" and "It's a punky reggae party it's gonna be alright." Punk was making friends in unexpected places.

As well as the Roxy, there was plenty of action to be found elsewhere around the city in 1977. I saw the Stranglers, Generation X, the Adverts and Siouxsie and the Banshees at my local Croydon Greyhound venue (now confirmed as a new wave club) and caught shows at the Marquee, the 100 Club and the Nashville Rooms.

In the winter of that year I also made my first stab at joining a punk band. Spotting a 'NEW WAVE BASS PLAYER WANTED' advert in the back pages of 'Melody Maker' - the only place to find a decent gig in the UK in the 1970's - I telephoned the given number and made arrangements for an audition.

The tryout was at a rehearsal studio in north London, a foul smelling and squalid little room with two amps and a drum kit set-up in a corner. One of the group greeted me as I stepped into this appropriately fetid environment (this was punk rock after all!) and I immediately recognised him as the ex-drummer of Generation X, John Towe.

Towe told me that his band was called the Rage, an outfit of his own creation, with a UK tour booked as support act to the Adverts and a small weekly wage available for the successful bassist candidate. It sounded the perfect start to a punk career, and as I pulled my bass guitar out of its case I determined to make a good impression.

The drummer got behind his kit, and a spiky haired guitarist with dyed eyebrows that gave him the appearance of a punky Groucho Marx, whipped-up a super-fast, MC5-ish riff and nodded for me to follow along as best I could. Towe joined in with a crash of his cymbals, and we sped through three or four numbers, 'till satisfied that he had got a grasp of my bassist abilities, the skin beater called time.

"Well you can play alright" he said.

"Thanks" I replied, and enquired "What's the prognosis?"

"Good. You're one of the best we've seen - you wouldn't believe the amount of Bozos we've had down here who didn't know one end of their bass from the other."

Ah, but I could very well believe it. Though punk righteously had little concern for advance technique and indulgent musicianship, this attitude had unfortunately been misconstrued by posers and the terminally talentless as an excuse to forego all the basic principles involved in learning an instrument. Some seemed to believe that a cool, 'SEX' bought look, and affected angry image should suffice.

On my way out I ran into another hopeful on his way in, dressed in a black vinyl bin-liner for a shirt, ripped bondage strides and safety-pin earrings carrying a battered cheap bass.

"Another Bozo" I thought.

I didn't get the gig with the Rage and it was just as well; half way through their tour with the Averts, Towe left his own band to play drums with the headliners, staying with them a couple of months before joining Mark Perry's Alternative TV. It wasn't to be the last time I would run into this drummer though. Two years later we would work together as the rhythm section for a touring/recording outfit with the Damned guitarist, Brian James.

During that time together I reminded him of the Rage audition.

"Now I remember" he said. *"Yeah, that's right you did good and we had you pegged as the man for the job."*

"So what happened" I asked.

"Well, just after you left a bloke in a bin-liner with a God-awful guitar turned up and though you were a better player, we figured he had a great punk image and gave him the gig."

"No way!" I said.

"Honest" he replied... *"Straight up!"*

* * * * *

Both Elvis Presley and Marc Bolan took their leave of this mortal coil in 1977. One, through prolonged and self-inflicted body abuse, the other in an instant, the victim of a car crash on an empty road - just like one of his heroes, James Dean. Their deaths symbolised the end of two rock 'n' roll eras; the pioneering rockabilly 1950's, and its weird and effeminate nephew, the glam rock of the early 1970's. The King was dead, and his corkscrewed poet-laureate had gone and joined him. We looked expectantly towards a new kind of monarchy.

The Sex Pistols had become a social phenomenon. They were at once admired, despised, ridiculed and feared, and had become the subject matter for a million opinions from a million and one cultural theorists. For good or bad, they were happening.

McLaren and Westwood were excited at their progress and determined to take full advantage of the notoriety. They decided a name change was again required for 430 Kings Road to mark this new, (so far) successful phase in their anti-establishment, anti-apathy war. 'SEX' was out, 'Seditionaries' was in.

REVOLTING!
SEDITIONARIES, SEX PISTOLS, A & M AND VIRGIN.

Whereas 'SEX' had been Sartorially Sleazy, McLaren and Westwood determined that Seditionaries would be high-tech and highly controversial. The new interior had a Spartan feel, with grey carpet, fluorescent lights, frosted windows and futuristic furniture, combined with blown up photographs of the smouldering remains of the German city of Dresden just after it had been bombed by the allies during the second World War.

A new range of Westwood designs were also unveiled. Pornographic T-shirts showing two cowboys with their dicks hanging out, and a black athlete with an unfeasibly large sexual organ. A tartan trousers and kilt ensemble covered in straps with matching footwear,...

VIVIENNE WESTWOOD: *"All those straps made you feel very wild. You felt like a highlander, very savage. When I did punk, I also think it was the most elegant thing. The boots with straps and everything."*

... a canvas jacket covered in zips, clips and straps, and the 'piece de resistance' of the collection - a beautiful garment made of muslin with ultra-long sleeves that hung past the fingers with a swastika and an upside down crucifix printed on the chest with the command 'DESTROY' emblazoned over them.

This piece of clothing which came to be known as the 'Destroy' shirt, embodied the whole movement. It was radical, daring and deliberately offensive - the upturned cross offended Christians and Conservatives, the swastika gave offence to Jews and Liberals. Pure Punk.

All of the new Seditionaries range featured a label that bore the Anarchy symbol (a capital A inside a black circle), and the legend *"For Soldiers, Prostitutes, Dykes and Punks"*.

The reconstructed store and these audacious designs were a testament to McLaren's and Westwood's optimism and their belief that punk had made a breakthrough, their movement now vital and strong enough to take on all taboos with impunity. But this was to be proved a false assumption - the establishment was about to strike back.

Even while the Sex Pistols had been on the road promoting their first record for the company on the ill fated 'Anarchy' tour, EMI's chairman, Sir John Read, had told reporters that it was possible the group's contract could be terminated. When this was relayed to one of the Pistols by a press hack the reported response was *"Tell him to go fuck himself!"* This of course only added to the pressure to drop the band.

The EMI press department was ordered to stop giving out information on the group, and the anti-Pistols noises coming from the record company board of directors reached a new crisis level. To

McLaren, with his visceral hatred and distrust of the music establishment, this had all the hallmarks of a plot to drop the group. He became convinced it was no longer a matter of if EMI dropped the band but when, and started making discreet telephone calls to other major labels with a new deal in mind.

Early in 1977 the Pistols took a trip to play three shows in the land of good Grass and Gouda, Holland. The dirt dishing British newspapers made sure there was another Sex Pistols outrage to share with their readership.

Claiming an air stewardess - who was not named - had told a reporter that the group and their entourage had vomited and spat at each other during the flight to Amsterdam, the 'London Evening News' ran a front page exclusive on the incident under the headline: 'REVOLTING!'. The story was immediately picked up by the rest of the tabloids, and once again a perfect opportunity had been provided for the voices of reaction to be raised in unison.

Tory MP Robert Adley wrote to EMI complaining that *"Your company is financing a bunch of ill-mannered louts who seem to cause offence wherever they go. Surely you could forgo the dubious privilege of sponsoring trash like the Sex Pistols."* The fact that the story was fraudulent and purely the invention of an unscrupulous tabloid journalist seemed to be of no consequence, EMI had their excuse and acted on it.

On the Pistols return to the UK on the 8th of January 1977 the band were formally dropped by the record label.

Despite his public protestations, McLaren was privately pleased. The Pistols and more importantly his company Glitterbest, had got to keep all of the record advance despite having delivered only one single, and two of the labels he had secretly been talking to, Polydor and A & M, were now offering other big advances for their services. The Great Rock 'N' Roll Swindle was about to be enacted.

That EMI split was not the only divorce in the air in the Sex Pistols camp. Johnny Rotten decided he could no longer work with Glen Matlock. Rotten had always considered the bassist too squeaky clean for the Pistols, and too musically adept and accommodating - he had even made friends with other punk musicians for Chrissakes! - and besides, he wanted his mate Sid Vicious in the group.

A *"sack Matlock"* campaign was instigated by the singer to which the bassist put up but a token resistance. Rotten's behind the scenes manoeuvres eventually got the tentative support of McLaren, Jones and Cook, and Matlock's fate was sealed - he received a £3000 pay-off and immediately started work on recruiting musicians for a group of his own.

McLaren's assistant and group tour manager Nils Stevenson was forced out of the Pistols/Glitterbest orbit at the same time. Malcolm, now firmly in control of all facets of the band's career, had come to regard Nils as an unnecessary addition to the payroll. He was offered a pay-off one tenth the size of Matlock's, and took it without argument; he desperately needed the £300, he was broke.

Vicious was in, Matlock and Stevenson out - the Sex Pistols saga entered a new and eventful phase.

On the 13th of February 1977, Sid Vicious performed his first duty as a Sex Pistol, a telephone interview with a Los Angeles radio station, while McLaren, having rejected the overtures of Polydor, CBS and Virgin, came to terms with A & M Records; a two year deal with a guaranteed advance of £75,000 per-annum.

In March, a limo containing all four Pistols and their manager glided to a halt at the central traffic island outside the London home of H. R. H. Queen Elizabeth the second, Buckingham Palace. A group of press photographers awaited them along with representatives of A & M who had set up a small table bearing a contract to be signed.

Snappers snapped, the Pistols signed, and Vicious obligingly stuck up two fingers in the direction of the royal residence before departing with the rest of the band for a press conference at a top London hotel. There, the foursome consumed large amounts of beer and vodka, and having given the press what they'd come for - sarcasm and insults - headed over to Wessex Studios to finish up some tracks they had been recording for the new label.

However, nothing but chaos was achieved that afternoon at Wessex. An alcohol induced fist fight between Rotten and Cook broke out within an hour of their arrival, during which the drummer, coming off the worse, sustained a blooded nose. The producer of the sessions, Chris Thomas, made a hasty exit leaving Jones to break up the fisticuffs just before the limo reappeared to take the band out once again to an A & M promotions meeting at the company's headquarters.

Somewhere on that ride, Vicious lost his shoes and badly cut his foot. The Pistols arrived at their new label's office building blooded, boozed-up and looking for trouble. They demanded more beer and wine which they drank down in extensive quantities, with Sid eventually being so drunk that he collapsed in a heap, unconscious, onto a promotions executive's desk. Rotten worked at reviving him by throwing wine in his face, and finally responding to this unorthodox first aid technique, the Pistols new bassist got up, staggered into another room and screamed at the female typist he found there *"My foot's bleeding, can you find a fucking plaster for me, you bitch!"* For an encore he smashed up the A & M gents toilets and took a shit in one of the office out-trays.

Not to be upstaged, Jones crashed into the ladies toilets, manhandling and making indecent suggestions to two women he found there. The women fled from the bathroom at top speed and alerted senior members of staff to the horrors that had befallen them. A & M director Derek Green immediately cancelled the meeting and ordered the band off the premises.

Now on a roll, they took cabs - the limo driver refused to take them - to a West End pub to continue their serious drinking, and at closing time made for the Speakeasy Club along with a bunch of punk friends they had run into. The Speakeasy had been a favourite hang-out for rock musicians, roadies and the music biz for some time; an 'old school' rock establishment, full of long haired, flared jean types, sipping on tequila sunrise and such.

That night, the personification of that 'old school' was present in the shape of the soft spoken, BBC TV 'Old Grey Whistle Test' presenter and DJ, Bob Harris. It was Harris who had dismissed the New York Dolls on his show as "Mock Rock" after their spine-jolting TV performance, and had shown disdain for the music being made by their punk rock off-spring. With Harris and the boozed-up Pistols in the same room, it was inevitable that trouble was afoot.

BOB HARRIS: *"I was in the Speakeasy that night with my friend George Nicholson. The Pistols had apparently caused mayhem at A & M and were continuing the celebrations when they ran into us. In their minds, I was the epitome of everything they hated. Jah Wobble (a friend of Vicious and Rotten) was with them and he asked me when the Pistols would be on Whistle Test. I said it wasn't something I wanted to discuss, and he took a swing at me. All hell broke loose. Sid Vicious slashed George on the head and wrist with a broken bottle. I was knocked to the floor and my back was cut. I found myself backed up against a wall with these guys coming towards me. I started trying to reason with them but, fortunately, about six guys stepped in between us, and we got out. I took George to Charing Cross Hospital in Hammersmith. He needed fourteen stitches."*

Though Harris and his friend may have had their night ruined by this incident, to Vicious and his mates the blood-letting was a perfect end to a perfect day. Just before lapsing into unconsciousness at Steve Jones' flat, Sid declared *"I've had the greatest time of my life. This is my first day and as far as I'm concerned it's great being in the Sex Pistols!"*

Back at A & M though, Derek Green was far from happy at the reports of this new Pistols atrocity. Harris was a good friend of Greens, and the record executive was naturally appalled that his buddy had been treated in this way by one of his own groups. The realisation dawned that he had signed an outfit with a genuine talent for mayhem and random violence.

Other rock bands he had dealt with had certainly used aggressive imagery and cultivated exaggerated hard men personas, but not wanting to bite the hand that fed them, they had generally acted with deference and some respect to the record company and wider music biz. The Sex Pistols though were something else. They truly didn't give a shit - they were dangerous.

The more Green thought about the wrecking of the A& M offices, the abuse, Harris' violent run-in with the group, the more he convinced himself he couldn't work with these people and they had to be dropped from the label. He received the full support of Herb Albert and Jerry Moss (Albert is the 'A', Moss the 'M' in A & M), for his decision to terminate the relationship and contacting McLaren later that day, told him the grim news.

One week after signing to A & M Records, and another £75,000 richer, the Sex Pistols were once again label-less, footloose and fancy free.

During their brief liaison with A & M, it had not been all alcoholic and aggressive action for the band, they had written and recorded a new single.

'God Save The Queen' was an anti-royalist anthem designed to cause maximum offence and outrage during the Queen's Silver Jubilee (twenty five years as the reigning monarch) celebrations; a glorious tirade against pomp, privilege and Britain's persisting imperial delusions. The opening lines to the song set the tone...

"God save the queen/And the fascist regime
It made you a moron/A potential H-bomb
God save the queen/She's not a human being
There is no future/In England's dreaming."

... over multi-tracked guitars and a powerful rhythm section.

A & M had already pressed up 25,000 copies of the record, and after jettisoning the group had no choice but to destroy and recycle the bulk of this treasonable vinyl. Those few copies that did survive immediately became expensive collectors items and are worth a small fortune today.

Though McLaren was genuinely surprised and shocked at Green's decision to axe the band, he quickly turned the circumstances round to his image advantage. Claiming the chaos and aggression of that week had been premeditated, a series of manoeuvres to force the company to drop the Pistols after a considerable cash injection, McLaren's Svengali-esque reputation was considerably enhanced. This Glitterbest spin on things was readily accepted by many in the media, and the myth of the rock 'n' roll swindle was established.

To show the world that the Pistols and what they represented were bigger and more important than either EMI or A & M, McLaren had them play a gig at London's Notre Dame Hall just after the A & M bombshell had exploded. It was Vicious' debut, and it was sold out. Having already made £125,000 from the EMI/A & M deals, Malcolm then got down to the more important business of working on adding to that sum by obtaining yet another advance from yet another record label.

It would be fair to say that from this point on McLaren saw the Pistols no longer as prophets, but as profits.

Polydor and CBS were approached - Polydor were uncertain with CBS being interested only if the band would sign for no advance. Other major labels made positive noises, but it was Virgin Records that were pushing the hardest.

McLaren didn't want to do business with the self-made millionaire Richard Branson and his company. After all, the Virgin label had been built on the mega-sales of the ultimate hippie-dippie, progressive rock album 'Tubular Bells', by a long haired and bearded muzo, Mike Oldfield. This was hardly the record company image the manager had in mind for his hippie hating, big, bad, punk monarchs, the Sex Pistols. Following rejections from five preferred labels, McLaren put aside his anti-Branson/Virgin prejudice and reached an agreement with the company. Branson for his part saw the acquisition of the Pistols as an opportunity to change for good the woolly, counter-culture image of his label. On the 12th of May 1977 contracts were signed for an advance payment to Glitterbest of £65,000. Manager and group were back in business.

Virgin concurred with McLaren that 'God Save The Queen' should be the first record release, and Jamie Reid was invited by the label to pitch some sleeve designs - Reid came up with the ultimate punk rock record cover.

Reproducing an official Cecil Beaton photograph of the Queen in blue and silver, the artist simply tore two strips out of the portrait where the reigning monarchs eyes and mouth should have been, and replaced them with the song title and the name of the group in his trademark ransom note lettering. He also produced an advertising poster with the same photo, sans the ripped out eyes and mouth, with one small addition - a safety pin could be seen sticking through Her Majesty's top lip. The effect was both shocking and compelling.

The single was released at the end of May, and as McLaren had intended, it did indeed give rise to lashings of hate, fear and loathing in the UK.

A TV advert for the forty-five was banned by the commercial station, and the airing of the record on British radio was confined to two consecutive plays on the late night John Peel show. Once again, packers of a Sex Pistols record threatened to go on strike rather than handle their product, and a host of record shops and chain stores refused to stock 'God Save The Queen'.

Even so, the UK music press recognised its quality and importance, with 'Melody Maker', 'NME', 'Sounds' and 'Record Mirror' giving it single of the week status, and the punk faithful flocking to those stores that did sell the record to buy in excess of 150,000 copies in seven days.

To counter the 'God Save The Queen' advertising embargo on the TV, radio and non-music press, McLaren decided to hire a boat, the appropriately named 'Queen Elizabeth', with a view to manufacturing some publicity. The idea was to have the Pistols play live as the craft made its way up and down the river Thames with an invited crew of punk faces, journalists and media types on board.

The 'Queen Elizabeth' set off from Charing Cross Pier on the evening of the 7th of June 1977, and as the famous silhouette of the Houses of Parliament came into view, the Sex Pistols took their places on the foredeck's makeshift stage and tore into a sulphate and hate inspired rendition of 'Anarchy In The UK'. Rotten was at his angry best; taunting, confronting, sarcastic and mesmerizing. The band played as if possessed while the assembled crowd stood and stared and understood that this was rock music at its most urgent and finest.

JORDAN: *"Rotten was in a terrible mood. Here was this anarchist group, the Sex Pistols, with people like Richard Branson on the boat that he didn't think should be there. In the end, he was furious: he just got to the limit."*

As this riveting performance continued, police launches activated by the sound of loud guitars on the river and by a tip off from the panicking owner of the craft, started to slowly encircle the hired boat. Loud hailers suddenly conveyed instructions from the river police for the 'Elizabeth' to return to the pier and for the music to cease. The Pistols, guests and captain under orders from McLaren, pointedly refused to obey the officer's commands, and as the band powered into 'No Fun', the forces of law and order cut off the vessels progress with their more mobile launches, compelling the good ship anarchy to dock back at its starting point.

Waiting for them on the jetty of Charing Cross Pier was a wall of blue uniforms. The boat party refused to emerge, and though the captain had turned off the power supply, Rotten continued to sing the words to 'No Fun' over Paul Cooks drum pattern. After thirty minutes the police started to physically remove and manhandle guests from the boat, and some started to fight back. McLaren called the police *"Fucking fascist bastards"* and was dragged by four burly officers into a police van where he received a good kicking for his troubles. All hell broke loose.

People were yanked down the gangplank by their hair and brutalised. Westwood was arrested along with Jamie Reid, and both suffered the same fate as McLaren at the hands of the police in the back of one of their windowless vehicles.

JAMIE REID: *"It was really vicious in the police van. Near my feet, on the floor, people were being sadistically kicked by these burly policemen who obviously got a perverted pleasure out of it. Very macho."*

Some of the guests and band made a run for it. A few were caught and roughed up a little, others were arrested and taken to Bow Street Police Station to spend an uncomfortable night in the cells, while a couple made good their escape. Whether by accident or design, the Sex Pistols were yet again front page news.

*   *   *   *   *

It's hard to imagine now in this new era of royal scandals, scams and dissatisfaction, just how incendiary and reviled 'God Save The Queen' was in that jubilee summer of 1977. Britain was in the grip of an ugly monarchist hysteria; only forelock tugging, servile, loyal discourse was acceptable, anything else was treasonable, even evil, and had to be gagged.

The Pistols single of course represented the antithesis of this uncritical, unthinking mood in the country. It was the *"wake up"* call for the spellbound millions, realism in the face of fantasy - an accusing finger pointing at an institution and a country that had lost their bearings and were suffering from severe delusions of grandeur. It was the anthem of the anti-jubilee minority - of those who refused to join in the mad parade.

The price paid for being in opposition was high. Though 'God Save

The Queen' sold over 200,000 copies - more than enough to make it the number one record in the UK charts in jubilee week - those who compiled the charts (the British Market Research Bureau), made sure that the single stayed at number two. Rod Stewart's 'First Cut Is The Deepest' was allowed to remain in the premiere position.

More seriously, on the streets of Britain it was now open season for punk bashing. The Teddy boys - xenophobic, intolerant and ultraconservative - saw the Pistols single as a direct attack on their revered Queen and country and declared war on the band and their followers.

CAPTAIN SENSIBLE: *"Britain's full of rednecks. The country is full of very conservative people frightened by anything that is remotely different. I got my teeth beaten down my neck in Croydon High Street... it was most unpleasant."*

I myself got jumped and beaten up by five stocky Teds in Croydon's Surrey Street Market that summer, but at least only feet and fists were used, some were not so lucky.

Rotten received several bad cuts from an assailant's flick knife and a teenage punk travelling home on the top deck of a London bus died from stab wounds he sustained from some moronic and brutal Ted vigilante's blade. Both Paul Cook and Jamie Reid got badly beaten that year, and hundred of punks up and down the country shared their experience as the tabloid press condoned and inflamed the anti-punk backlash: *'PUNISH THE PUNKS'* ran a memorable headline in the big circulation 'Daily Mirror'.

These Ted/punk wars would continue well into the 1980's and caught on in other nations where the two youth tribes existed. It resulted in many casualties and reached a point where those involved didn't even know what they were fighting about - it was mindless.

The optimism that had existed for the survival, effect and expansion of the movement at the start of 1977 evaporated as these random acts of violence and the media/establishment backlash accelerated towards the end of that year.

'God Save The Queen' had lit the bonfires of ignorance, prejudice and hatred in Britain, it provoked a reaction in the country like no other rock record before or since. It was British punk's finest moment and I was fiercely proud of it. I still am.

MALCOLM McLAREN: *"'God Save The Queen' was the most English, angst ridden, toughest, motherfucking rock song that has ever been written... no question!"*

Over in the USA, the emergence of the new wave had seen nowhere near the resistance and hostility that the UK version had aroused. There was no equivalent of the Sex Pistols/Grundy outrage on American TV screens to activate that country's (so called) moral majority. No 'shock, horror' tabloid newspaper revelations or Sid Vicious clones opening up journalist skulls - nothing to catapult punk into the mainstream consciousness of the Land of the Free and the Brave.

Most of those who had been exposed to the new music assumed it was of British origin, having read of the strange and terrible events surrounding those weird looking Limey's the Sex Pistols, the Clash and the Damned in 'Rolling Stone' or the super-straight 'Time' magazine. In the minds of the majority of the American public, punks, punk rock and punk fashion was synonymous with London, the Sex Pistols and the Union Jack.

Though Yankee punk had certainly not had the sensational media coverage that its UK cousin had received, it nevertheless continued to grow and evolve at a slow and steady pace. While New York's CBGB's had nurtured new wave careers, the industrial cities of Cleveland and Akron had both given birth to a fistful of bands that were not so far removed from the new approach and sound of the Big Apple groups.

Cleveland's new scene revolved around that city's very own equivalent to CBGB's, a club for unsigned, underground acts called the Viking Saloon. During the mid-1970's, the Saloon turned over its stage to three hard driving rock 'n' roll outfits with snotty and loud intentions: Rocket from the Tombs, the Electric Eels and the Mirrors. All three memorably shared the bill together at a 'Special Extermination Night' showcase at the club in 1974, and together, all three would integrate and sonically reduce into two outstanding bands...

PERE UBU: From the pool of musicians that made-up the personnel of Rockets, Eels and Mirrors came the experimental and influential outfit Pere Ubu. Formed by ex-Tombs guitarist Peter Laughner after that band's demise in 1975, Ubu's initial line up also featured David Thomas - vocals, Tom Herman - keyboards, Tim Wright - bass, Allen Ravenstine - synthesizer/sax and Scott Krauss - drums.

Making their debut at the Viking Saloon on new years eve 1975/ 1976, they submitted two of their most well received titles for single record releases - the haunting '30 Seconds Over Tokyo' and 'Final Solution'. Calling on the influences of Captain Beefheart, Frank Zappa and Roxy Music, Ubu followed up with the release of two further forty-fives, 'Street Waves' and 'The Modern Dance' and an album - also titled 'The Modern Dance' (1977) - becoming the first Cleveland new wave group to play both Max's Kansas City and CBGB's.

The LP's 'Dub Housing' (1978), and 'Datapanik In The Year Zero' (1979) followed, winning critical acclaim for their distinctive compositions and artistic invention. Though attaining a substantial following and gaining the adoration of the critics, Ubu failed to achieve strong sales and by their 1982 album release 'Song Of The Bailing Man' the frustrations and anxiety at the lack of progress of the band began to tell.

Kraus left the line-up, and Thomas split to make a solo LP, 'The Sound Of The Sand', leaving the remaining members to search out new projects. In 1987, Pere Ubu reformed to play a reunion concert in Cleveland, their intuitive and artistic approach having already influenced and entertained for over a decade.

THE DEAD BOYS: Whereas Pere Ubu had the reputation of being both cerebral and artistic in their 'modus operandi', Cleveland's own Dead Boys were more a case of combustible and autistic in theirs! The brainchild of ex-Rocket from the Tombs and Electric Eels members Stiv Bators - vocals, and Cheetah Chrome - guitar, the Dead Boys also comprised Johnny Blitz - drums, Jimmy Zero - rhythm guitar and Jeff Magnum - bass. Having played a handful of shows as Frankenstein in and around Ohio, the band made a name change sure to offend, and resettled in New York City in 1976 quickly becoming firm support-slot favourites at Hilly's CBGBs.

Signing to the Ramones record label Sire in 1977, the Dead Boys released their aptly titled debut LP 'Young Loud And Snotty' that same year which featured 'Sonic Reducer', an album cut that was recognised as a classic punk rock anthem on both sides of the Atlantic. Soon after their first record release, Stiv and his deceased compatriots teamed up with the UK outfit that had the most similarity to their snarling sound for a double bill at CBGBs, the Damned.

A friendship was formed between Bators and Damned guitarist Brian James that night, that would pay musical dividends in the future. But before the Dead Boys' demise and Bators' departure in 1980, the band managed one further LP with 'We Have Come For Your Children'; a fine testament to the DB's brand of Stooges-esque, good time, punk.

In another part of the state of Ohio, the town of Akron had also fathered some interesting new music and performers in the early to mid 1970's. Most of these outfits, like the Bizarros, had self-destructed by 1977, but one band persevered and made a great contribution to the art-school, angular wing of the American movement.

DEVO: Originally formed in 1972, Mark Mothersbaugh - vocals / keyboards, Bob Mothersbaugh - guitar, Jerry Casale - bass, Alan Myers - drums and Bob Casale - 2nd guitar, shortened their group name from De-evolution in the mid-1970's and made a world wide impact with their debut single 'Jocko Homo'.

The surreal and gripping video that accompanied this release earned them a reputation as one of the first truly multimedia new wave acts, with their marketing and visual side playing a primary part in their success. 'Come Back Jonee', their second forty-five, had an equally David Lynch-esque promotional video and as with their debut proved a minor USA and UK hit. Two relatively successful albums followed, 'Q: Are We Not Men? A: We Are Devo!' (1978), and 'Duty Now For The Future' (1979), plus their biggest selling single release, a quirky and inspired reworking of the Rolling Stones classic '(I Cant Get No) Satisfaction'.

The LP's 'Freedom Of Choice' (1980) and 'New Traditionals' (1981) saw the arrival of a more synthesiser orientated dance sound though their visual output continued its experimental tradition; the video for 'Freedom Of Choice' featured dancing chocolate donuts and the band sporting plastic flowerpots for hats. Their mid-1980's single 'Whip It Up' sold over a million copies worldwide and the Akron eccentrics continued to release records and entertain audiences up to their dissolution at the end of the 1980's.

Though other cities across the USA were slowly spawning a new generation of music, New York was still, nevertheless, the undoubted Yankee-punk capital. The Big Apple was the place to go to when kick-starting a new wave profession and CBGB's and Max's were still the country's leading venues.

These clubs, Hilly's in particular, had continued to launch the careers of a mixed bag of new outfits, some New York born and bred, others out-of-towners...

THE DICTATORS: Formed in the early 1970's in Detroit, the Dictators - 'Handsome' Dick Manitoba - vocals, Scott 'Top Ten' Kempner and Ross 'The Boss' Funichello - guitars, Andy Shernoff - bass and Stu 'Boy' King - drums - moved to NY in 1974 and sadly got overlooked at the onset of American music revolution in favour of outfits like the Ramones and Television, even though their fast and furious sound had all the hallmarks of the genre.

Releasing a debut album on Epic Records in 1975, 'The Dictators Go Girl Crazy', featuring such entertaining tracks as '(I Live For) Cars And Girls' and 'Teengenerate', the band were unceremoniously dropped by the label soon after and found themselves in the rock wilderness for two years. Elektra picked them up and funded their second and third LP's 'Manifest Destiny' (1977) and 'Bloodbrothers' (1978), and likewise dropped them when neither of these two records managed to sell in reasonable quantities.

Disbanding in 1979 they would reform on and off throughout the 1980's, releasing a live cassette album 'Fuck 'Em If They Can't Take A Joke', before going their separate ways for good to form various heavy rock combinations.

THE HEARTBREAKERS: After making the break with the New York Dolls, Johnny Thunders - guitar/vocals and Jerry Nolan - drums, joined forces with ex-Television bassist Richard Hell to play some fine but erratic rock 'n' roll in the clubs (notably CBGB's) and bars of NY City.

Not at all happy with his new musical companions' obsessive interest in drugs and drug taking, Hell quit the band in 1976 and was replaced by Billy Rath along with the addition of Walter Lure on rhythm guitar to the line-up. Writing about his interests - girls, lost love, liquor and drugs, drugs and more drugs! - Thunders penned the classic Heartbreakers anthem 'Chinese Rocks' (his favourite brand of smack) with Dee Dee Ramone, containing the lines...

"I'm living on Chinese Rocks/All my best things are in hock"
"I'm living on Chinese Rocks/Everything is in the pawn shop!"

... which appeared on the debut album 'L.A.M.F.' ('Like A Mother Fucker') in 1977.

Supporting the Sex Pistols on their ill-fated 'Anarchy' tour, they earned themselves a loyal following in the UK and were embraced by the nascent British punk movement playing regularly at the Roxy Club and other London venues. 'Live At Max's Kansas City' (1978) was their follow up long player, but too much junkie business meant the band never really capitalised on their releases - too junk sick to play, hopeless timekeeping, regular O.D's, cancelled tours and recording engagements, with Nolan finally picking up his sticks and walking soon after the live LP's release.

Thunders turned to a solo career and delivered, with the help of guest musicians from the Only Ones and the Sex Pistols, one of the best records of the late 1970's in the audio shape of 'So Alone' (1978). It was his finest moment.

Kicking his nasty little habit before inevitably going back to his vein destroying ways, Thunders would occasionally get the Heartbreakers line-up back together again to do a tour, or make a half arsed attempt at recording a new LP. Nothing much came of any of it. With his legendary and natural flair for overdosing and collapsibility, Johnny dug out a slim existence playing the world's dives to an ever decreasing audience, most of whom had come to watch him fall off stage or collapse in a heap on the drum-riser after just one number or so - a regular occurrence at a Thunders show.

In 1991, after two decades of playing rock 'n' roll, Johnny Thunders died in New Orleans under mysterious, drug related circumstances. For a while, he had been considered America's great white, new wave hope... a real heavyweight contender, but I guess Johnny knew better. One of his favourite self-penned songs was titled 'Born To Loose'.

THE VOIDOIDS: Having left the Heartbreakers in 1976, Richard Hell set about putting together an outfit in his own image. The result, with the aid of Ivan Julian and Bob Quine - guitars, and Marc Bell - drums, was the Voidoids.

More direct and rough edged than his former band Television, Hell added the songs to the Voidoids set that his former friend Tom Verlaine had eventually forced from the TV repertoire such as the prophetic 'Blank Generation' and the anthemic 'Love Comes In Spurts'. Using CBGB's as a spring board, Hell and his Voidoids pulled in the crowds and secured a record deal with little delay with Sire Records.

The LP 'Blank Generation' (1977), was the first and last vinyl offering from that association. Bell left to change his surname to Ramone joining up with Forest Hill's finest punk rock "*bruddas*". Quine left to take up lucrative session work, and Hell was left to carry on, label-less, with numerous line-up changes and variations to his creation.

Turning to acting and writing for a while, Hell musically re-emerged with two albums in the 1980's, 'Destiny Street' (1982) and 'R.I.P' (1985), before heading back to the creative shadows. A widely overlooked but important figure in the punk rock story, Hell never received the recognition he deserved. His ripped-up clothing - mainly as the result of fights with his volatile girlfriend rather than an intended fashion statement - and slashed T-shirts bearing felt-tipped slogans such as 'MAKE ME!' or 'BLANK GENERATION' greatly influenced Malcolm McLaren and Vivienne Westwood's future designs - the pair met Hell on their first trip to New York together in the mid-1970's.

Maybe if Richard Hell had accepted McLaren's invitation to go to

Left: Born to loose - Johnny Thunders' Heartbreakers (1977) / Photograph © Alvin Gibbs

London to front his fledgling Sex Pistols his role in new wave history would have been greater, but on the other hand...

TALKING HEADS: Without doubt the most artistically and commercially successful, critically acclaimed group to emerge from the CBGB's, New York New Wave scene, David Byrne - vocals/guitar, Tina Weymouth - bass, and Chris Frantz - drums, started their idiosyncratic musical journey on the island of Manhattan in 1975.

After appearing on numerous occasions at NY's premier punk joints and giving a good account of themselves, they added keyboard player Jerry Harrison to their line-up and signed to the Sire label in late 1976. Their debut record, the weirdly titled 'Love Goes To Building On Fire' (1977), had the critics drooling with positive adjectives as did their maiden LP 'Talking Heads '77'. The follow up single 'Psycho Killer' is widely recognised as one of the finest songs to emerge from the American wing of genre.

'More Songs About Buildings And Food' (1978), kept the journalistic praise a-rollin' and secured impressive sales worldwide proving that the Heads highly intelligent, art-school-informed compositions had massive crossover appeal. 'Fear Of Music' (1979), kept up the momentum, and their 1980 album release 'Remain In The Light' spawned a world wide hit with the rhythmically compelling, lyrically brilliant 'Once In A Lifetime'.

LP's 'The Name Of This Band Is Talking Heads' (1982), 'Speaking In Tongues' (1983) and 'Stop Making Sense' (1984) followed, racking up more credibility, bigger sales and wholesale music press admiration for the group, and adding two more big selling forty-fives in 'Burning Down The House' and 'Road To Nowhere' to their hit list. Byrne's trademark, deranged, jerky dance and oversized suits were displayed to good effect on the film 'Stop Making Sense', and a second foray into celluloid territory resulted in the 1986 movie 'True Stories'.

Offshoot ventures included film soundtracks and an album collaboration with ex-Roxy Music keyboard player Brian Eno for Byrne, and a sideline band with a hit single for Weymouth and Frantz, the Tom Tom Club. In 1991, the Talking Heads sojourn came to an end with the official announcement of the break up of this wonderfully eccentric and efficacious collaboration.

By 1978 a significant handful of New York/CBGB's outfits were making headway into mainstream territory. Blondie had enjoyed considerable success with their second and third album releases 'Plastic Letters' and 'Parallel Lines', from which three hit singles had emerged: 'Denis', '(I'm

Always Touched By Your) Presence Dear' and 'Heart Of Glass', with Debbie Harry in the process having become an American heart-throb.

Patti Smith had scored her own hit with the Bruce Springsteen composition 'Because The Night', and her album 'Easter' was a substantial seller.

The Ramones and Television had not managed to duplicate the kind of approval and saleability that Blondie, Smith and Talking Heads had achieved, but nevertheless did good business in the live arena with their record output selling in unspectacular but steady numbers.

Still, despite these new wave success stories, the American charts were still top heavy with releases from the likes of the Bee Gees, the Rolling Stones, Wings and Donna Summer. The big money and sales were still being garnered by the old wave not the new, and it would be many years before that situation would change.

* * * * *

As well as this transatlantic alliance, a number of outfits had emerged worldwide by 1978 influenced by the UK/USA punk scene, and looking to spearhead a new music movement in their own individual nations.

Australia had sent out an early contender in Brisbane's THE SAINTS. Formed in 1975, Chris Bailey - vocals/guitar, Kym Bradshaw - bass, Ed Kuepper - guitar and Ivor Hay - drums, received positive reviews for their debut album 'I'm Stranded' (1977) in the British music press, after which they moved to London and attained a cult status. Two follow-up LP's, 'Eternally Yours' and 'Prehistoric Sounds' (both 1978) were released by the group before they dissolved into obscurity in 1979. Other early Antipodean punk acts with vinyl output include THE VICTIMS - 'Television Addict' (1978), was a fine forty-five - THE SCIENTISTS and RADIO BIRDMAN.

New Zealand's fledgling new wave scene found a friend in independent record label Flying Nun who nurtured the careers of THE SAME, THE ENEMY and THE CLEAN.

As well as unconvincing outfit STINKY TOYS, France also produced the more adept LIZZY MERCIER DESCLOUDS and industrial-punk combo METAL URBAIN - their 'Paris Maquis', 'Hysterie Connective' and 'Ultra Violence' singles are all recommended.

SUZANNES from Holland released 'De 1000 Idioten' EP in 1978, which featured such sneering compositions as 'Teenage Abortion' and 'New Disease', while Switzerland sneezed-up all female new wavers KLEENEX that same year.

Across the border from the land of the Ramones and the Voidoids, Canada, duly influenced by its neighbours, gave the movement its spin on this punk rock thing in 1977 in the shapes and sounds of THE DIODES - great self titled debut LP on Columbia Records - and psycho (as in certifiable) punk band THE VILETONES - listen to their singles 'Swastika Girl' and 'Screaming Fist' and you'll know what I mean!

Ireland's RADIATORS FROM SPACE delivered a fine debut 45' in 'Television Screen' for the Chiswick label and turned a few heads with their 1977 album 'Tube Heart'. The land of Joyce and Wilde also did us proud by nurturing the hugely popular BOOMTOWN RATS. Bob Geldof and his band had a UK chart success with their first self-titled LP and scored Top Twenty hits with the late 1970's singles 'Looking After Number One' and 'Mary Of The Fourth Form'. Their urban protest song 'Rat Trap' gave them their first UK number one and the follow up album 'A Tonic For The Troops' (1978) received critical acclaim and excellent sales figures. Slowly substituting a more commercial new wave look for their original punky image, the Rats finest moment came in the shape of the brilliant number one 45' 'I Dont Like Mondays' which was based on the true-life tale of an American teenage girl who had shot and killed her school headmaster and seriously wounded eight of her classmates.

By the end of 1977, punk had established a firm bridgehead in the music industries of the UK and USA, and was fast becoming a global affair. However, as the year gave way to a new twelve month cycle, the movement was about to experience a series of events that would see it become leaderless, despondent and close to collapse. It was to be a year of disintegration, depravity, and for one particular mixed up punk girl from the city of Philadelphia - Death.

7
EVER GET THE FEELING
YOU'VE BEEN CHEATED?
VICIOUS

"Everybody is going to fall apart, disintegrate, all character structures based on tradition and uprightness and so-called morality will slowly rot away, people will get the hives right in their hearts, great crabs will cling to their brains..."
Jack Kerouac, 'The Town & The City' (1950).

"My kingdom is one of discord!"
Bela Bartok (1881-1945).

Malcolm McLaren and the Sex Pistols had opened up a Pandora's Box with the release of 'God Save The Queen'. The extreme loathing and aggression this record provoked towards the faction persisted in the UK throughout the remainder of 1977 and into the new year. Punk had become the scapegoat for a society's ills, punks, the whipping boys and girls, for a section of the populous whose lack of education, comprehension and sophistication left susceptible to tabloid manipulation and unable to pinpoint their true enemy.

The establishment had been challenged and the clampdown was under way. Punk kept its head down, took some body blows, and came up gritting its teeth to land a couple of wild shots of its own - punk was down but not out.

As well as without, within the rock music industry itself, the new wave had managed to alienate and make enemies of a number of important and not so important musicians, managers, MD's, A & R men, DJ's and journalists who had careers curtailed, stalled or threatened by its insurgency.

Second division progressive rock acts such as Greenslade, the Groundhogs, the George Hatcher Band, Racing Cars and Widowmaker had all been caught up in the whirlwind of generational change, dropped by their labels to make way for the new-bloods and as a result had large axes to grind. The wailing and gnashing of teeth could also be heard coming from those at the top of the rock 'n' roll ladder as well as from those on the lower rungs.

When A & M had signed up the Sex Pistols, the Carpenters, ex-Yes player Rick Wakeman and Peter Frampton (the company's biggest selling artist at the time), had all contacted Derek Green to protest at having to share the same label with such un-musical and depraved monsters. Likewise, the musicians and managers of such established rock outfits as Jethro Tull, the Eagles, Led Zeppelin and that man of the blues himself, Eric Clapton, had all slammed the new band as unaccomplished and malicious. Naturally, they all completely missed the point, though in the case of Led Zeppelin you can kind of understand their hostility - after all, they did have two of their members turned away from London's Roxy Club with a sharp *"Fuck off!"*

The Roxy Club had folded in the spring of 1977, but its successor, the Vortex, had opened for business that summer in Wardour Street, hosting a debut concert that featured Siouxsie and the Banshees along with Adam and the Ants, the Slits and a new band, SHAM 69. Sham's front man, Jimmy Pursey, was a rabble-rousing, new wave evangelist who preached punk solidarity and strong resistance to the anti-movement clamp down. He had ambitions to lead the crusade and wanted to be taken seriously as a cultural theorist and social commentator. He would not have long to wait to accomplish his first ambition.

Filmed in 1977 for cinema release the following year, punk had surfaced in a feature film for the first time in independent English director Derek Jarman's 'Jubilee'. Jarman had already made a name for himself as a provocative, outrageous movie maker with his debut feature; a controversial, homo-erotic depiction of the life of Christian martyr Saint Sebastiane, in 1976. 'Jubilee' would significantly add to his apostate credentials with its vision of an oppressed, cynical and ultra-violent England as seen through the eyes of its main protagonist Kid, played by Adam Ant.

As well as Ant, Jarman used such punk notables with little or no acting experience as Wayne County, Chelsea's Gene October, McLaren's ex-Art School friend/lover Helen Wallington-Lloyd, Toyah Willcox (excellent as the orange haired 'Mad') and 'SEX'/Seditionaries store assistant, Jordan. This cast of film amateurs appeared alongside such experienced actors as Jenny Runacre and 'Rocky Horror Show' creator Richard O'Brien to produce a movie that captured the mood of 1977 punk England superbly.

Infatuated by the genre, Jarman's next film 'The Tempest' (1979), was an adventurous, Shakespearean-punk 'tour de force' - a blend that had been pre-empted in 'Jubilee' with the figure of Queen Elizabeth 1st soliloquizing throughout the movie having been transported to the future by the sixteenth century metaphysician John Dee.

However, Derek Jarman wasn't the only one interested in putting punk onto celluloid. Malcolm McLaren had visited Los Angeles and talked to the director of such cult, soft porn movies as 'Faster Pussycat - Kill, Kill!' and 'Ultravixen', Russ Meyer, about directorial duties for a proposed film starring the Sex Pistols. Despite the fall-out from their anti-monarchy single, McLaren was determined that the Pistols should not be seen to retreat from such adversity and a big screen debut would be a perfect counter strike and moral booster for the band.

The violence directed towards the foursome had taken its toll. Rotten had become defensive and paranoid, and Vicious had turned to hard drugs to help him cope with life in the media spotlight. Despite his plans for a movie, McLaren decided the scarred and scared combo had to escape from the home troubles that were threatening to destroy them, and booked a Pistols short tour of Scandinavia as a means of getting them away from it all.

It was not to be. Stockholm had a large and fanatical home grown Teddy boy contingent, who, having read and watched on Swedish TV the reports of the Teds versus punk wars over in the UK, decided it was their duty to do their bit for the founding chapter of their youth cult and turned up at the Pistols gig on-mass. Within minutes they had smashed up the venue and were getting into bloody skirmishes with the Swede punks. Rotten and the band had to have a police escort to their hotel where they barricaded themselves into their rooms for the rest of the night from the gangs of Teds who had discovered their whereabouts and marched along the corridors looking for them. British punk rock had been successfully exported abroad along with the violent behaviour of its detractors.

In England during the years 1977/78, it wasn't just Teds and punks who were engaging in street battles. Rival football supporters fought on and off the terraces, police fought with picketing Trade Unionists and rioters at the Notting Hill Carnival, Socialists fought with Fascists, while skinheads and other natural born thugs fought with whoever was handy - it was as if we were in the midst of a second English Civil War.

The ultra-right racist National Front party had been gaining electoral support throughout the mid-nineteen seventies. High unemployment, rising crime and recession had led an increasing amount of British to look to extreme explanations and solutions to the country's problems.

Like Hitler, a National Front hero, the NF leader John Tyndall had managed to convince a desperate and despondent minority of the population that one particular section of society was responsible for all the nation's problems. Hitler had used the Jews as his scapegoats, for Tyndall and his retarded cronies it was the immigrants who were to blame.

By the Jubilee summer they had turned from being an ugly joke into a serious threat. When the NF goose stepped (metaphorically speaking) threateningly through the largely Asian populated Brick Lane section of Lewisham in 1977, they were met by bricks and bottles from a coalition of anti-fascist activists who took this threat very seriously indeed. Among the organisations affiliated to this Anti-Nazi League formed in 1976, was an association that drew its main body of support from punk/new wave/reggae bands and musicians, Rock Against Racism.

POWER IN THE DARKNESS
ROCK AGAINST RACISM AND THE TOM ROBINSON BAND

Two incidents took place in 1976 that led directly to the formation of Rock Against Racism. In the February of that year, David Bowie returned to London from Los Angeles dressed like one of Oswald Mosley's Blackshirts (1930's British Fascists), and made a Nazi salute to the gathered press from an open topped car as it sped him away from Victoria train station. He later tried to explain away his behaviour as a visual statement relaying his belief that Britain was about to become a Fascist state, a conviction that he partly blamed on his prodigious cocaine consumption and resulting paranoid mind-set. To many who were truly worried about the rise of the neo-Nazis in the UK in the mid-1970's, this was seen as simply an irresponsible and provocative act.

Some months later, Eric Clapton - the plunderer of black music - spoke up in favour of the anti-immigration speeches and stance of Tory politician Enoch Powell at a concert in Birmingham - a Midlands city with a large population of West Indians and Asians.

At the Birmingham Odeon that night was Caryl Phillips, one of the UK's finest black playwright and novelist, who as a fan of Clapton's had gone to the concert with friends expecting an enjoyable time. Instead, the event turned out to be one the most painful experiences of his teenage years.

CARYL PHILLIPS: *"Clapton went into a rap about Enoch. His initial line was 'Enoch's right - I think we should send them all back'. I dont think he said 'nigger', I think he said 'wogs'. He definitely said, 'Keep Britain white'. Nobody cheered, but after he'd played another song, he did the same again. It was extraordinary - he stood there being overtly and offensively racist. I was completely and utterly mystified as to why this man playing black music should behave this way."*

Also a witness to Clapton's outburst that same night was photographer Red Saunders, who, horrified at the implications - one of music's biggest stars condoning racism - sent a letter of protest to the UK's music press which was also signed by David Widgery, one time editor of 'OZ' & 'Socialist Worker', and fellow rock snapper Syd Sheldon. It ended: *"We want to organise a rank and file movement against the racist poison in music. We urge support for Rock Against Racism."*

That support was immediately forthcoming from a host of punk and reggae outfits and artists that included the Clash, Sham 69, Misty In Roots, Steel Pulse and black poet Linton Kwesi Johnston. The punks were particularly keen to get involved.

As a result of the casual use of the swastika in punk fashion, many on the outside assumed the movement had neo-Nazi connotations. This was quite untrue of course, the Nazi symbol had only been used in a punk context to shock and challenge taboos, it was never intended to show solidarity with the politically far-right, and to alter this misconception many from the movement were quick to align themselves to the anti-Fascist/racist RAR.

SIOUXSIE SIOUX: *"One of my accoutrements was an arm band with a swastika. It was purely out of high camp and nothing else."*

Side by side with its sister organisation the Anti-Nazi League, Rock Against Racism led the rock 'n' roll resistance to the upswing in ultra-right views in the UK from the mid-1970's through to the early 1980's, by promoting black/white unity concerts, events, protests and through the articles, interviews and editorials of its magazine 'Temporary Hoarding'. One of this publication's first interview was with Johnny Rotten who made it clear that he detested the National Front and added: *"I hate racial prejudice, and any prejudice. I'm a pacifist by nature."*

The leader of the Clash summed up his band's reasons for actively supporting RAR this way...

JOE STRUMMER: *"For better or worse, we felt we had a mission. For Human Rights and against Racism. For democracy and freedom and against Fascism. For good against evil."*

I suspect these words would be echoed by the vast majority of those who heeded the Rock Against Racism call to fight the spread of the inhuman Fascist creed with their guitars as well as with their hearts and fists.

In the 1930's and 1940's, the folk singer and political activist Woody Guthrie had the legend *'THIS INSTRUMENT KILLS FASCISTS'* painted on the back of his acoustic guitar. In the 1970's, RAR revived that worthwhile musical aim and tradition, and helped kill (metaphorically speaking again of course!) enough Fascists to have put a wide smile on the late Woody's weathered face.

As more musicians became politicised and actively involved in RAR, a band appeared that would become identified with that organisation more than any other.

Tom Robinson had started off a musical career with an acoustic rock outfit called Cafe Society. Signed to the Kinks' record company Konk in 1974, a debut self-titled album was released the following year, but discord between the label and group led to Robinson's breakaway and the formation of the Tom Robinson Band with himself as bassist/singer/front man in 1976.

Openly gay, Robinson had his band, Danny Kustow - guitar, Mark Ambler - keyboards and Dolphin Taylor - drums, embrace a number of left wing and radical causes which included the National Abortion Campaign, Feminism, gay rights, and support of one parent families, though their main preoccupation was always the anti-Fascist movement.

TOM ROBINSON: *"The thing that really shocked me was when an NF manifesto dropped through my letter-box along with other parties, during the '77 local elections. I thought 'bloody hell, we're talking Nazis here.' With a couple of the other members of the band, I went down to Lewisham to join the ANL in trying to stop the NF march. You knew it was serious when you actually saw those guys walking down the road, with their vision of a future of blonde blue-eyed boys and master-races."*

Though TRB's politics were radical, their sound certainly was not; most of their material was made-up of mainstream rock cliches with soapbox sloganeering lyrics to compensate. Despite this, and the fact that their image - shoulder length hair, clean jeans, white shirts worn with a carefully paint speckled tie and the occasional boiler-suit for an attempt at street credibility - was a half hearted and unconvincing stab at punk fashion, they still managed to be adopted with Robinson even becoming the movement's political spokesman for a while.

EMI, having been seen to be reactionary and out of touch in their decision to drop the Sex Pistols, decided they were just the outfit to restore some much needed credibility to the label and signed them up in 1977. Their first record release '2-4-6-8 Motorway', was a classic sing-along pop/rock single without a political message in sight, that cruised into the UK Top Ten. It proved a kind of Trojan horse for their more overtly ideological follow-up forty fives - the homosexual anthem 'Glad To Be Gay', the anti-racist rant 'Up Against The Wall', and the politically potent maiden LP 'Power In The Darkness'.

With their 'right on' credentials, TRB became the house band to the ANL and RAR appearing at many of their sponsored concerts, carnivals, demos and even using the back cover of their debut album as a recruiting poster for the organisation. Next to the RAR emblem (a red star in a black circle), the sleeve notes explained: *"Rock Against Racism is a campaign supported by rock fans and musicians alike, including TRB"*, and went on to declare *"We want rebel music, street music. Music that breaks down people's fear of one another. Crisis music. Now music. Music that knows who the real enemy is."*

The most remarkable aspect of this Robinson's RAR avocation piece though, was the fact that EMI had paid for it.

By 1980, with the most right wing British prime minister this century installed at number ten Downing Street, the NF/Fascist threat receded and so did the fortunes of the Tom Robinson Band and Rock Against Racism. Both formally disbanded shortly after Margaret Thatcher had begun her fist term of office. Their contributions are incalculable.

Together they reintroduced political awareness, radicalism and ideology into music, at a time when it became vitally important that musicians use their influence to argue and stand for, as Joe Strummer had eloquently put it: *"... democracy and freedom against Fascism. For good against evil."*

They helped change the cynical *"Who cares?"* attitudes of the young and politically naive, and laid the foundations for contemporary music's involvement in such notable causes and events as the Red Wedge, pro-Labour party 'Jobs For Youth' package tour, the Live Aid festival and record, Amnesty International's 'Conspiracy Of Hope' tour and the Anti-Apartheid festivals, concerts and records, notably '(Free) Nelson Mandela' by the Specials, throughout the 1980's.

* * * * *

I certainly wore my Rock Against Racism badge with pride, and attended a number of their concerts and carnivals including the first in London's Victoria Park in 1978, with Sham 69, Misty In Roots, Tom Robinson Band and Aswad on a bill that was headlined by the mighty fine Clash. That same year, I made a further stab at getting into a punk outfit after clocking another 'Melody Maker' advert that held promise.

As a group name wasn't mentioned in the advert at all, I was delighted to find on arrival at the rehearsal studio that the outfit I was auditioning for was the *"near-legendary"* ('Sounds' journalist Gary Bushell's description, not mine) Users who already had two excellent pieces of speedo-punk vinyl under their belts, the singles 'Sick Of You' and 'Kicks In Style'. They seemed dejected at the large number of duff candidates they had already seen, but bucked-up after we had played through a bunch of songs together and discovered that I knew my way round my instrument.

After half a hour or so of going over their material with a couple of Stooges and MC5 covers thrown in for good measure, we looked at each other and smiled, and singer James Haight called the proceedings to a halt. They got me a cup of coffee, huddled for a few seconds together in a corner of the room, turned to face me and announced that I had the bassist's job if I wanted it.

My career as a punk musician had begun in earnest - I resigned from my day job the following morning.

Over the next twelve months we rehearsed, first at the audition studio, then in the front room of my home in Sydenham, south London, where we composed new material and went on to play a bunch of dates, mainly supports, at colleges, universities, the Marquee, Nashville Rooms and a new capital city venue, the Music Machine. As the other three members of the band lived in Cambridge and most of our rehearsals and gigs were in London, James, Chris 'Panic' Free - guitar, and Andrew Bor - drums, moved into a spare room at the house I rented from my girlfriend's parents so we could save the travel time and spend it more productively. It proved to be a mistake.

At first things went well. With daily rehearsals the band got a lot tighter and we could take care of the running of our own label, Warped Records, more efficiently. The Sex Pistols soundman and 'Anarchy In The UK' producer Dave Goodman set up his eight-track recording machine and desk in my kitchen and spent several nights capturing the hard and fast sounds being relayed from the front room for a prospective Users album. At the same time though, some things were not so good.

It became a bit obvious that James, Chris and Andrew were into certain specific Jamaican and Moroccan plants and substances in a big way. Though I was not adverse to an occasional toke myself, their constant use of these intoxicants were beginning to effect their playing and common sense - on one occasion all three went to Cambridge for a party and turned up wasted and a week late for a gig we had booked as support act to Gene October's Chelsea at the Marquee.

They became lethargic, lard-headed and even more forgetful, spending less of their time playing, and more of their time locked in their room with their home-made bong (a device for the smoking of hash) and drugged ciggies. On the odd occasion that I wanted to get stoned, all I had to do was walk past their door and inhale. In the end I confronted them with an ultimatum: *"Get your shit together or fuck off!"*

Well with a name like the Users you didn't think they were gonna change on my account did ya? Having played a number of good and not so good gigs around town, recorded an album that would never see the light of day with Dave Goodman, and got some valuable experience regarding the effects of Marijuana and Hashish on young minds, I parted company from the Users and dipped back into the 'Melody Maker' to see what I could find. It was just as well that my relationship with the Users ended when it did.

Some six months after parting with them I ran into James, Chris and Andrew in a club in London. They were all wearing porkpie hats, two-tone suits and Fred Perry shirts and had changed their collective name to the Vespas or some such nonsense having decided the Mod revival of 1979 was the future. Like so many who had attached themselves to the movement at its inception, they turned out ultimately to be punk dilettantes and fashion thrill seekers simply riding on the latest bandwagon.

*   *   *   *   *

Out in the wider scene things were similarly unstable. Those supreme advocates and supporters of all things punk, NME's Tony Parsons and Julie Burchill, had written a book that effectively pronounced the Last Rights over the (as they now saw it) rotting corpse of the new wave. Released in 1978, 'The Boy Looked At Johnny' - subtitled 'The Obituary Of Rock And Roll' - told the story of a failed revolution, the punk revolution. 'Rolling Stone' magazine had this to say about it...

"Burchill and Parsons are scabrous, wrong-headed, insulting, condescending, xenophobic, cut-throat, dogmatic, obfuscating, insipid - sometimes all in the same sentence - which makes them a lot like their subject, punk rock... I find them inspiring. Acts of insurrection like this one keep rock alive."

At the same time that Parsons and Burchill were burying punk, the mentor of that movement and manager of its acknowledged leading rock group was about to set into motion a sequence of events that would result in the very real burial of one of his charges. Tragedy and horror were looking for a Sex Pistol.

FREAKSHOW
THE END OF THE SEX PISTOLS, SID AND NANCY.

The single 'Pretty Vacant' had followed 'God Save The Queen' into the UK charts. It had a catchy opening guitar sequence, a pounding floor tom drum and powerchord build-up, followed by a contained verse into cranked-up chorus - a classic heavy rock arrangement. The B-side was a multi-guitar layered and metallic reworking of their Iggy Pop and the Stooges favourite 'No Fun'.

A promotional video was recorded on the stage of the Marquee Club and despite McLaren's strong objections, the band agreed with Virgin that it should be shown on 'Top Of The Pops'.

The following week, after getting a record into the higher reaches of the charts for a third time, the Sex Pistols were back on the nation's TV screens.

Badly miming the words to 'Pretty Vacant', Rotten was resplendent in a Westwood Destroy shirt and bondage strides; his icon face glowering at the unseen audience, the whole movement right there in his eyes. Steve Jones threw rock star poses with his Les Paul guitar wearing a knotted handkerchief - working class wally style - on his head, while to his right Vicious had accessorised a leather jacket and trouser combination with his battered, knee high Fender bass and trademark sneer. On the drum kit Paul Cook was being... well... Paul Cook. You could almost hear the collective sigh of relief from the watching nation when the band disappeared from our flickering screens to be followed onto the show by the insipid and safe disco outfit Hot Chocolate.

The row between McLaren and the band - primarily Rotten - over broadcast of the video on TOTP's was indicative of the breakdown in relations between the manager and his clients. Jones and Cook felt he was spending too much energy on the proposed movie and not enough on getting them gigs and the trappings of rock stardom that went with

Left: Never mind the bollocks! - Johnny Rotten (Sex Pistol) / (1978)
Photograph © Rex Features

them - hotels, limos, booze and birds. New boy Vicious had taken up with a notorious American groupie, Nancy Spungeon, for occasional sex and more importantly needle sharing, and likewise wished to get back out on the road where drugs were more freely available, to satisfy his new habit. Rotten was the most dissatisfied of the lot. He openly blamed McLaren's Machiavellian manoeuvres for the hate and violence directed towards the group and distrusted him. Rotten was no longer happy to be a Sex Pistol, it was *no fun* any more.

McLaren for his part was no longer interested in managing a rock 'n' roll band. His main preoccupation was the raising of the funds for the movie that had been provisionally titled 'Who Killed Bambi'. After tapping a number of sources that included Virgin and Twentieth Century Fox, he realised he still had a shortfall in the budget and decided that it would have to be made up from the revenue of the first Pistols album.

The LP, skilfully produced by Chris Thomas, was in the bag. McLaren once again invited Jamie Reid to provide the artwork, and with the working title of the record 'God Save The Sex Pistols' being dropped in favour of the more controversial 'Never Mind The Bollocks', he turned in a cover of vibrant simplicity; Reid's favourite ransom-note lettering for the band's name on a cerise pink strip with the title in bold, black print over a day-glo' yellow background.

Starting with what would be the Sex Pistols final single 'Holidays In The Sun' - a cut of wit and power - 'Never Mind The Bollocks' proved to be one of the finest rock records of the decade. All three singles were included, 'Anarchy In The UK', 'God Save The Queen' and 'Pretty Vacant', along with a searing, sneering put down of their first record company in 'EMI'. 'Problems', 'Seventeen' and 'Bodies' were all Dolls-esque pieces of savage teenage angst, with 'No Feelings', 'New York' and 'Liar' showcasing Jones' fanfare of guitars, Rotten's venomous vocals and the rhythm section's relentless exuberance to good measure. A heroic record, a rock 'n' roll classic.

Released in the Autumn of 1977, the LP was predictably banned from certain record shops and chain stores. This time the word 'Bollocks' was the excuse along with the discovery that the 'F' word appeared on the record on a couple of tracks. The tabloids did their best to drum-up more anger and aggression towards the band with headlines like the Sun's *SEX PISTOLS IN A NEW FOUR LETTER STORM*', and window displays featuring the sleeve in stores that did stock the record were forced to remove them by the police and threatened with prosecution under an obscure nineteenth century act of parliament.

One store manager was even arrested after he refused to stop displaying the sleeve, and Richard Branson was eventually forced to go to court to win the right to be able to publicise the Pistols album in his own record shops. With the help of one of England's finest liberal QC's, John Mortimer, who argued that 'Bollocks' was a good Anglo-Saxon word used freely in literature for centuries, Branson won his case. Despite all the continuing hostility towards the Pistols and their first Long Player, the record still managed to jump into the UK album chart at number four its week of release.

McLaren meanwhile had been too busy with his movie project to notice the fuss. Russ Meyer had gone cold on the idea, and Malcolm had begun negotiations with director Jonathan Kaplan. To keep the band out of his hair he organised a string of small club dates in Holland and the UK to promote 'Bollocks', and it was during these performances that it became apparent how bad a musician Vicious actually was in comparison with the ex-Pistols bassist Glenn Matlock.

MALCOLM MCLAREN: *"Sid's playing was so bad that we'd hide someone behind the speakers to play his bass parts. It was usually a roadie. We'd have to tape up the amp so Sid couldn't tell it was turned off, but the audience would have known soon enough - he made such a horrible racket they'd all have wondered what was going on!"*

Matlock had no such need for subterfuge, his bass playing was superb and was shown to good effect with his new band, the EMI signed Rich Kids. With the assistance of Midge Ure - vocals/guitar (one time member of one hit wonder Slick and considered as a candidate by McLaren for front man of the Pistols before Rotten came along), Steve New - lead guitar (also considered for the Pistols but eventually rejected because he refused to cut his hair), and Rusty Egan - drums, Matlock and his Rich Kids came on like a new wave Monkees with their debut self-titled single.

"I'm talking 'bout rich kids/Guys too much for you
They got so much feeling/And something special to do
Because they're rich kids/You had better beware
The thing with rich kids you see is... they're all there!"
'Rich Kids' (1978)

Matlock's bubblegum-cum-punk sound started a 'Power Pop' movement in 1978 that pretty much fizzled out by the end of 1979. The Rich Kids follow up single and album were produced by ex-Bowie guitarist Mick Ronson and titled 'Ghost Of Princes In Towers' - two finely crafted and entertaining new generation pop/rock records. Live, the band were flash and loud and I enjoyed them immensely the half dozen times I saw them play in the capital, but as squabbles between the band members increased (especially between Matlock and Ure), the bassist's attempt at creating a Small Faces for the new wave came to nothing, disbanding in 1979.

Matlock went on to form the Spectres with ex-Tom Robinson Band members Danny Kustow and Mark Ambler before playing with Iggy Pop, while Ure and Egan joined forces with Steve Strange to form the new romantic outfit Visage after which Ure made his big move to lead singer of Ultravox. Steve New's continuing involvement with hard drugs insured he never did anything of musical significance again... But enough of this sidetracking, back to the Pistols.

Despite Vicious' lack of musical ability and his new intravenous hobby, McLaren was desperate to sell more 'Bollocks' units for film revenue, and having made a deal for the release of the record in the USA put together a tour that would see the Pistols playing that country for the first time. There were problems though.

At first the American Embassy in London refused to issue visas. All four members of the group had convictions, with Jones the clear winner in the arrest stakes with a criminal record as long as his arm. However, after many arguments and legal representations, visas were issued, and the undisputed heavy weight champions of punk prepared to do battle in a country that had never witnessed their like before.

Punk had nowhere near the impact on the American contemporary music scene as it had on the UK's, its influence in that country in 1978 being pretty much negligible. Apart from New York, Los Angeles, San Francisco and a couple of other scattered States-side cities, punk was still an unknown commodity. Rock dinosaurs still ruled in the arenas, disco and soul still filled the airways, and without the aid of MTV (introduced in 1981), most of those who had heard about punk had been exposed to it in the few sensationalist and uninformed articles - complete with photos of weird looking, swastika wearing Limey mutants - in 'Time' and 'Newsweek' magazines.

Warner Brothers then, had the dubious privilege of releasing 'Never Mind The Bollocks' in disco (Bee Gees, Rose Royce, Donna Summers) and soft rock (Eagles, Fleetwood Mac, Linda Ronstadt) obsessed America. The record company was both excited and apprehensive about the ability of the Sex Pistols and their first album to make a decisive impact on an American audio landscape so dominated by music conservatism. 'Never Mind The Bollocks' entered the Billboard Charts at number one hundred and eight.

Sex Pistols and entourage landed in a cold New York City on January 3rd 1978. Two days later they were back on a plane flying south to Atlanta, Georgia to play their first show; McLaren had engineered the tour to ensure that his band performed most of their gigs in the unsophisticated southern states where he rightly figured they were bound to cause a bigger stir. This was the tactic he had used for the New York Dolls on their infamous 'Red Leather' tour: maximum confrontation, maximum agitation, maximum retaliation - with a bit of luck some redneck might even take a shot at one of them, which in turn would lead to more hype and coverage.

Their debut American gig was played out for a six hundred strong crowd of journalists, TV camera men, Christian fundamentalist Satan seekers, vice squad officers and the vaguely interested - all totally in the dark as to what to expect from these four skinny, strangely dressed Englishmen. What they got was a tuneless, hellish noise.

The Pistols were plenty nervous, and nerves always affected their playing for the worse. Rotten summed up the general consensus with a question to the rapidly dwindling crowd: *"Aren't we the worst thing you've ever seen?"* he asked.

In Memphis, Vicious scored some drugs and in his mind-scrambled state decided some deep cuts in his arm from a flick-knife were what was needed. He was found by the Pistols tour manager sitting on the edge of the Holiday Inn Hotel swimming pool dripping blood into the water, totally oblivious to the horrified reactions of the other guests.

McLaren couldn't control him and Rotten directly blamed the manager for that, deciding the best way to register his disapproval was to stop communicating with Malcolm altogether.

San Antonio saw them play to a couple of thousand long haired 'Good ol' boy' redneck Texans at Randy's Rodeo Ballroom. The majority of the crowd had come to taunt the band and start fights, and the Pistols were more than up for the showdown.

Vicious' opening line of *"You cowboys are all a bunch of faggots!"* didn't exactly endear the group to the assembled stetsons, and one of the biggest of the brutes decided to register his objection to Sid's assertion by knocking out some of the bass players teeth. However, as he tried to get up onto the stage to deliver his knuckle sandwich, Vicious hit him over the head with his trusty Fender bass guitar to which Rotten dryly observed: *"Oh dear... Sid seems to have dropped his bass... what a pity!"* From then on it was madness; beer cans flew, fist fights erupted,

Vicious spurted blood from a nasty wound caused by a Jack Daniels bottle hitting him full in the face - the Pistols loved it.

Following the next Baton Rouge gig the tour party squabbles resumed with Jones and Cook - annoyed at Vicious' crazy behaviour and Rotten's new lease of apathy - deciding to travel separately, both flying to Dallas for the next gig rather than taking the band bus. Back on stage the chaos continued.

During the Dallas Longhorn Ballroom show, Vicious had his nose broken from a headbutt by a demented fan who had made the trip to Texas from Los Angeles especially to deliver this gesture of affection. Not satisfied with the blood flow from his smashed snotter, Sid used a broken beer bottle to make deep cuts in his chest, a successful attempt to get more claret flowing. No longer even trying to play his instrument, arms aloft watching the blood collect in pools at his feet, all eyes were on the completely out of control figure of Sid Vicious. Rotten looked at this hellish apparition and pointing him out for audience approval sneered: *"Look at that... a living circus."*

PAUL COOK: *"We were getting screamed at, all manner of things thrown at us on stage. I though someone was gonna get killed or something. We thought the FBI were following us, Malcolm thought the CIA were after us, and relationships in the band deteriorated day by day."*

JOHN LYDON: *"It was a juggernaut out of control running down hill with no breaks. There was just nothing you could do. The people who were in positions of power, from the management on downwards, were deliberately letting these things happen."*

The Cain's Ballrom in Tulsa came next, but by this time the main concern of the touring party was no longer the show to be played or the promotion of a record. Preventing Vicious killing himself or, more likely, being killed by some gun toting redneck became the main objective.

On January 13th they reached their final destination, San Francisco. While resting up before the last show of the tour in the city by the bay, McLaren came up with an idea that he was sure would propel the band into an even higher 'Shock, Horror, Outrage!' bracket, back home in the UK, Warner Brothers had agreed to McLaren's request for funds to cover a trip for the band to the Brazilian city of Rio de Janeiro - home of the notorious runaway Great Train Robber Ronnie Biggs.

Biggs had been part of a gang that had successfully stolen one million pounds in one of the most famous British crimes of the 1960's.

Having evaded the law in the UK, he had made it to South America where he cannily avoided deportation by getting a Brazilian women pregnant, and by the late 1970's had become something of a Rio tourist attraction. McLaren's plan was to get the band to record with Biggs; a collaboration that was guaranteed to detonate an explosion of outrage in the British tabloids and needle the establishment still further.

Rotten was appalled at the scheme. He had had enough of McLaren's cynical manipulations and their violent repercussions, and understood all too well what this new scam could lead to: more beatings, increased police harassment and a greater hatred of the band all round. Johnny tried to talk Jones and Cook - Vicious was too drug demented to bother with - out of participating in McLaren's potentially dangerous plan, but the guitarist and drummer wouldn't listen. They looked upon Biggs as an English folk hero and were up for the travel.

Rotten immediately moved out of the band's hotel and set up his own HQ across town - the split in the group was now irreversible. The Sex Pistols were getting ready to play their last gig together with a singer who's only desire was to get the event over with so he could quit his job, a guitarist and drummer who were too intellectually challenged and under the thumb of their Svengali-like manager to think through the possible negative results in the Biggs/Rio scam, and a bass player full of heroin on a mission of self-destruction.

The SF Winterlands punk showcase began with local outfit the Nuns, and another home-grown band, the Avengers, to follow. When the Pistols took to the stage, expectations were high but began to quickly diminish when the appalling quality of the sound left the crowd straining to make sense of what was actually being played.

Vicious had no interest in his instrument any more, he had become the 'Too Fast To Live, Too Young To Die' legend made flesh - a living (just), breathing , rock 'n' roll cliche. Jones and Cook bashed through the songs vaguely aware of how awful the results were, while Rotten did nothing to hide his contempt for the proceedings, asking the audience at one point: *"Oh bollocks, why should I carry on?"*

On that Californian evening of January 15th, 1978, Rotten brought 'No Fun', the final song of the band's set, to a finish and spat out his last words as a Sex Pistol *"Ever get the feeling you've been cheated"*, before leaving the stage.

PAUL COOK: *"I dont think we were so naive as to believe we were going to change the world through music, but we definitely wanted to give people a different outlook and attitude towards life and music. We just wanted to shake things up really."*

GLEN MATLOCK: *"The Pistols were really the last great rock 'n' roll band."*

Following the Winterlands fiasco, Vicious overdosed in SF and ended up in New York's Jamaica hospital with pallid flesh and breath like dead snakes after mixing methadone and valiums just before his post OD flight from the West to East Coast.

By contrast, Rotten had ended up in the sun-drenched island of Jamaica to rest up and share ganja joints with his reggae heroes, having had a brief confrontation with McLaren, Jones and Cook in their SF hotel and a short trip to Manhattan where he spilled the beans about the Sex Pistols split to one of the city's daily newspapers, 'The New York Post'. Within hours of the piece appearing in print, the break-up of the band received worldwide coverage. When a British journalist caught up with him in Kingston, Jamaica, the ex-singer of the Pistols told him he would no longer answer to the name Johnny Rotten; from now on he was to be addressed only by his real name, John Lydon.

Jones, Cook and McLaren meanwhile had met up with Ronnie Biggs in Rio and got him to supply the vocals to two songs intended for a single release: the tasteless piece of wank that was 'Belsen Was A Gas', and 'A Punk Prayer'. With these recordings in the bag they returned to London where Malcolm inevitably returned his attentions back to his beloved project, the elusive Sex Pistols film.

When Vicious was well enough to function again, he joined McLaren in Paris to shoot a scene for the movie that was now being directed by a young British film student, Julian Temple. Staged in an empty Parisian theatre, the scene called for Sid, dressed in punk regalia and a formal evening jacket, to croon, in his own demented fashion, the nightclub/ cabaret circuit standard 'My Way' to an audience of middle-aged and wealthy looking patrons.

As the song progressed, electric guitars, bass and drums were added to the soundtrack and Vicious' vocals turned into a sneering recital of his past misdeeds. Towards the end of the scene, Sid pulled out a handgun, shot selected members of his audience and made good his escape up an enormous set of under-lit scenery stairs - just like the kind you see in the classic Hollywood musicals - where he delivered a two fingered salute and a final sneer for the camera before disappearing from view.

It was to be Sid Vicious' most memorable performance, an enduring testament to his ultra-punk snotty charm and Yob From Hell persona.

Against McLaren's strict instructions, Vicious had brought his girlfriend with him for the Parisian filming. Born and raised in Philadelphia before being attracted to the bright lights of NY, a one time problem child and teenage runaway, the girl of Sid's dreams was the twenty year old smack addict Nancy Spungeon.

PHOTOGRAPHER: (To Vicious, 1978) *"Your basic nature is going to get you in a lot of trouble."*
SID VICIOUS: (To photographer) "My *basic nature is going to kill me in six months."*

Nancy had flown to London in 1977, in pursuit of Heartbreakers drummer Jerry Nolan. A bunch of New York new wave outfits were turning up in the city that year to play the famed Roxy Club in the hope of ingratiating themselves with the Brit-punks. Among them were Wayne County and his new band the Electric Chairs, Cherry Vanilla - horny, biker girl singer with pop-rock backing group - and of course that Daddy of the Down 'N' Dirty, *"Noo Yawk"*, raw rock style, Johnny Thunders with his Heartbreakers.

Nolan was in enough trouble with drugs as it was, and the Heartbreakers road manager and crew being wise to Nancy's game - Spungeon was a well known groupie and junkie prostitute - made sure she got nowhere near their skin-beater with her bag of bad medicine. Nancy did what she always did when a sexual target was proving hard to pin down... she found another.

Vicious had been a New York Dolls fan and worshipped the ground Thunders walked upon. He used Johnny as a blueprint for the construction of his hard drinking, super-wasted, quick fisted, punk rock star image. Despite his bravado and given surname, with Sid though, it was always more image than truth.

JOHN LYDON: *"He believed his own publicity. He was called Vicious because he was such a wanker. He couldn't fight his way out of a crisp bag."*

As a Sex Pistol, Vicious had direct access to his hero. He started hanging out with Thunders and the Heartbreakers, and through the association met Spungeon who was always around the band in the hope of getting to Nolan.

Sid and Nancy hit it off immediately. It was inevitable, karmic, a romance made in hell. Nancy introduced Sid to sex and a cornucopia of drugs. Within months of being together she had Sid hooked on heroin and their love affair began in earnest.

John Lydon teamed up with old friend turned bassist, Jah Wobble, ex-Clash and Flowers Of Romance guitarist Keith Levine and Canadian drummer Jim Walker, to form his own band, Public Image Limited. Releasing a debut, self-titled single and album in 1978 on the Virgin label, the PIL sound was as remote from the Sex Pistols guttersnipe rock 'n' roll attack as could be. Lydon had not just changed name, he was also determined to change musical direction and reinvent his own public Image. With heroes like Captain Beefheart and Can as his compositional guides rather than the Stooges or the Dolls, the process had begun.

A Lydon free Sex Pistols record emerged soon after the formation of PIL. Biggs, Jones and Cook's recording of 'A Punk Prayer' had been released as a double A-sided single with Vicious' wonderful punk-meets-Sinatra pastiche 'My Way'.

The Temple/McLaren movie that the song had been lifted from was in the can, complete with specially filmed scenes, old super-eight and live footage, with Malcolm as the narrator putting his own spin on the Sex Pistols phenomena and sowing the seeds for his personal legend. It would be released with the title 'The Great Rock 'n' Roll Swindle'. Two more Vicious set-pieces appeared in the movie - Sid playing the cartoon renegade and singing punked-up versions of dead rockabilly hero Eddie Cochran's 'Something Else' and 'C'mon Everybody'.

Sid and Nancy though, were hurting. Their short-term switch from heroin to methadone, in the hope of kicking the habit, had not worked out as expected - they got hooked on methadone instead - and Vicious' tough-nut reputation got him into nightly bar brawls in London.

I saw them both one evening in 1978, propped up against the Marquee Club bar looking like a couple of homeless street people who had found someone's wallet and had decided to swop the cold alleys and cheap cider for a night in the warm and some whisky. Both were sporting death-white tans and were gaunt of face and ugly-thin. Both had assorted bruises and cuts and Sid had one eye that was badly fucked up and half closed; a souvenir from some horror show filthy fighter who wanted to try his luck with a man named Vicious and now had something to brag about.

After the Pistols split, Sid had wanted to form a band with Johnny Thunders and call it the Living Dead. Studying them that night from across the room I could see why. They looked for all the world like a couple of ghouls from a George A. Romero zombie flick. They already looked dead.

In an attempt to break the cycle of drugs and violence that had become their daily existence in London, Vicious raised some funds by

Left: He did it his way! - Ultra-Punk Sid Vicious (Sex Pistols) / (1978)
Photograph © Rex Features

playing a show with backing group Rat Scabies, Steve New and Glen Matlock at a new punk orientated venue, the Electric Ballroom in Camden, and split to New York with Nancy.

Checking into the Chelsea Hotel (where else!) on their arrival, both went to work on their dream of a successful solo career for Sid, and a healthier lifestyle for them both. Nancy became Sid's manager and set up some gigs at Max's Kansas City with the Heartbreakers rhythm section and the Clash's Mick Jones on guitar as his backing band.

Despite their high hopes for a Vicious re-launch, it was soon apparent that there were no takers. His set was a series of punk cliches with a smattering of obvious covers - yet another version of Iggy's 'Search And Destroy' and 'I Wanna Be Your Dog' - and Nancy's loud mouthed and aggressive attitude to those outside of Sid's inner circle of friends made sure the music biz and press were well and truly alienated.

The fights began again, and with the realisation that the real problem was not what city they inhabited but their own destructive natures, a deep depression descended and the couple turned to heroin once more.

On October 11th 1978, Nancy had a drug dealer bring over some Tuinol as they were having trouble sleeping on junk, and that evening they took a bunch of the capsules and washed them down with cheap booze. As the effect of the drug started to take a hold on them, Nancy started to complain to Sid that he had not scored some smack for the following day. Sid was in no mood to go looking for 'H' but Nancy kept insisting he do something about it in increasingly urgent and aggressive tones.

Though having taken nine Tuinol - enough to have killed off most people - Sid finally relented and staggered downstairs to the room of another well known junkie Chelsea Hotel resident. There was no reply to his insistent knock, so he started to scream and kick at the door in desperation. A black bellhop, alerted by the noise, confronted Vicious in the corridor, and told him to shut up before he woke more residents with his banging around and yelling. Sid insulted him, called him a nigger and suchlike, and rightly enraged, the bellhop hit him hard on the nose knocking Vicious on to his leather-clad arse.

Sid got up and made his way back to room 100 with a bleeding, swollen nose, and without the drug both he and Nancy so badly needed. Nancy called him an arsehole and a wimp and Sid told her to shut the fuck up. She wouldn't.

The haranguing went on for some time before, in a frenzy of vitriol and expletives, Nancy climbed out from the bed dressed in just her panties and bra and struck Sid across the freshly broken nose. In a blind rage, with the intense pain from the blow rendering him oblivious to his actions, Sid picked up a five inch long hunting knife they kept for their protection by the bedside, and lunged at the only thing he loved in the world.

Sid and Nancy met in a deadly embrace. Nancy pulled away and made back for the bed, Sid joined her trying to smooth things over, pleading with her to stop the provocation, to treat him right. They kissed, wrapped their arms around each other and drifted off into a Tuinol induced sleep.

Sid woke on the morning of the 12th to find a pool of dark blood where Nancy had been. He followed a trail of the bodily fluid to the bathroom where he was confronted with the dead body of Nancy Spungeon, soaked in her own blood, the hunting knife still embedded in her abdomen. Vicious called the police and admitted to the killing: *"I did it because I'm a dirty dog"* he told them.

While the corpse of his lover was being carried from the scene of the crime, Sid was 'cuffed and taken to the local police station on 51st Street and charged with second degree murder.

The news broke worldwide soon after. This was just what the tabloids had been waiting for; the proof that their depictions of punk and its leaders as dangerous and immoral had been justified and accurate all along. Punk had thrown up its own Charlie Manson and the British press especially, had a field-day.

McLaren flew into NY with Sid's mother Ann Beverley, and started raising money for a court case. Vicious was released from Rikers Island prison on $50,000 bail - provided thanks to pressure from Malcolm by Virgin Records - weak and in physical pain having been forced to go cold turkey in Rikers, the interminable muscle aches and spasms still attacking his grieving body.

Sid was in some spiritual pain too. While in prison he had been forced to take a journey into his own darkness. He had killed the only person he ever really loved, the only person who had shown him love in return, he was left with nothing but the myth of his own empty stardom - he wanted to die.

On October 22nd, he tried to commit suicide by taking vast amounts of Methadone and slashing up his arm with a razor blade. McLaren found him in his hotel room with old mother Vicious sitting beside him seemingly unconcerned as Sid lay close to the point of bleeding to death. McLaren refused Sid's request to get something to finish him off (preferably heroin) and called for an ambulance instead. He survived, but it wasn't long after his recovery that the stubborn, self destructive streak in his nature made sure some more blood was spilled.

In a Manhattan nightclub, on some R & R after his self-imposed brush with death, Vicious got into a fight with Patti Smith's brother Todd; allegedly because Sid was groping his girlfriend. Punches were thrown, but Sid being a dirty fighter didn't leave it at that. Picking up a broken bottle and plunging it into Todd's skull, he was removed from the premises soon after by the police and locked back up in the tough Rikers Island prison, where a young, skinny and arrogant punk Limey with a name like Vicious only brought out the worse in the numerous professionally violent inmates - the real thing.

On February 2nd 1979, Sid Vicious finally got out and joined his Nancy. Having been forced to clean up again at Rikers, his detoxed body was liable to rebel against even small doses of heavily cut heroin. The day he left the prison he went to his new girlfriend - Michelle Robinson, a club pick-up and another maladjusted, mixed up kid - with his mother, and took two large hits of almost one hundred percent pure 'H'.

Sid turned blue but recovered some minutes later to assure Ma Vicious and Robinson that he was OK and was gonna sleep it off. Sometime during the night he got up, went through his mothers handbag, found the rest of the smack she had purchased for him and shot up the lot. It was the final act in a cruel drama. Sid's heart literally exploded - he was twenty one years old and had pitifully done it his way.

MALCOLM McLAREN: *"I though Sid was wonderful... he could have become a huge star in Las Vegas."*

JOHN LYDON: *"It was a shame he bought the whole hog - sex, drugs and death... what a pity!"*

* * * * *

Sid's choice of poison was not a typical punk drug. Heroin was considered the preserve of the old guard, along with all the other hippy narcotics and potions such as LSD, downers, marijuana and hashish - passive drugs conducive to staying in and mellowing out.

By contrast, the main chemical preference of the punks was for speed pills, amphetamine sulphate and other uppers, action drugs that gave the user the ability to operate over long hours and didn't diminish aggression. Even those in the movement who had at one time rubbished drugs as a fad of the past, found them a necessary part of their work once the pressure was on.

MICK JONES: *"We did the band's first interview and me being all young and naive, I blamed bands taking too many drugs for the great mid-1970's drought in rock. I recall saying it really well. And a year or so later, I found myself doing just as many drugs as them! Y' know, taking drugs as a way of life, to feel good in the morning, to get through the day. I was so into speed, I mean, I dont even recall making the first album!"*

JULIE BURCHILL: *"'The Boy Looked At Johnny' was a nightmare. Speed damage. That book was entirely written on speed and it was shockingly bad."*

With or without the aid of drugs, by 1979 punk was coming off the rails. The Pistols had crashed and the two other bands of the punk elite, the Clash and the Damned were losing control.

Strummer's combo had swopped street credibility for blatant commercial considerations with their second album release 'Give Them Enough Rope'. Having given in to record company pressure with the hope of infiltrating the American market, they agreed to use Blue Oyster Cults producer and heavy rock specialist Sandy Pearlman, and turned in an LP of almost mainstream sounding rock tunes.

The British music press slated it, and hard-core punk fans once again cried *"Sell out!"* Unconcerned by the accusation, the Clash concentrated their efforts in the USA, touring that country repeatedly throughout 1979 and into the new decade.

Likewise, the Damned follow up long player 'Music For Pleasure' was also produced by a figure from the once detested old wave, the reviled Pink Floyd's Nick Mason no less, and was similarly mauled by the critics. Friction between the band members led to first the departure of drummer Scabies and then in 1978, their main songwriter and guitarist Brian James.

With the Clash having virtually emigrated to America and the Damned coming apart at the seams, a vacancy appeared for British punk leadership. Sham 69's Hersham Boy singer and rabble-rouser Jimmy Pursey had been waiting in the wings for just such an opportunity. He waltzed centre stage into the spotlight and took up the mantle of movement spokesman with his *"Kids united, not divided"* message and his populist punk rhetoric. Pursey's dream was to bring together all of the UK's youth cults so they could work shoulder to shoulder to change society instead of fighting each other. It was a worthy but impossible ambition.

Unfortunately, one youth cult in particular had decided to adopt Sham as their own, and turned to violent measures when confronted by others who also dared to lay a claim on the foursome - the skinheads.

Skinheads had been around since the late 1960's, a working class mod mutation and reaction against the middle class long haired, counter-culture types who frequented the country's universities and art schools at that time. Their uniform consisted of shaved or closely cropped hair, straight leg jeans, two tone or stay-press trousers worn with braces, Ben Sherman button down shirts with Crombie coats or short padded 'rucking' jackets, and their famed steel toe capped Doc Marten boots - more a weapon than a fashion statement.

Skinheads political affiliations were mainly right wing - immigrant bashing was one of their regular entertainments which was bizarre as their musical preferences were West Indian ska, blue beat and reggae. A good skinhead was always ready to ruck, ready to *"Put the boot in"* and dish out a bit of aggro. Most of the trouble on the football terraces in the late 1960's and 1970's was caused by skins - believe me I was there! - and the worst thing in the world at that time was for a tough looking skin with his hardnut mates behind him to confront you with the question *"What you looking at John?"* Chances were your name wasn't John and you were moments away from a severe beating.

I was a skinhead from 1969 to 1971. There really wasn't any other choice at my school, unless of course you wanted to get the shit kicked out of you everyday - the place was swarming with them. It was a case of self-preservation.

Skins kept a low profile throughout the years 1972 to 1976, but with the increase in right-wing activity and the youth cults revival of the mid-seventies, they made a comeback with their habits unchanged. Turning up regularly at Sham 69 gigs in their hundreds, making Nazi salutes, beating up punks and causing as much *"bovver"* as possible, Pursey did his best to make Sham's skin following understand that their violent behaviour was making it impossible for the band to play live. This was as much use as trying to reason with a pack of psychotic rottweilers.

Despite Sham's appearance at the first Rock Against Racism carnival, and Pursey's insistence that his band hated violence and was anti-Fascist, the ugly ultra-right skinheads continued to turn up and spill blood at their performances. Promoters understandably shunned the group and by 1979 their reputation was so bad that literally no one wanted to put on a Sham 69 show.

Pursey's dream of solidarity between the youth-cults had turned into a Nazi-bonehead, steel toe capped nightmare. Despondent and fearful that more blood would be spilt if Sham persisted, Jimmy called it a day and retired from the field of battle. Their brief career spawned three albums, 'Tell Us The Truth', 'That's Life' (both 1978), and

'Adventures Of The Hersham Boys' (1979), along with a more realistic attitude to what the movement could and could not achieve.

With Sham's demise the leadership was up for grabs again and there were some obvious contenders.

Inspired by a Clash performance in Belfast in 1977, Jake Burns - vocals/guitar, Ali McMordie - bass, Henry Cluney - rhythm guitar and Brian Falloon - drums, adopted the title of a Vibrators track and became Northern Ireland's foremost punk rock band as STIFF LITTLE FINGERS.

Releasing a single, 'Suspect Device', on their own Rigit Digits label, their lyrics dealt with the realities of existence in sectarian riven, war-torn Ulster, allied to a sturdy and strident sound. John Peel championed them on his BBC radio show, and the band's second single, the brilliant 'Alternative Ulster', and debut album 'Inflammable Material' (1979), sold well and earned them a large following on mainland Britain as well as in their native Belfast.

Another Irish outfit was also in the running. Feargal Sharkey - vocals, Michael Bradley - bass, Billy Doherty - drums and John & Damian O'Neil - guitars, better known as THE UNDERTONES had been another pet Peel band that had made a big impression with their debut single 'Teenage Kicks'. Less punk more pop than SLF, they never the less gained accolades from the pogoing hordes, and after breaking into the UK charts with such forty-fives of acerbic wit and humour as 'Jimmy Jimmy' and 'My Perfect Cousin' looked set to step into the breach.

Both Stiff Little Fingers and the Undertones had the right credentials for the move to punk's pole position, but across the Irish Sea in London, a band specialising in two minute bursts of blistering R & B informed rock were about to be recognised as the new standard bearers of the tribe. That band was THE UK SUBS - short for United Kingdom Subversives.

I first became aware of just how fanatical their following was at a concert at London's Lyceum Ballroom in 1979, where as support act to Generation X they had blown the headliners off stage. Just about every punk in the Lyceum that night had UK SUBS spray painted onto the back of their leather jackets, many also sporting Subs badges, T-shirts, bum-flaps (so called because they clipped to the back of your bondage trousers and covered your arse) and armbands.

As the houselights went down in preparation for the Subs arrival on stage, a deafening chant of *"UK Subs, UK Subs, UK Subs!"* went up from the three thousand strong crowd who proceeded to go pogo crazy on mass at the opening chords of the band's first number. They never stopped.

All through the set the punks energetically showed their adoration of the group, and their allegiance was clear. Poor Generation X didn't stand a chance. They were met with contempt, beer cans and a non-stop chorus of *"UK Subs!"* from the audience.

When they finally got the message and bolted for the wings, I nipped backstage to say hello to a roadie friend and passed the Subs dressing room. Mick Jones was in there having just come back from yet another Stateside visit with the Clash. *"Looks as if you lot have taken over from us"* he said to Subs singer Charlie Harper. *"Yeah"* agreed Harper, *"Looks as though you're right."*

* * * * *

As well as new British punk leadership, 1979 also gave us a couple of short lived fringe movements that ultimately produced no more than three of four bands of any worth.

A movie released that year, based on the story behind the Who concept album 'Quadrophenia', starring a young English actor Phil Daniels had sparked off a mod revival with the added assistance of the look and Rickenbacker led sound of the Jam. Lacklustre bands like Secret Affair, the Merton Parkers, and the Lambrettas put on shark skin suits and loafers in the hope nobody would noticed how bad their music was, and gave some berks in pork pie hats an excuse to recreate the mid-1960's mods versus rockers battles on Brighton Beach that Easter. The whole silly business was over within less than twelve months.

At the same time a much more interesting ska/blue beat/rude boy revival was under way. It was given the name 'Two Tone' by the press because of the healthy mix of both black and white musicians in its principal bands and it provided us with such fine combos as the Specials, the Beat and those nutty Camden boy geniuses, Madness.

Two tone's contribution to British popular music, unlike the mod's feeble efforts, was lasting and substantial. Both movements, especially two tone, collected disenchanted ex-punk rockers to their fold during their heyday. But many of these were fair-weather fashion punks and bandwagon jumpers who in turn would become new romantics in the early 1980's when that tawdry attempt at glamour became 'a la mode'.

Back in the harsh world of punk rock, the departure of Brian James from the Damned was to have a direct effect on my own future. Having released a one off single with his band Tanz Der Youth, James decided at the beginning of 1979 that a new name and line-up was urgently required to stop him slipping into musical oblivion. It was at this point that I stepped into the picture to help him in his enquiries.

SMASH IT UP!
BRIAN JAMES, HIS BRAINS AND THE POLICE.

After my split with the Users, the back pages of 'Melody Maker' once again yielded up a couple of interesting situations vacant. After telephoning some of the advertised numbers, I managed to set myself up with three bass playing auditions for the following day.

The first was with a new band called the Original Mirrors which featured the ex-Big In Japan guitarist Ian Broudie. Their music was interesting but nowhere near the Stooges-esque sound that I was looking for, and after just two numbers both parties decided they were unsuited. None too worried at this outcome I headed to my next assignation.

This time I was to try out for 'Jubilee' actress turned singer, Toyah Wilcox's band. Toyah was very friendly and chatty, I liked her a lot but once again the music on offer was not what I had in mind. We played around with some numbers but it was all in vain. I told her it wasn't my thing, she understood and I headed off to audition number three hoping this was not going to be a totally wasted day.

As I walked into the rehearsal room for my last appointment I concluded that this time there was a definite chance of musical satisfaction. Standing behind a low-slung SG guitar was Brian James and beside him, the ex-guitarist/vocalist of the Physicals, Alan Lee-Shaw, who's Dolls/MC5 inspired 'All Sexed Up' EP had been nearly played to death on my turntable. Behind them, sat at his drum kit was the man who had passed me over at my first punk band audition, ex-Chelsea, Gen X, Rage etc., etc., John Towe.

After the formalities, James quickly showed me the chords to a new song of his called 'Living In Sin'. Seconds later, on his count, the rest of the band joined in and we tore through a set that included some of Brian's well loved Damned compositions such as 'New Rose', 'Neat, Neat, Neat' and 'Sick Of Being Sick'. The interaction was good, I knew I had made a favourable impression and after the playing stopped, James took me aside and told me I was definitely in the running, though he still had a few more players to see. I left with my fingers crossed.

The next day Brian James telephoned me to ask if I'd join his new outfit. He explained we would go out as Brian James and the Brains and that there was recording and touring opportunities aplenty - I immediately agreed to be one of his Brains. That evening the band got together to rehearse, and manager Miles Copeland turned up to check out the new boy.

Copeland, an American who's first involvement with the music business had been as an agent and manager for British progressive rock band Wishbone Ash, had been looking after James' career since he had split from the Damned. His other interests included the running of two record companies with the help of Mark Perry, Step Forward and Deptford Fun City, plus his own solo-run recording enterprise, the Illegal label. Gene October and Chelsea were also managed by him, as was his brother Stewart's band THE POLICE.

Formed in 1977, the Police had originally consisted of ex-Curved Air member Stewart on drums, Henry Padovani - vocals/guitar and Newcastle teacher/jazz buff turned new waver Sting (real name Gordon Sumner) - bass. Releasing a single, 'Fall Out', on Miles' Illegal label that same year, they had been treated as pretty much a bad joke by the majority of punk rockers who diagnosed they were old farts in punk clothing: bleached blonde hair with the roots showing and self consciously worn leather jackets and boiler suit combinations.

STING: *"At first I didn't take being in the Police seriously at all... being in the band seemed like a big joke. It was dire and I was appalled, but I went along with it."*

The departure of Padovani and the arrival of ace ex-Soft Machine and Kevin Coyne band guitarist Andy Summers saw Sting's move to lead vocals and the group move away from their early unconvincing speedo-punk style to a more refined sub-reggae and rock-pop sound. This immediately put them into the desirable commercial/crossover/new wave category, and in 1978 Miles negotiated a world wide deal for the band with A & M records on the strength of his clients' obvious potential and the label's need to sign up a punkish act sharply after the Pistols fiasco.

Their debut single for A & M 'Roxanne', failed to make an impression when first released, but on the back of the UK chart success of their follow up 'Can't Stand Losing You', it was re-released and sold in large enough quantities to make the band a household name. First two LP's 'Outlandos D'Amour' and 'Regatta De Blanc' dominated the British album charts in the late seventies from which the number one singles 'Message In A Bottle' and 'Walking On The Moon' were lifted.

By 1979 then, the Police were no longer considered a joke. They had metamorphosed into the most commercially successful outfit to ride in on the back of the movement. They already had a huge following throughout Europe and had started to lay down the foundations for

Left: Brian James & The Brains (1979) / Photograph © Alvin Gibbs

their considerable future success in the USA - they seemed to be growing in stature by the day.

I was well pleased to be associated with the manager of such a thriving and famous concern, and despite his success with the Police, Miles turned out to be an easy going and unpretentious chap, getting the drinks in after the rehearsal and assuring us he would set up some support gigs for BJ and the Brains with Sting and the boys.

Our first batch of dates were not quite as glamourous as that though. Lots of university and Poly dates supporting all manner of outfits - the Stranglers, the Beat, the Mirrors and punk poet John Cooper Clarke among them - plus London headliners at the Nashville rooms, Dingwalls, the Marquee, the 100 Club and the Fulham Greyhound; all the usual rock 'n' roll dives.

But Miles was true to his word, and after we'd recorded the single 'Dancing On Sand' for Illegal Records, he fixed us up with a European tour as special guests with the Police to promote the record. Our first show in the German city of Hanover playing to a four thousand strong crowd of Police worshipping, fired up Deutschlanders. It didn't go according to plan.

I guess the essential problem was that the BJ and the Brains sound was a touch too hard edged and rampant for the taste of an audience looking forward to such accessible pieces of pop-rock as Stings' 'De Do Do Do De Da Da Da' and 'Roxanne'. The opening song left them slightly dazed, though a smattering of applause was forthcoming at its conclusion and a small contingent of leather and studs, spiky dyed haired Hanoverian punks looked vaguely excited and as if they wanted more.

By the middle of the set though, they had been removed by the venue's security staff for over exuberance leaving us to face an audience who had taken a definite dislike to us - some with their hands over their ears, some chanting for the Police - without any support. Brian decided enough was enough and tried another approach - insults.

"You Krauts wouldn't know good music if it kicked you up the arse with a leather jackboot!" he sneered through the microphone. This didn't go down too well with the crowd, so encouraged Brian continued... *"No don't put your arms up, you lot being good Germans and all we might get the wrong impression."*

More negative reactions. Alan Lee-Shaw got into the spirit of things by shouting *"Take that square-heads!"* and singing portions of 'Springtime For Hitler' to them after each successive song, and by the penultimate number in our set the increasingly hostile crowd looked set to storm the stage.

It was at this point that Brian concluded the proceedings with his Euro-unity 'piece de resistance'. First posing the question to the fist waving audience *"Who's this then?"*, he proceeded to goose-step across the stage while making a rigid Nazi salute and shouting *"Sieg heil!"* Heading back to the mic he snapped his heels and finished his act and our show with the words *"Well then you sausage eating shite, who's for invading Poland?"*

All hell broke loose. Cans of beer and schnaps bottles rained down on us, and a couple of enraged audience members got up onto the stage determined to inflict some GBH on our Brian. We made a hasty exit and left our roadies and the bouncers to deal with it.

Back in the dressing room Mr. James was well pleased.

"The primary objective of any rock 'n' roll act is to provoke a reaction" he declared, astutely concluding *"They won't forget us in a hurry"*.

The Police and the promoter of the show had a different slant on things.

"What have you bastards done to our audience?" demanded an amiable but slightly concerned Sting when we ran into him backstage.

"Just warming the buggers up for you like we're supposed to do" I insisted.

The promoter by contrast was livid and suggested we split to our hotel before the Police finished their set as there could be problems for us if we ran into certain members of the crowd while loading out after the show. It was good advice.

We had a two day stop over at our promoter's booked hotel, a five star Sheraton in the heart of Hanover, before we were due to drive off to the next Police support gig. Despite knowing full well that all extras should have been paid for out of PD's (Per diems - a daily cash allowance provided for each member of the band from our gig money), we never the less ran up an astronomical bill charging all food, booze (the bulk of the expense) and overseas telephone calls to the promoter's tab. Each taking it in turn to sign the checks under the 'nom de plume' Jack English.

The hotel staff finally got a bit suspicious on the afternoon of our departure when Mr. Jack English signed for two bottles of wine at the bar, a three course meal in the restaurant and some room service snacks simultaneously, but by that time it was all a bit too late for them to check if this was above board with the promoter. There was also the question of the expensive repairs that were necessary to the swanky suite I had shared with John Towe.

On the last night, John and I had chatted up some local frauleins in the bar, and having ordered all manner of beer and booze, had taken them to our room. Brian and Alan, alerted by the sounds of carry on from our suite next door and having also acquired some female company, stopped by to join in with the merry making.

The end result of the ensuing riotous behaviour included two beds that had collapsed and were no longer usable, one destroyed television set (a rock 'n' roll classic), a shattered bathroom mirror, a smashed sink along with numerous broken table-lamps, chairs and glasses scattered over a seriously wine, beer and brandy stained carpet.

While our nervous wreck of a Tour Manager tried to reassure the distinctly worried Sheraton desk clerk with cries of *"Not to worry, the promoter will pay for all damages"* and *"Jack English is a man of his word... all debts will be met in full"* and such like, we (the band) crept off to our van, started the engine and once our TM had managed to join us, made a fast getaway.

On the way to the next gig in the city of Kiel, we stopped at an autobahn service station so that our trusty TM could call the promoter to get directions for the venue while the rest of us got a coffee. He came back looking pale and serious and we rightly figured the promoter must have been in contact with the Hanover Sheraton.

"The news is not good" he stammered.

"Well then" I said *"Let's have it straight."*

"You're off the Police tour" he finally blurted out *"The promoter has completely freaked. Your abuse of the audience was bad enough - apparently it took the Police a good half hour to calm them down, to get the fighting to stop and restore order - but then when he was confronted with a bill of close to £3000 at the Sheraton for our two days stay he went fucking crazy and chucked us off the rest of the gigs."*

Brian's succinct observation on these developments was *"They've no sense of humour whatsoever these Germans have they?"*

No indeed, but all was not lost - another call, this time long distance to Miles in London, saw us fixed up with some alternative Euro dates. We played a cracking show in the French city of Lyon opening up for two tone heroes the Beat and headed off to Paris where we were assured we had a gig at the famed Montmartre venue, Le Palace. There we warmed up the crowd for a newly emerged CBGB's second wave American punkabilly outfit THE CRAMPS.

Comprising of Lux Interior - vocals, 'Poison' Ivy Rorschach - bass, Nick Knox - drums and Bryan Gregory - guitar, the Cramps came on in leather and lace, Lux looking like a disinterred Elvis, Ivy, gum chewing and super-sexy in stiletto heels and fishnet stockings, playing voodoo tinged tracks from their debut LP 'Songs The Lord Taught Us'. It was a great night.

Back in Blighty we got our hands slapped by our manager who

told us bluntly that we would have trouble getting gigs in Europe again after the facts of our Hanover debacle became common knowledge, but didn't really matter anyway.

A few weeks later Brian James was offered an American tour as guitarist for Iggy Pop in a pick-up band that included ex-Sex Pistol Glen Matlock on bass. However, Miles kept paying our wages and Brian assured us that his gig with Iggy was temporary and he would return to work with us Brains as soon as the tour was over.

To keep in shape Towe, Lee-Shaw and I went out as support act to hard rockers Thin Lizzy on a short UK jaunt, and sure enough Brian rejoined us with the idea that we should change the band's name and add a front man/singer to get round the Continental blacklisting of BJ and the Brains. One Nelson Rockefeller (real name John Milner - James made him change his name to something more exotic) was added to the line-up, and the inspired group name the Hellions was adopted.

We played some more shows around the capital, got some good and not so good reviews in the press, and generally seemed to be going nowhere fast. Towe was the first to leave. We had become friends and enjoyed working together and despite a prized Reading Festival appearance coming up I didn't really want to be slogging around as Brian's bass player any longer. I asked John to give me a call if he discovered any interesting bassist gigs up for grabs, and he promised to contact me as soon as he found something suitable.

Later in the week that Towe left the Hellions, I went to see a movie with my girlfriend at our local cinema. The main film was a critically acclaimed British picture about life in a brutal borstal titled 'Scum'. The B-movie was a Julian Temple directed film, a spoof on a war time propaganda documentary starring the UK Subs, called 'Punk Can Take It'.

As I watched the live footage of the Subs in action in front of their fanatical following I suddenly became aware that my girlfriend and I were the only two people in the cinema. This struck me as strange and significant, a strong feeling that the two of us alone in the cavernous cinema building with those images being played out on the screen had personal meaning.

No more than two days later I got a telephone call from John Towe.

"What do you think of the UK Subs?" he asked.

"That's funny" I replied *"I just saw them in their own film a couple of days ago."*

" Yeah?... well it's like this, I ran into the Subs guitarist Nicky Garratt at the Marquee Club last night and he said they were looking for a bassist to

replace Paul Slack. I recommended your good self and gave him your phone number - expect a call at any time."

I thanked John for his recommendation unaware at the time that the information I had just received would change my whole life.

8
SECOND WAVE
THE SUBVERSIVES

"In my own country I am in a far-off land.
I am strong but have no force or power.
I win all yet remain a loser.
At break of day I say good night.
When I lie down I have a great fear, of falling."
François Villon (1431-1463)

"A wave on a beach when it rolls in doesn't suddenly stop it
tapers out. Nothing ever suddenly stops in music."
Nicky Garratt, UK Subs (1980).

On March 28th 1979, a British general election was called when the Labour government lost a parliamentary vote of confidence. After a winter of discontent, strikes and disruptions, and with the aid of a Saatchi & Saatchi inspired advertising campaign that featured a poster depicting a dole-queue with the slogan *'LABOUR ISN'T WORKING'* - to highlight the fact that there were over a million unemployed in the country - the Conservatives came to power and Margaret Thatcher became Britain's first woman prime minister.

Two years on, the unemployment figures had doubled, legislation was proposed to neutralise the trade unions, cuts were announced for state spending on the NHS, social security, schools and public transport, and social unrest was rife with nationwide anti-government demonstrations and inner-city riots. Thatcher and her government became immensely unpopular and punk suddenly acquired a new relevance and vitality.

A second wave of outfits emerged, fully equipped musically, lyrically and politically for the harsh economic and social conditions.

Those that had ridden the punk wagon because it was fashionable and cool had long since jumped back off to join one or other of the new trends, with those that remained essentially being punk fundamentalists. The whole of the movement went back to basics.

For many, punk died the day the Sex Pistols imploded, for others, it was the fateful night Vicious had injected that deadly amount of heroin into his vein. Some even believed it was a case of 'fini la guerre' when the Clash signed to CBS, but this is all nonsense. What actually happened in 1979, was that punk didn't die, it simply became unfashionable.

Punk no longer appealed to middle class art students and the chattering 'demi monde'. It reverted back into the hands of the great unwashed and the guttersnipes, and although it still maintained a reasonable degree of media attention, in terms of spirit and demeanour, punk went underground.

At the forefront of this new attitude was a band that had the necessary ingredients to lead the pack, the United Kingdom Subversives.

BRAND NEW AGE
RIDING THE SECOND WAVE WITH THE UK SUBS.

> *"The UK Subs are really something else. The UK Subs have a string of hit singles and albums. The UK Subs are punks, albeit mature ones who walk it like they talk it. The UK Subs play loud, snotty and regressively. The UK Subs are gods to the Pavlovian masses whose mouths freely salivate to the beat boys."*
> 'Record Mirror' (1980).

After a series of failed recruiting experiments, a UK Subs line-up was finalised by singer/front man Charlie Harper in 1976. Harper (real name David Perez), had been a vocalist on the fringes of the music biz since the 1960's, first busking around Europe with his harmonica and an acoustic guitarist, and then, after teaching Rod Stewart the finer points of blues-harp playing and hanging out with the Rolling Stones, playing bass and singing in his own R & B combos.

In the early 1970's, Charlie took to the London pubs and clubs with the soon-to-be Thin Lizzy guitarist Scott Gorham in a popular blues outfit called Fast Buck. At Fast Buck's demise and the coming of the new wave, Harper pulled in Nicky Garratt - guitar, Paul Slack - bass and Pete Davies for the drums, and together they hit the road as support act to any punk group that would have them.

Left: Born a rocker, die a rocker - Charlie Harper (UK Subs) / (1981)
Photograph © Alvin Gibbs

CHARLIE HARPER: *"To me punk was an excuse for fanatics to have their say, people like me who never had a chance before, people who have just been laughed at. Blokes like me who've just been through life being sneered at, fingers pointing saying 'That's the local nut-case'. When punk came along it was the best thing that ever happened to me... I was accepted."*

By 1978, they had gained for themselves a reputation as an unpretentious, hard working foursome with a growing following, and were given the chance to release their first vinyl by the indie label Pinnacle in the shape of the revved-up R & B forty-five 'C.I.D.'

John Peel loved it and gave it numerous plays on his show. Sales were good and the Subs were seen to be blowing off the stage each and every band they opened for. Gem Records, a subsidiary of major label RCA, took note and signed Harper's men to a multi-album deal in 1979 - their debut LP was appropriately titled 'Another Kind Of Blues'.

To the surprise of everybody except the Subs, 'Another Kind Of Blues' became a Top Twenty album, with the 45's 'Stranglehold' and 'Tomorrow's Girls' denting the lower reaches of the Top Forty singles chart. Their following had grown to large and fanatical proportions, and despite a few minor problems with a handful of ex-Sham 69 right-wing skins who had latched onto the Subs after the Hersham boys capitulation, promoters UK and Europe wide were keen to book their tours and make a buck.

The release of the follow up album 'Brand New Age' and singles 'Warhead' and 'Teenage' saw the band chart once again and gave them the ability to be beamed into millions of British homes via their appearances on 'Top Of The Pops'. However, during the UK leg of the tour to promote the new LP, a rift opened up between the slightly arrogant and fame-affected Slack and Davies and the more down to Earth and idealistic Harper and Garratt.

Tempers flared, and fists were thrown one night after a show with Slack and Davies coming off worse, and the next day it became a question of the rhythm section rushing to quit before they could be sacked. A replacement drummer was found in Yorkshireman Steve Roberts who had come to Harper and Garratt's attention as a member of Subs support act Cyanide, and with this new sticksman in place Charlie and Nicky focused on finding a replacement bassist to complete their UK Subs mark II line-up. It's at this time that your humble writer entered the UK Subs story stage left.

Following John Towe's recommendation, Nicky Garratt telephoned me to ask questions and make a judgement on my viability as a possible

Right: The UK Subs (Mark II) - from left to right: Nicky Garratt, Charlie Harper, Steve Roberts and Alvin Gibbs / (1981) Photograph © Alvin Gibbs

UK Sub. I guess I checked out OK as he finished our conversation with an invitation for a playing audition that week.

It was at a rehearsal room in south London where after a drink and a chat, during which time I discovered how affable and intelligent both Harper and Garratt were despite their hard-line reputations, we got down to making some noise. Nicky would call out the title of a song, give me the key and on a drum count from Steve Roberts we piledrived through a set of spine-snapping, super-loud numbers. After twenty or so pieces of this uncompromising punk rock, Nicky took off his Gibson SG and brought the audition to a close.

I figured I'd done alright but it was hard to tell, Harper and Garratt were hardly displaying their hearts on their sleeves, and there was the usual post audition talk of *"Well we've seen about twenty people and we've still got another fifty or so to see, so we will let you know... thanks for coming."* Putting my bass away in its case I said my farewells and headed off down some stairs for the exit. Just as I got to the door, Roberts appeared at the top of the stairway and shouted *"Hang on mate!"* in a broad northern accent. Seconds later he had reached me and with a wide smile on his face said *"Me, Charlie and Nicky want you to join... what do you say?"* I was kind of taken aback at this but managed to blurt out *"Sure... love to... is that it then?"*

"Yeah that's it. We will call you tomorrow to set up a meeting with our management" concluded Steve.

That night, I took John Towe to the Marquee as a thank you and opened just about every bottle in the club. I had become a UK Sub.

My first duty as the new Subs bassist was a debut show at the three thousand capacity London venue the Music Machine. The place was packed to the rafters with the band;s very vocal pogo a-go-go following and we went down a storm - Steve and I achieving total acceptance from the dyed-spikey haired, leather-loving crowd.

Next up was the making of a new album. A live record 'Crash Course', featuring a Rainbow theatre performance from the final tour with Slack and Davies had just been released and entered the UK album charts at number eight. The management wanted a follow up Long Player as soon as possible to capitalise on this chart success.

Charlie and Nicky had a bunch of songs written, and I had a few to throw into the pot so material was no problem. The main cause for concern though was who was going to produce the record. Guy Stevens was mentioned.

Stevens had been the volatile and idiosyncratic producer of such Island Records artistes as Mott The Hoople, Free and Spooky Tooth during the late 1960's and early 1970's. By the later part of the decade, the drugs - Stevens had been a heavy speed user for many years - his addiction to alcohol and the resulting ill health combined with a nervous condition had led to the work drying up. He became a recluse, living with his mother, and reliving former glories with those who would listen. I met him in 1978.

Having gone for a drink one evening at a local pub with my girlfriend we became aware of a manic looking man with receding, frizzy black hair studying a tatty book and shouting aloud *"Yeah, Montgomery Clift was rock 'n' roll... very rock 'n' roll, yeah, Yeah, YEAH!"* and other such strange statements, alone at a table across from ours. After a while he started looking in our direction and we did what most of you would probably have done in the same situation, we ignored him and prayed he wouldn't bother us.

Naturally our prayers went unanswered. He shuffled over to our table, dropped down onto an empty seat next to me and exclaimed *"You're a musician, don't deny it, you're a musician, I can see it in your eyes!"* I didn't deny it and we got to talking.

The tatty book was a biography of dead movie star Monty Clift, one of my favourite film actors and obviously also well loved by this down and out looking character: *"He was the best, the BEST... sensitive, articula:e, better than that fucking right wing arsehole John Wayne or Gary 'fucking' Cooper!"* he screamed.

Agreeing with him and figuring this man was harmless enough I offered to buy him a drink and asked his name.

"It's Guy Stevens" he informed me.

"Really?, that's funny, one of my favourite glam rock bands Mott The Hoople had a mentor and producer named Guy Stevens" I informed him.

"Yeah I know" he replied *"I am that man."*

After buying him several beers and quizzing him on his days with the Hoople, Guy came back to my girlfriend's flat to drink some more and kept us both enthralled with his life/rock 'n' roll tales - among them Stevens' journey to the USA in 1964 to successfully get Chuck Berry out of jail, plus a host of other fascinating exploits - till the early hours of the next morning. It was the start of a friendship.

Guy's mother's house was just a fifteen minute walk from my place, so most evenings when I wasn't rehearsing with the Users, or later with the Brains, I'd go over and take him to the pub for a drink (or ten), or hang out in his room sipping wine and listening to his favourite records - Bob Dylan, Stones, Muddy Waters and other blues greats - talking music and making plans to some day work on a record together. It was a friendship that was not always easy.

Once he came by my place pretty drunk after the pubs closed to watch Hitchcock's 'Psycho', and just five minutes into the movie launched himself off the couch screaming *"Anthony Perkins... Anthony Perkins is God... Fucking Goooddd"* and proceeded to smash a dining chair into a dozen pieces of useless wood which pissed me off and scared the hell out of my girlfriend. I tried calming him down but he wouldn't have it, he kept yelling around and looking for more furniture to break, and in the end I was forced to physically remove him from the premises.

Another time he rang my doorbell at four am, once again in a state of some inebriation, and having got out of bed to let him in, I ended up with a smashed window - Guy managed to loose the grip on a wine bottle he was waving around to Mott's 'Wildlife' album - a bunch of broken glasses, and another dining chair reduced to match wood for my troubles. I was thankfully over at his place when a surprise telephone call came from Joe Strummer inviting Guy to produce the Clash follow-up LP to the critically panned 'Give Them Enough Rope'. He accepted and celebrated by smashing whatever was at hand with a large hammer he kept for beating out a rhythm when he listened to music.

Guy put his unique production skills to work on the Clash city foursome's 'London Calling' record...

JOE STRUMMER: *"Guy would come into the studio yelling and put on a recording of the Arsenal Cup Final then stand in front of the speakers with his arms outstretched, waving a scarf to and fro and joining with the chants. And that was how the day would begin, cranked full volume. We thought it was great."*

... he sure wasn't a technical producer but he knew how to set up an atmosphere and get results. During the recording of a Strummer/Jones composition 'Clampdown', Guy decided there wasn't enough urgency to the take, so having pulled out a length of rope from his briefcase (dont ask!), he tied one end to the back-rest of a collapsible metal chair and took it out with him to the live room where the band were intently playing. Next thing the Clash knew, a metal chair was being swung perilously close to their skulls by their demented producer who screamed at them *"NOW play it you fuckers... play for your lives... PLAY! PLAY! PLAY!"*

Strummer and the boys kept their heads down and did what they were told. Luckily no one was decapitated, and when it came time to listen back to the take it was by far the best one of a batch, Guy had injected just the right degree of jeopardy for the track.

JOE STRUMMER: *"Guy's contribution was to give a crazed edge to proceedings."*

He also influenced them lyrically. To follow is a verse of the album cut 'The Right Profile'...

"Say where did I see this guy?/In Red River?/
Or maybe A Place In The Sun?/ Maybe the Misfits?/
Or From Here To Eternity?...
Everybody say' what's he like?/Everybody say' is he alright?/
Everybody say' he sure look funny!...
That's Montgomery Clift honey!"

Guy's Clift obsession had been Strummer's inspiration.

The Clash had no doubt chosen Stevens to provide the band with some much required credibility after their blatant submission to commercial needs as demonstrated by the hire of the slick, rock biz insider and safe pair of hands Sandy Pearlman to produce 'Give Them Enough Rope'. Guy, by contrast, was a risky outsider with a dangerous approach to record making. He was considered a brave and inspired choice by the music press, if not by CBS, and 'London Calling' received far better reviews than their previous album as a consequence and paradoxically also proved more commercially successful. The gamble had paid off.

Guy, for his part, made some money and found himself back in demand with a new generation of musicians. It didn't last very long though.

When I took the rest of the Subs to meet him to discuss producing our album he had lapsed back into his more extreme manic, alcoholic tendencies: slurring his words, jumping around and screaming stuff like *"Yeah, Jerry Lee Lewis, that's who you guys should sound like... the KILLER!"* and spitting more flecks of spittle into peoples faces as the words emerged than was usual. A nervous skin complaint had also made a serious comeback - he looked and sounded awful.

Totally unimpressed with the Jerry Lee Lewis idea and Guy's crazed behaviour, Charlie, Nicky and Steve though he would be entirely the wrong man for the job and said so. I was disappointed, I really wanted to make a record with Guy, it was something we had planned to do since we had first become friends, but I also knew they were right, in the condition he was in it would never have worked. We looked around for another producer.

I only saw Guy a couple of times after that disastrous meeting. Each time he looked and sounded a little worse than the time before, and on the last occasion his mother Lilian said it would be best if I left after I had spent just five fruitless minutes in his company as he was really too drugged-up to speak.

On August 29th 1981, Guy Stevens overdosed on the prescription drugs he was taking to reduce his alcohol dependency. I regret to say I never made it to his funeral, I had UK Subs business to attend to and I didn't get away in time and I still feel guilty about that. Two of my most prized possessions are a 'London Calling' album and copy of the book 'The Denial Of Death', both given to me by him and both with dedications ending *"With love, your friend Guy Stevens"*.

Well, the Subs did eventually find a suitable producer in the shape of glam rock superstar Gary Glitter's co-writer and producer Mike Leander. We felt the Spector-esque wall of sound he achieved on Glitter's records would contrast well with our stripped-down, street punk compositions. On some of the more accessible album cuts it proved a successful marriage, on some of the hard-core, hell-for-leather tracks it proved a mess and Nicky was called upon to re-mix them with a more tougher overall sound.

A single was released from the sessions in 1980, 'Party In Paris', and I experienced my first UK Subs European and British tours to promote it that same year. Halfway through the UK leg of our promotional sojourn we were informed that 'Paris' had reached number thirty seven in the charts and we had to make a flying detour (literally) to London to appear on that week's episode of 'Top Of The Pops'. It was at the studios that I came to understand just how fanatical the UK Subs following actually was.

A three hundred strong gang of devotees had been turning up to each of our shows, gig to gig, city to city since the start of the tour. Instead of heading for the next town we were due to play, they loyally, on-mass, hitched, drove and bunked trains and buses across the nation to the BBC TV studios in Shepherds Bush to support us.

About a hundred and fifty of them made it in to see us - the rest being locked out by a fearful BBC producer - resulting in a studio more used to an audience of would-be disco divas, permed haired and open shirt 'lads' and overdressed and underwhelmed Essex girls, being overrun by our contingent of red/green/orange and mohican haired toughs - dressed to kill in their studded leather and bondage wear finest.

Two other acts with punk connections were also on the show that night. THE CURE, Robert Smith - guitar/vocals, Lol Tolhurst - drums and Simon Gallup - bass, had issued a debut record, the 'Killing An Arab' single on the Small Wonder indie label in 1978. By 1980 they had altered their original basic punk sound for a more considered, darker approach with a notable deadpan vocal delivery from Smith. With his striking jet black spiked hair, eye make-up and smudged lipstick visage, Smith would go on to lead his band to phenomenal success in both Europe and the USA with a string of big selling LP's: 'Faith' (1981), 'Pornography' (1982), 'The Top' (1984), 'Kiss Me, Kiss Me, Kiss Me' (1987) among them, and hit singles 'The Love Cats', 'Boys Dont Cry', 'Why Cant I Be You?' and 'Just Like Heaven'. They were to perform the minor chart success 'A Forest' for the studio and TV audience that evening.

Also sharing the T.O.T.P's bill was the newly reinvented Adam and the Ants. After hiring the services of Malcolm McLaren as an image consultant, Adam and his backing outfit were given a radical new look and sound by the former Pistols maestro. Out went the punk garb and riffs, to be replaced by a mixture of Red Indian, pirate and classic rock 'n' roll imagery complete with new pop, heavy-percussion compositions that owed more to Gary Glitter and Marc Bolan than to the Clash or the Pistols. Adam had gone mainstream.

It was a sensible move as far as I was concerned, but to a number of our hardcore followers it was seen as betrayal. I could sense trouble was a-brewing.

Our (mimed) performance of 'Party In Paris' for the TV cameras proved a colourful spectacle with the massed Subs zealots pogoing in unison at the front of our stage, their multicoloured heads bobbing up and down like some kind of kaleidoscopic sea. Captain Sensible taking time off from the Damned, had joined us to pretend to play the keyboards having played them for real on the record, and finished things off by pushing the hired Hammond organ over and diving into the crowd. Despite the fear in his eyes, the BBC floor manager seemed pleased, and we passed Adam and his Ants as they made their way to the stage to perform their hit forty-five 'Dog Eat Dog' and got down to some serious drinking in the cheap, subsidised Beeb bar.

ADAM ANT: *"We did 'Top Of The Pops', bang, one week 200,000 sales. We were ready. Man, we'd waited a long time. People say they liked me when I did 'Dirk Wears White Socks' (Adam's pure punk phase) but it went down hill after that. No you didn't! So few copies were sold I could've gone round to punters' houses and put them through their letterboxes personally."*

Back in the studio Adam was getting some stick from our supporters, but being the trooper he is put in a professional performance despite the heckling and made his way back to the dressing room. In a corridor outside the studio, Adam's guitarist Marco Pirroni and Adam's then girlfriend, the actress Amanda Donahue, were confronted by a couple

of tough looking Subs fans who had decided that verbal abuse was not enough. Punches and kicks rained down on Adam and Pirroni and they were knocked to the ground - a knife was produced and if it wasn't for Donahue's swift punch to the blade wielding assailant's jaw, the incident could have had a much more serious outcome.

A couple of security guards eventually appeared and the Subs thugs made a run for it. Despite the fact that we were merrily downing beers in the bar, completely oblivious to the assault, the band was blamed for the attack and the BBC banned the UK Subs from appearing on the show for a whole year. Punk violence was once again the subject of newspaper articles and my band unjustifiably acquired a roughhouse reputation which stuck with us for many years.

Adam recovered from his beating, and with ex-'SEX' and 'Seditionaries' staffer Jordan as his personal manager went on to be an international pop star. His 'Kings Of The Wild Frontier' (1980) and 'Prince Charming' (1981) albums were both big sellers and he succeeded in getting two forty-fives into the number one spot - 'Stand And Deliver' and 'Prince Charming'. The Ants promo videos were creative and influential at a time when the medium was just starting to be taken seriously by the music industry, and Adam's dandy image was a prototype for the early 1980's New Romantic fashion movement. In 1982 Adam took up a solo career that saw his move into movie and TV acting as well as continued record making.

Just a year on from the imposition of our 'Top Of The Pops' ban, we were invited back to perform our single 'Keep On Running' - into the UK single charts at number twenty five - on the show, our past indiscretions finally forgiven by the mighty BBC. It was 1981, and after a solid year of British, European and Scandinavian touring, we were looking to experiment a bit with our music and image and had identified why there was a ceiling on the UK Subs success and popularity. The problem was crossover potential.

Whenever we released a record, our considerable following would go out on mass over the first couple of weeks to purchase enough copies to push the LP or single into the higher reaches of the charts. By the third week though, the sales would start to dry up and the title would start to slip, eventually, within a few weeks, to drop out of the top sixty.

The Mike Leander produced album of the previous year 'Diminished Responsibility' (1980), provided a fine case study for this frustrating dilemma. Entering the UK album charts at number fifteen its first week of release, it had dropped to eighteen by the second week.

Left: Prince charming - Adam Ant / (1981) Photograph © Rex Features

Come the third it was at twenty one, and by the fourth, had gone down to forty where it held its position for a heroic fourteen days before dropping once more to number sixty six. After two months it had disappeared from the UK Top One Hundred altogether.

Our record company thought an image change and a more accessible sound could secure the Subs a larger audience and bolster our fan base for greater sales and sustained chart success - it had certainly worked for the Police and Adam and the Ants - and with this in mind we appeared on Top Of The Pops with a combination of punk classics: studded leather belts, wristbands, bootstraps and motorcycle trousers, mixed in with new romantic attire: frilly dress shirts, suede Chelsea boots and silk scarves worn as waist sashes. This had been the sartorial mix of the Subs Scandinavian support band of that year, Hanoi Rocks, much admired by Charlie, Nicky, Steve and myself.

'Keep On Running' was also something of a departure from the usual UK Subs forty-five. Produced by Peter Collins, who had previously worked with chart toppers the Beat, it was a Police-esque pop/rock song penned by Charlie and I with extreme radio friendliness in mind.

Despite the band being up for it, this tactic was in fact very dangerous. There was a very good chance that by changing our tried and tested formula, not only would we not succeed in attracting a wider audience, but we could very easily alienate and lose our existing hardcore following. It was a risky strategy but one I thought was essential if the band wished to survive.

A breed of distinctly un-punk, new wave sounding outfits had emerged in the early 1980's to attain substantial success in Britain and Europe, with America enthusiastically beckoning. As well as the Police, Elvis Costello, Joe Jackson and Squeeze, ex-'SEX' shop assistant and 'NME' journalist Chrissie Hynde had also scored big with her band THE PRETENDERS. Their 'Brass In Pocket' single had reached the number one position in 1980, and the debut self-titled album had all the ingredients for acclaim from a wider audience.

RAT SCABIES: *"I was very surprised when I finally heard her first single because it was something everybody had sort of waited for. She had been this loud Yank hanging out, so everyone wanted to know what she was gonna do and everyone was sort of 'This isn't punk rock is it?' And everyone kind of went 'oh!'"*

DON LETTS: *"It was obviously against the grain of what we in our hip circle were into at the time. But you couldn't deny that voice and I was knocked for six. I've got to admit that I couldn't believe this was coming out of that scraggy, loud mouthed, aggressive bitch!"*

The follow up LP, 'Pretenders II', yielded more melodic new wave tunes and Hynde and her band started to make deep inroads into the American market. Guitarist James Honeyman-Scott's death from a cocaine overdose quickly followed by sacked Bassist Pete Farndon's fatal heroin OD in 1982 proved a near terminal blow to Hynde and drummer Martin Chamber's Pretender ambitions. But in 1984 they returned to the breach with a new line-up and the international chart topping album 'Learning To Crawl'. Another string of forty-five hits followed: '2000 Miles', 'Thin Line Between Love And Hate', 'Middle Of The Road' and 'Back On The Chain Gang'.

Straight British punk had rapidly been overtaken by a more easily digested sound, and along with the Police and Pretenders a new generation of rock-pop bands such as Simple Minds, Psychedelic Furs and A Flock Of Seagulls, synth-pop acts Human League, Soft Cell, OMD, Ultravox, Gary Numan and Depeche Mode had begun their largely successful bid for chart domination and international approval.

To survive, I, along with Nicky Garratt especially, felt the UK Subs could ill afford not to take risks. The sales of UK hardcore records were rapidly drying up, and 'Keep On Running' was but the first stage in a plan to revive the band's career. With only a week or so before the single's release we had run into yet another band with a redesigned new wave sound that were fast becoming press darlings and contenders for stardom.

We had just filmed a video for 'Running' on the sound stage of a London studio, and the band that was due to follow us to record their promo looked somewhat nervous to be in such close proximity to the infamous UK Subs. As I walked past the singer on my way to the dressing room I clocked the look of apprehension on his face and went out of my way to put him at ease, shaking his hand, wishing him luck etc. He thanked me, wished me luck back in his soft Irish accent, and took to the stage with the rest of his band to commence filming. They were called U2 and though I didn't know it at the time, they represented the future of rock 'n' roll while we merely symbolised the past.

* * * * *

Many a first wave punk outfit had fallen by the wayside by the early years of the Greed Is Good decade, dropped by labels who were on the look out for more fashionable and commercial commodities to sell. However, some had survived and prospered, and a few were even experiencing a renaissance of sorts.

Siouxsie and her Banshees continued to have Top Ten albums: 'Juju' (1981), 'A Kiss In The Dreamhouse' (1982), 'Nocturne' (1983), and singles, 'Dear Prudence' and 'Swimming Horses', together with well attended concert tours and intercontinental respect. In fact Siouxsie's popularity was such that she even succeeded in having hit records with her side line project, also featuring drummer Budgie, the Creatures.

America never took to the Banshees in the same way it had embraced the Police, Pretenders etc., but even there, a country Siouxsie had openly declared she detested, the band could still do good business in the major cities and be guaranteed reasonable record sales.

Her dramatic voodoo doll imagery and sound, along with Robert Smith and the Cure's similar approach - Smith had in fact once played with Siouxsie as a temporary Banshees guitarist - also gave life to a 1980's music and fashion punk offshoot, 'Goth'.

Goths were easily identified by their dyed raven backcombed hair, heavy use of make-up, horror show black apparel and skull & crucifix accessories. They had their own capital city HQ in the Batcave Club, and their bands included such theatrical inventions as Bauhaus, Alien Sex Fiend, the Bolshoi, Southern Death Cult (later to metamorphose into platinum purveyors of post-Led Zeppelin metallic riffing the Cult), Gene Loves Jezebel and Sex Gang Children among them. Goth was especially big in the cities and towns of the UK Midlands, and elements of its sound and style can be readily observed in the hardcore Death Metal outfits of the late 1980's and 1990's.

While the Banshees and the Cure had been influencing a new strand of essentially punk influenced self expression, those movement originals the Damned had delved into rock 'n' roll's past to find inspiration for their eighties compositional endeavours. After the exuberant metallic attack of 1979's 'Machine Gun Etiquette', the band, with a reinstated Rat Scabies and Captain Sensible taking up lead guitar duties, had turned to 1960's psychedelia to flavour their 'Black Album' (1980), 'Strawberries' (1982) and 'Phantasmagoria' (1985), vinyl long players.

Ex-Damned guitarist and my old touring buddy Brian James, had disbanded his Hellions and with ex-Dead Boys lead singer Stiv Bators as the Iggy-esque front man, ex-Sham 69 bassist Dave Treganna, and ex-Barracudas drummer Nicky Turner, had formed the goth-punk rock 'n' roll band LORDS OF THE NEW CHURCH in 1981. Managed by Miles Copeland, the group issued their debut 'Lords Of The New

Church' LP in 1983, quickly followed by 'Is Nothing Sacred' that same year. The Lords built up a healthy following touring these dark-side rock albums with their apocalyptic imagery and anti-religious rhetoric, a project that would finally run out of interest and artistic steam in the late 1980's.

Those who had served with the Sex Pistols had also resurfaced in new guises. Ex-Johnny Rotten, John Lydon had forged a credible post Pistols career with Public Image Limited. Their 'Metal Box' (1979), 'Au Printemps' (1980), 'Flowers Of Romance' (1981) and 'This Is What You Want, This Is What You Get' (1984), albums generally received good reviews and sales though some of their live performances proved a little too 'avant garde' for audiences. One memorable show at the New York Ritz in 1981 saw Lydon and his band playing behind a cinema screen, a theatrical device that was not appreciated by the Ritz crowd. A small riot ensued, Lydon and the musicians finally being forced to flee the stage under a torrent of beer bottles. Lydon left London in that same year to live in New York, before relocating in the mid-1980's to the sunnier climes of Los Angeles, California.

Whereas Lydon had opted for an experimental sound with PIL, ex-partners Steve Jones and Paul Cook went for more of the multi-layered metallic guitars with their new band, the Professionals. Having recruited ex-Subway Sect bassist Paul Myers and second guitarist Ray McVeigh to their cause, they recorded a self-titled debut album in 1980 and took to the road for its promotion. During a States-side visit, the group were involved in a high speed car crash that saw all the members in an American hospital with various broken bones for some weeks. On making a full recovery they reconvened in London and recorded the appropriately titled second LP 'I Didn't See It Coming' (1981).

With neither critical acclaim nor worthwhile sales to show for their efforts, the Professionals folded in 1982 and following the example of his former front man Lydon, Jones moved to the USA also setting up home in Los Angeles. Cook remained in London where he involved himself in various projects of no great significance.

It didn't take Malcolm McLaren long to find a new protegee and a new sales pitch. Having discovered a fourteen year old Burmese girl singing in a north London launderette, McLaren's mind effortlessly slipped into Machiavellian mode and in jig time he had signed up Annabella Lu Win and constructed a backing band to compliment her discreet visual and vocal charms. With former Adam and the Ants members David Barbarossa - drums, Mathew Ashman - guitar and Leigh Gorman - bass, on board, the venture was given the collective name BOW WOW WOW and a deal was signed with EMI Records in 1980.

Using ethnic drum patterns mixed in with rockabilly style guitars as a backdrop for Lu Win's frankly limited vocal talents, the main focus of attention was not on the music but on McLaren's promotional stunts for the band that hinted at paedophilia and centred on the nubile fourteen year old's jailbait potential.

In a re-run of the Pistols/EMI debacle of 1977, the label quickly became unhappy at Malcolm's methods and Bow Wow Wow were effectively dropped. McLaren secured them a deal with RCA soon after and their debut LP, the curiously titled 'See Jungle! See Jungle! Go Join Your Gang, Yeah, City All Over! Go Ape Crazy!' was released in 1981. By this time 'Seditionaries' had been replaced by another McLaren-Westwood clothing store 'World's End', which featured Vivienne's new dandy highwayman, pirate and redskin designs made famous by Adam Ant. Dressed in these 'World's End' garments (McLaren was still determined to sell a lot of trousers!), Lu Win and the band took to touring and promoting their maiden record but found that McLaren's manipulations were having a detrimental effect on their chances of success.

His decision to have Annabella semi-naked on the album sleeve, a pastiche of the Manet painting 'Déjeuner sur l' herbe', led to more raised eyebrows and did nothing to help the band in their quest to be taken seriously. Despite a Top Twenty single in 'I Want Candy' (1982), a second album of the same name, and a third and final attempt at critical acceptance in the shape of the 1983 LP 'When The Going Gets Tough, The Tough Gets Going', Bow Wow Wow collectively handed in their notice to their manager at the tail end of 1983 and moved on to new musical ventures.

Deciding anything they could do (his clients), he could do better, McLaren took up a new career as a recording star. The fact that he could not sing and had no technical knowledge of music didn't appear to present a problem for our Malcolm, and on securing a record deal in 1983 he released his first album 'Duck Rock' - an interesting mix of ethnic African rhythms and North American Hillbilly music - to some acclaim. Two hit singles were pulled from the record 'Buffalo Girls' and 'Double Dutch', and McLaren turned to American dance culture to inform his follow up LP of 1984 'Would Ya Like More Scratchin'?'. His third album 'Fans' (1984), showcased his successful merging of opera and rock 'n' roll styles and produced a superb version of Puccini's tearjerking masterpiece 'Madame Butterfly' which became another hit forty-five for Malcolm when released that same year.

Having broken up both his romantic and business partnership with Vivienne Westwood by this time, McLaren followed in the footsteps of former Sex Pistols John Lydon and Steve Jones - both litigants in an ongoing lawsuit against their ex-manager for misuse of band's revenues - swapping London for Los Angeles and taking up with the glamourous American movie star Lauren Hutton.

Westwood meanwhile went to Italy to work in that country's fashion industry and learned the finer points of clothing manufacture, distribution and construction. Returning to London in the mid-1980's she started her own fashion house dedicated to her highly original and creative inventions and laid the foundations for a very successful garment design and manufacturing business.

By the early 1980's, constant touring of the USA had begun to pay off big dividends for the Clash. Having changed their radical punk image for a more classic rock 'n' roll look - rockabilly quiff haircuts, biker leather trousers, baggy demob suits, turned-up collar 1950's style shirts worn with string ties and suede waistcoats - Strummer and gang nevertheless demonstrated their continuing devotion to left wing politics by naming their epic fourth LP 'Sandinista!' in support of the Communist revolutionaries who had taken power in Nicaragua.

From the Westway to Broadway - the band played an unprecedented seventeen consecutive shows at Bond's theatre on Broadway and Times Square in New York in 1981 to promote the record, and received rave reviews and a front cover on America's foremost music magazine 'Rolling Stone' for their considerable efforts.

Despite the departure of drummer Topper Headon (heroin addiction strikes again!) the band found a solid replacement in their former sticksman Terry Chimes and toured their most successful release to date, the superb 'Combat Rock' long player. This record gave the Clash two 1982 USA/UK hit singles in 'Should I Stay Or Should I Go?' and 'Rock The Casbah', and led to the group playing their biggest and most prestigious gig as support act to the Who at the 60,000 capacity New York Shea Stadium.

By 1983 the Clash were on the cusp of attaining superstar status in the USA, but the criticism that the band had received from some quarters of the music press back home regarding what some journalists saw as their unseemly conversion from anti-rock establishment radicals to pro-rock establishment realists, had affected some members more than others. Strummer, always keen to maintain his street credentials, took these accusations to heart and started to complain that things had got out of hand. Jones, on the other hand, felt this was all nonsense, he firmly believed that the Clash should be as big as they possibly could be and had no time for the ghetto mentality of some journalists as he had sharply demonstrated at a press conference before the Bond's dates.

JOURNALIST: (In demanding tones) *"Paul Weller of the Jam has accused you of selling out. What constitutes a sell-out to the Clash?"*

MICK JONES: (Deadpan) *"What happens, is that all the tickets go on sale for a concert and people go and buy them, and if as many go and buy them as there are tickets, that constitutes a sell-out."*

This difference of opinion between Strummer and Jones led to arguments and bitterness, and following a Strummer interview during which he accused his guitarist and co-songwriter of laziness, Jones quit the Clash. Strummer and Simonon continued with a new guitarist and drummer and went on to make the disappointing 1985 album 'Cut The Crap'.

Jones enlisted the services of the ex-Roxy DJ turned film maker, Don Letts - Letts had directed the Clash's 'London Calling' promo video and made a documentary called 'The Punk Movie'- on keyboard duties, Dan Donovan - second keyboard, Greg Roberts - drums and Leo Williams - bass, and took to recording and touring as BIG AUDIO DYNAMITE.

Apart from the Clash and the Police, only the ex-Generation X singer turned solo artist and New York 'habitue' Billy Idol, had come close to platinum album status and genuine international rock stardom. In pure commercial terms, punk's first wave had been a dismal failure.

Britain's second wave then had no real hope of succeeding where those before them had failed, and for the most part weren't even concerned with trying. The larger percentage of second wavers were simply content with satisfying the needs of the punk purists and had no ambitions to join the mainstream of rock 'n' roll, challenge the establishment, nor change the world. Despite its anti-government political posturing, its menacing sound and style, by the 1980's punk had become essentially conservative in nature. There were also other distinct differences between the first and second generation of punk.

The most obvious was a stylistic change. Bondage strides, ties worn with paint flecked white shirts and safety pins were no longer stylish, having been replaced by disintegrating blue jeans - a fashion innovations adopted in the 1990's by that bastard son of punk, Grunge. Or camouflage combat trousers along with punk band promo T-shirts, more tattoos and an alternative to the dyed spiky haircut, the Mohican or Mohawk: hair-sprayed high on the scalp and inspired by Robert De Niro's look in the movie 'Taxi Driver'.

Right: Second wavers The Exploited / (1981) Photograph © Rex Features

---

Other things remained the same though. The Kings Road still served as the main artery to the body punk with a constant flow of peacocks, posers and hustlers who would charge 50p to have their photographs taken by tourists and punk audiences still showed their appreciation by spiting at their groups. This was one of the nightmares of being a UK Sub.

Each night on tour I would walk off stage covered in gob and flem - it was always greener and nastier in the winter months! - and though I almost got used to it after being in the band a year or so there would still be the odd occasion when the whole thing would turn my stomach. One nightmare of a night, someone's well aimed gob landed in my mouth when I was singing backing vocals. A decision had to be made as to whether to spit the stuff back out - looking at what had just entered my mouth could very well make me vomit - or swallow - I wouldn't have to look at someone else's flem at least but there could be health risks. Joe Strummer had encountered an identical problem during a Clash gig, decided to swallow and ended up with hepatitis B.

With this in mind I spat the substance back out onto the stage, vomited behind my amplifier and promptly returned to the fray like nothing had happened. It was all in the line of duty, but enough of these gob and vomit tales, let me introduce you to a few of my fellow second wavers.

PUNK'S NOT DEAD
THE EXPLOITED AND OTHER POST PISTOLS STORIES.

Whereas the initial wave of UK punk outfits had overwhelmingly emerged from London, by the early-1980's the trend setting capital had written punk off as deeply unfashionable and it was predominantly left to the provincial towns and cities to provide the new recruits for the second assault. One of the most abrasive bands from this new batch came from the far north of the country, Scotland's own...

... THE EXPLOITED: Formed in 1980 by Mohican sporting ex-British army soldier Wattie along with Big John - guitar, Dru Stix - drums and Gary - bass (the Exploited weren't big on surnames), this band specialised in discordant, super-fast bursts of sound with sloganeering and lyrical cliches of the worst kind covering themes such as government corruption, Police brutality and unemployment.

Right: Mick Jones contemplating life without The Clash / Photograph © Bob Gruen

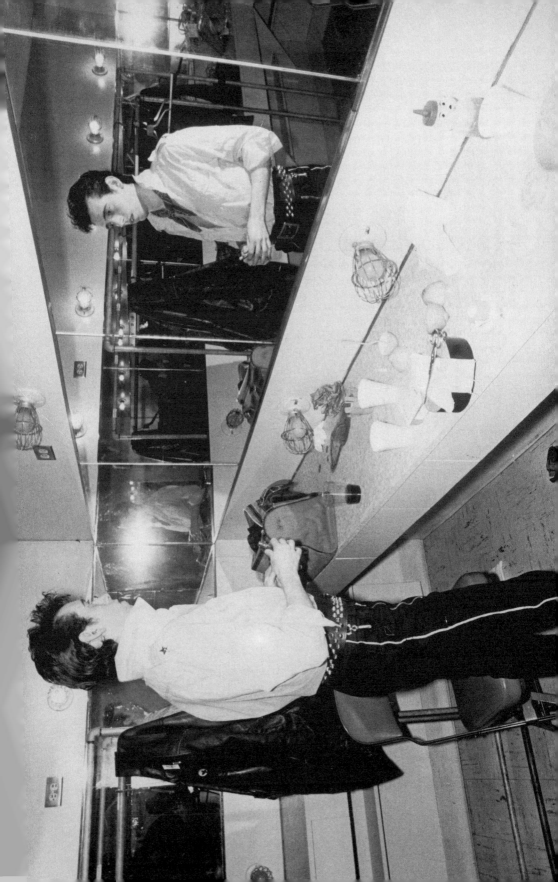

Despite, or rather, because of the unsophisticated nature of the band's approach and material, Wattie and the Exploited became embraced as truly authentic by the hardcore troops of tomorrow and gained a considerable following as a result. Their 'Punk's Not Dead' debut LP sold in surprisingly large quantities in the UK and entered the Top Ten of the albums charts, and by 1982 they had even surpassed the popularity of the UK Subs, taking over as second wave leaders while we attempted to seek our fame and fortune in the USA.

WATTIE ('Sounds', 1981): *"The Damned and the UK Subs are the only originals left. The main punk bands now are us, Discharge and Vice Squad. It's starting to get really good again. At the last few gigs there's been more and more punks turning up, the newer bands having started a new generation of punks. That's why I hate bands like Spandau Ballet, they're shit, they all used to be punks when it was fashionable."*

'Troops Of Tomorrow' (1982) and 'Let's Start A War' (1983) were their follow up vinyl offerings, but with the departure of the excellent guitarist Big John, the group's sound lost its vital attack, a malady which a succession of replacement guitarists were unable to cure. By 1984 they were a spent force with a dwindling audience reduced to playing the more unsavoury clubs and pubs around Britain to survive and where they continued to insist to a handful of die-hards that punk was still not dead.

ANGELIC UPSTARTS: A product of the UK's north-east, the Upstarts were led by fiery vocalist Mensi. Another hard-line outfit in the mould of the Exploited, their sound was a similar barrage of hard and fast playing laced with anti-Thatcher, anti-police, social commentary lyrics - 'The Murder Of Liddle Towers' protesting the death of a man who was held in police custody was their first record in 1979.

Two good albums were forthcoming in 'Teenage Warning' (1979) and 'We Gotta Get Out Of This Place' (1980) and despite some gig trouble with a right wing following which the band were quick to ridicule and disown, by 1981, the Upstarts were also snapping at the heels of the Subs and looking to acquire a leadership role. Despite a left wing bias, Mensi was not prepared to slavishly follow the left's line on every issue. His 'Last Night Another Soldier' took up an anti-Irish Republican/IRA stance. 'Guns For The Afghan Rebels' riled against the Communist backed Afghanistan government and called for the arming of the anti-Communist Mujahedeen Islamic resistance fighters - two positions that were considered those of the political right.

Come the mid-1980's though, the band and the second wave had lost all momentum and were in retreat. Mensi called *"Last orders"* for the band in 1986.

THE COCKNEY REJECTS: Formed in 1979 the Rejects, Jeff 'Stinky' Turner - vocals, Micky Geggus - guitar, Vince Riordan - bass and Keith Warrington - Drums, were at the forefront of a hard-line second wave offshoot called Oi Oi. This was the tag given to a host of punk-skin, working class hooligan rock bands by 'Sounds' journalist Gary Bushell, and included such unattractive outfits as the 4-skins, the Gonads, Skrewdriver and Infa-Riot.

The Rejects far outstripped them all in popularity and commercial success, managing to place two singles in the UK Top Forty - 'The Greatest Cockney Ripoff' (# 21), and the West Ham football team anthem 'I'm Forever Blowing Bubbles' (# 35), and also charting their first two albums 'Greatest Hits Volume 1' and 'Volume 2' (both 1980). Inarticulate, arrogant, with a quick fisted reputation, the group soon became trapped by their violent renown and skinhead following, eventually turning to heavy rock in the hope of finding a new audience.

It didn't work. Heavy metal merchants were not impressed by their Oi past and considered them opportunist bandwagon jumpers while their original supporters looked upon this change of style as disloyal and deserted them. By 1983 it was a case of Cockney Rejects R.I.P.

THE RUTS: Influenced by the Clash's successful blend of punk and reggae, Malcolm Owen - vocals, Paul Fox - guitars, John Jennings - bass and Dave Ruffy - drums formed the Ruts and immediately jumped to the fore of the movement with their brilliant UK Top Ten single 'Babylon's Burning' (1979). Three more superb singles followed in 'Something That I Said', 'Staring At The Rude Boys' and 'West One (Shine On Me)', (all 1980) along with albums 'The Crack' (1979) and 'Grin And Bear It' (1980).

However, on July 14th 1980, the momentum that would have no doubt taken the Ruts to stardom came to a halt with the premature death of Malcolm Owen. Found cold and blue in his bath by his mother, Owen had been a long term heroin user and had been battling for some time to kick the habit. The rest of the Ruts, operating as Ruts DC, opted to continue with new boy Gary Barnacle, but the spirit had gone and after one LP 'Animal Now' (1981) the band folded.

For me, without doubt the most talented group to emerge from the second wave soup. Check out their records and weep at the loss of such a great rock band.

CRASS: Formed in an Epping commune by anarchists Steve Ignorant and Penny Rimbaud, Crass' discordant, off-beat sound was always secondary to their subject matter - strident feminists, anti-government, pro-animal rights etc., etc. Releasing records on their own Crass label - no major company would touch them with a barge pole - they took to playing small venues all over the UK and became the leaders of the ultra-fundamentalist wing of the movement. They accused just about every vaguely successful punk band of "Selling Out" and presumptuously and sanctimoniously claimed to be keeping what they considered to be the true punk ethos alive.

With this extreme doctrine present throughout their recordings - 'The Feeding Of The 5,000' (1979), 'Stations Of The Crass' (1980), 'Penis Envy' (1981), 'Yes Sir I Will' (1982) and 'Christ The Album' (1983), they inspired a batch of similar minded outfits in their own image, some of whom they signed to their label - Conflict, Poison Girls, Rudimentary Peni and Flux Of Pink Indians. Two compilation albums of Crass label bands 'Bullshit Detectors 1 & 2' appeared in the early 1980's, and during the latter part of the decade, Ignorant abandoned Crass to join London anarchists and label mates Conflict, effectively bringing his original group's career to a end.

THE SKIDS: Jettisoning to UK prominence with the Top Ten single 'Into The Valley' on signing to Virgin records in 1979, Richard Jobson - vocals, Stuart Adamson - guitar, Willie Simpson - bass and Tom Kellichan - drums, blended the vital energy of punk with pop sensibilities and came up with a commercially promising sound.

Albums 'Scared To Dance', 'Days In Europa' (both 1979) and 'Absolute Game' (1980), all enjoyed chart success, and two further hit singles were forthcoming in 'Masquerade' and 'Working For The Yankee Dollar' before Adamson took the decision to go his own way. Without his former guitarist and songwriting partner, Jobson eventually found the added creative pressures on him unacceptable and putting paid to the Skids in 1982 went on to form the Armoury Show with ex-Banshees guitarist John McGeoch.

Adamson meanwhile had found suitable candidates for his new project Big Country and went on to have substantial success with the group in the mid-1980's.

VICE SQUAD: With second wave sex symbol Beki Bondage (real name Rebecca Bond) as their front women, Dave Bateman - guitar, Mark Hambly - bass and Shane Baldwin - drums, found a strong supporter in 'Sounds' writer Gary Bushell who raved about their 'Last

Rocker' debut EP in the pages of the music weekly. As a result, EMI signed the band and a load of cliche nonsense duly emerged in their debut LP 'No Cause For Concern' (1981).

I saw this band over a dozen times when they were the support act for a UK Subs British tour and I couldn't see their appeal at all. Ripped-off riffs played fast and badly with Ms. Bondage whining over the top about police brutality and perils of modern urban life, stuffed - she was overweight and really not at all sexy - into a leather outfit that just may have looked erotic on a women half her skirt size.

'Stand Strong Stand Proud' (1982), was a somewhat better album than their first offering but still singularly failed to impress all apart from Mr. Bushell and suffered poor sales as a result. Dismayed, Bondage took her whip and handcuffs elsewhere, signing a solo deal with EMI and forming the band Ligotage with ex-Subs drummer Steve Roberts before pulling together a fresh set of musicians for Beki and the Bombshells - two projects that failed to pay either artistic or commercial dividends. Vice Squad continued with new female singer Lia and released their final record in 1985, the LP 'Shot Away'.

KILLING JOKE: From 2nd division second wavers to a genuine 1st division outfit. Jaz Coleman - vocals/keyboards, 'Geordie' Walker - guitar, Martin 'Youth' Glover - bass and Paul Ferguson - drums, came to prominence with their hypnotic 1980 single release 'Wardance' on their own Malicious Damage label.

Their debut self-titled album brought them more accolades, and Coleman's mesmeric, psychotic stage presence guaranteed Joke's reputation as a fine live act. Two more excellent LP's followed in 'What's This For...!' (1981) and 'Revelations' (1982), before Coleman's fascination with the occult got the better of him. Proclaiming the end of the world was at hand, he left the group to sit out the apocalypse in Iceland. When it became clear he had made an error in his prediction of Earth's imminent demise, the singer returned to London and his band, recording the sublime hit single 'Love Like Blood' and album 'Night Time' with new bassist Paul Raven.

Killing Joke, with Youth back on board, continue to tour and record to this day, a tasty outfit thoroughly deserving their longevity.

TENPOLE TUDOR: Having appeared in 'The Great Rock 'N' Roll Swindle' Sex Pistols movie singing a deranged version of a song entitled 'Who Killed Bambi', the very eccentric Edward Tudor-Pole joined forces with Bob Kingston - guitar, Dick Crippen - bass and Gary Long - drums, to form Tenpole Tudor.

Signing to Stiff Records in 1980, the band's finest moment came with the release of their UK hit single, the rousing 'Swords Of A Thousand Men'. Debut LP 'Eddie, Old Bob, Dick And Gary' (1981) followed and the Tudors made a colourful addition to the gig circuit with their medieval clothing - Tudor-Pole's stage gear consisted of a complete suit of armour - playing their shambolic punk-pop tunes to a small but adoring following.

Within a couple of years however the group had become utterly unfashionable and Eddie left the band to take up acting and earned parts in the movies 'Straight To Hell', 'Absolute Beginners' and 'Walker' and can now be seen hosting a British TV quiz show called 'The Crystal Maze'.

GBH: Very angry, very metallic 1980's outfit with multicoloured Mohicans and hardcore image. GBH comprised of Cal - vocals, Jock - guitar, Ross - bass and Wilf - drums (another band not big on surnames). Their albums: 'Why?' (1980), 'Never Again', 'Hear Nothing, See Nothing, Say Nothing' (both 1981), 'City Baby Attacked By Rats' (1982), 'City Babies Revenge' (1983) and 'Leather, Bristles, Studs And Acne' (1984), are all angst-ridden testaments to their sound which in the latter part of the decade turned even more metallic in nature and influenced a number of thrash metal and heavy metal acts of the late 1980's and 1990's.

UK DECAY: Influenced by the noise of early Adam and the Ants, John 'Abbo' Abbott - vocals, Steve Spon - guitar, Martyn 'Segovia' Smith - bass and Steve Harle - drums, came up with their own goth-punk approach and made a name for themselves in the movement with their 1979 debut record 'Carcrash'.

Regularly appearing in the UK Independent charts with such releases as albums 'For Madmen Only' (1981), 'A Night For Celebration' (1983) and EP's 'The Black Cat' and 'Rising From The Dread', the band's forte was always their live performances which earned them a healthy following across the country and looked likely to propel them into the second wave 1st division. At the height of their popularity though, bassist Segovia left the band and despite a replacement being found - Eddie Branch - Abbo decided Decay's halcyon days were over and had the group play a final, farewell concert at the Klub Foot in London, 1983.

The above represents a small selection of the UK's second wave punk outfits. There are many more I could have profiled such as ANTI-

---

PASTI, PETER AND THE TEST TUBE BABIES, METEORS (punk-rockabilly hybrid), ADDICTS, RUBELLA BALLET, THE WALL, THE OUTCASTS (Northern Ireland 1980's punk), DISORDER, DISCHARGE, THEATRE OF HATE and CHRON-GEN.

*****

In December 1981, I had participated as the UK Subs bass player in an all punk Christmas festival at the cavernous Queen's Hall in Leeds. Sharing the top of the bill with us were the Damned, Exploited and Bow Wow Wow with groups of the calibre of Vice Squad, Chelsea and GBH somewhere below. Also on the bill that night was a new American band, representatives of the emerging West Coast hardcore faction, with a tattooed, bare chested singer who delivered his lyrics with total commitment and focus, while his musical companions tore the roof off the venue with some superfine, super-fast punk rock. I was well impressed.

Turning to Captain Sensible who stood beside me at the edge of the stage I asked him who this Yankee combo was. *"Their singer's name is Henry Rollins, they're from California and they're called Black Flag"* he said.

9
BLACK FLAGS
AND DEAD PRESIDENTS
AMERICAN WEST COAST PUNK

*"It is the accent of languages that determines
the melody of each nation."*
Jean-Jacques Rousseau (1767).

*"They're the Wild Bill Hickoks, the Billy the Kids - they're the
last American heroes we have, man!"*
Ed Roth 'Go Get Those Punks', Newsweek' (1965).

As the proprietor of the coolest music club in early 1970's Los Angeles, Rodney Bingenheimer and his English Disco had introduced that influential West Coast city to the sounds of glam rock by exclusively playing the records of UK glitz and glitter groups such as T. Rex, Sweet, Roxy Music, Bowie and Slade, along with their American counterparts Alice Cooper and the New York Dolls. By the mid-1970's he had his own weekend radio show on KROQ California and had expanded his interests to the new music emerging on the East Coast as exemplified by the Ramones, Blondie and Television. In playing the debut vinyl output from these bands he became the first DJ to expose the West Coast to the American new wave.

It was also Bingenheimer who turned over the KROQ airwaves to two of LA's primary punk bands in the shape of the NERVES and the WEIRDOS; two outfits that were as much, if not more, influenced by the Damned's 1977 LA Starwood club debut and the English punk scene as by the New York CBGB's combos.

Shortly after that Damned performance and the formation of the city's first new wave groups, Los Angeles got its first fanzine in 'Slash', established by punk convert Steve Samiof and featuring an interview with the Damned's Dave Vanian in its maiden issue. Following the example of the UK's 'Sniffin' Glue', 'Slash' became a news sheet and twisted cheerleader for the burgeoning West Coast chapter of the movement and prompted Kim Fowley, a Californian McLaren-esque type figure, to promote a series of 'punk only' showcases at the famed Whiskey A-Go-Go rock club on Sunset Boulevard.

Fowley had been the manager of the all-girl group THE RUNAWAYS - a Suzie Quatro style rock-pop act of the mid-1970's that had kicked off the career of guitarist/vocalist Joan Jett. Going solo in 1979, Jett and her backing band the BLACKHEARTS had huge international success with the 1982 album and single (a total of seven weeks at the number one spot in the USA) 'I Love Rock 'n' Roll', and Fowley was desperately looking around for another act to practise his talents on.

The Whiskey shows were his opportunity to discover fresh talents, but to Fowley's chagrin the quality of the bands he showcased was generally poor. Only LA outfits the DILS and the GERMS, featuring a charismatic singer and future Hollywood punk star by the name of Darby Crash, came across as the genuine new wave article among a crowd of long haired, sub-heavy rock acts wearing carefully ripped T-shirts and wrap-around shades as some kind of evidence of their conversion to the new style. Fowley eventually pulled out of the promotion of the Whiskey punk shows and the new breed had to look elsewhere to find a gig.

In September 1977, Akron art terrorists Devo visited LA to play the downtown Myron's Ballroom with the Dils and Weirdos as their opening acts. Having by then been fully exposed to the ways of English punk through TV and press reports, many in the audience turned up in regulation bondage strides, ripped shirts and safety pins, sporting spiky haircuts and attempting their own version of the pogo. The news spread fast. San Diego sent its own home-grown outfit the ZEROS to play the Big Orange that fall, while San Francisco breathed life into the AVENGERS, the NUNS and CRIME.

A very peculiar Bay area collective that had been formed as far back as 1971 were also embraced by the SF new music enthusiasts at this time. With their bizarre vinyl offering 'Third Reich Rock 'N' Roll', THE RESIDENTS refused to reveal their true identities, appearing in publicity prints in a variety of surreal disguises; the most famous is a photo of the band beside the Golden Gate Bridge with huge bloodshot eyeballs for faces, dressed in matching tuxedos complete with top hats.

Despite a rapidly growing scene, LA still had very few venues for punk bands to play. London had its Roxy Club, New York had its CBGB's and it soon became apparent to the Los Angeleno new wavers that a permanent home and HQ was also required for their branch of the movement to provide independence and to consolidate the expanding 'milieu'.

A subterranean Cavern-like club, the Masque, opened in late 1977 and immediately turned over its stage to a host of un-refined Californian bands. Like any authentic punk club, the Masque was small, seedy and environmentally unsavoury but it provided a much needed focus for the sect, made converts and produced some bands of note...

THE DICKIES: Quickly established themselves as a Masque Club favourite with their humorous covers of Led Zeppelin, Black Sabbath, Moody Blues and Monkees songs and TV show theme tunes. Dressed in a variety of bizarre stage outfits (Gorilla suits were a usual choice) Leonard Phillips - vocals, Stan Lee - guitar, Chuck Wagon - keyboards and Karlos Kaballero - drums, caught the eye of a number of Angeleno A & R men, eventually signing to A & M Records in 1978 and releasing their debut album 'The Incredible Shrinking Dickies' that same year. Their original material was Ramones-esque in flavour and delivery - two minute, buzzsaw guitar wonders that were much in evidence on their follow up LP's 'Dawn Of The Dickies' (1979) and 'Stukas Over Disneyland' (1983).

THE AVENGERS: Always seemed to go down well with the pogo crazy Masque crowd. Along with Crime and the Nuns, Penelope Housten - vocals, Greg Westermark - guitar, Johnathan Postal - bass and Danny Furious - drums, were at the forefront of the emerging San Francisco faction. Musically fast and furious, the Avengers released their maiden record, the single 'Car Crash' in 1977, and the following year were chosen along with the Nuns as one of the support acts for the Sex Pistols at their West Coast debut at San Francisco's Winterland Ballroom. As a result of meeting the Pistols, Steve Jones was recruited to produce their follow up EP 'The American In Me'. By 1979, the band's interminable disputes and personnel changes led to the Avengers' demise with a posthumous album of their work 'The Avengers 1977-1979' being released in 1983.

X: Another band that made its name at the Masque, X was formed in LA in 1977 and consisted of Exene Cervenka - vocals, Billy Zoom - guitar, John Doe - bass and D. J Bonebrake - drums. With an appealing mix of punked-up rockabilly, R & B, and straight rock 'n' roll styles in their unique sound, the band released their first vinyl, the forty-five 'Adult Books' in 1978.
Gaining a considerable live reputation, they came to the attention of leading West Coast's indie label Slash Records who snapped them

up and procured the former Doors keyboard player Ray Manzarek to produce their glorious debut album 'Los Angeles' (1980) and equally brilliant follow up 'Wild Gift' (1981). 'Wild Gift' was voted album of the year in both 'The New York Times' and 'The Los Angeles Times' establishing the band as a major American talent and setting X on a course that most believed would lead to worldwide acceptance and success.

By the mid-1980's though, things started to unravel, their promise never to be fulfilled. Cervenka took a break from vocal duties to work on a book of poetry with Lydia Lunch - 'Adulterers Anonymous', published in 1982 - and Doe took to playing with Black Flags Henry Rollins in a country influenced group called the Knitters. Losing vital momentum through the time spent on these sideline projects, X went on to release a string of inconsistent records until their disolvement in 1988.

While the Masque was showcasing fresh talent, the first new wave West Coast vinyl appeared in the form of the Germs' forty-five 'Forming' (on their own What? label), and the Dils' single release 'I Hate The Rich'. At the same time, a brace of new and influential fanzines became available around town, 'Flipside, 'Lobotomy', 'Generation X' (named after the Billy Idol led combo), and 'Raw Power' - spreading the word, giving a literary voice to the scene.

However, come 1978, the Californian movement suffered a couple of painful blows that left it in a state of some depression. First, the disaster that had been the debut and final San Francisco Sex Pistols performance had left a bad taste in the mouths of those who had witnessed the band in its death throws. Their acknowledged and revered leaders - the West Coast was always more enamoured with the English bands than the American East Coast outfits - had self destructed before their very eyes and this led to genuine fears that the genre itself was in danger of imploding.

Secondly, the Masque was closed down by the Fire Department as a danger to the public, leaving LA punk without a club to call its own. Many suspected it was the movement itself that was seen as the real danger and the American anti-punk clampdown was under way. This apprehension was all but confirmed when LA police officers started to turn up regularly at punk shows throwing their weight around, insulting the clientele and looking for excuses to make arrests. It seemed the UK's establishments concerted efforts to put down the rebellion had been duplicated 6,000 miles away by the equally reactionary Californian institutions.

With the Masque out of action, an associate of Kim Fowley's, Michele Myer, reintroduced the Whiskey weekend punk nights, and even that bastion of long-haired, heavy metal music the Troubadour had a new wave evening for a time. Both experiments came to a quick end when each club owner decided the bands and audiences were too aggressive - once again the search for a new regular venue was on.

The San Francisco new wave fared better with its choice of the Mabuhay Gardens as a permanent club for its bands, opening up for business with gigs from the Nuns and Crime and offering up its stage to a youthful batch of Frisco mutant rockers such as the SLEEPERS, NEGATIVE TREND and the OFFS.

As the Mabuhay swung into action in the north, back in the southern part of the state a punk enthusiast and jewellery designer by the name of Paul Greenstein had, on a whim, asked the proprietor of an LA Chinese restaurant-cum-bar if she would be prepared to have bands playing there on a once a week basis. She agreed. Both the proprietor and the restaurant were called Madame Wong and X opened the venue with a memorable performance in late 1978.

Wong's would go on to become the home for a crop of less punk, more new wave-pop orientated groups such as the MOTELS, OINGO BOINGO, the KNACK and an all girl band that had dropped their early angry punk look and sound in favour of a more commercially acceptable image and approach, the GO-GO'S.

The reopening of the Masque in 1979 provided once again an appropriate environment for the more harder-edged acts to flourish. FEAR - a band that had taken on the leadership of the hard-core wing of the LA scene - became regulars at the new Masque, as did an outfit that would constantly make the 405 mile journey from San Francisco to grace its stage. This band was destined to be the West Coast's most famous new wave sons...

THE DEAD KENNEDYS: Led by vocalist Jello Biafra, with 'East Bay' Ray Glasser - guitar, Klaus Floride - bass, and Darren Peligro - drums, the Kennedys achieved immediate notoriety with their debut single 'California Uber Alles' in 1979. Released on their own Alternative Tentacles label 'Uber Alles' was a hilarious lampooning of the Liberal and laid-back Californian governor Jerry Brown's presidential aspirations...

"I am Governor Jerry Brown/My aura smiles and never frowns
Soon I will be president/Carter's power will soon go away
I will be Fuhrer one day/I will command all of you

Your kids will meditate in school.
Zen Fascists will control you/100% natural
You will jog for the master race/And always wear a happy face
Close your eyes it can't happen here/Big Bro' on white horse is near
The hippies won't come back you say/Mellow out or you will pay
Now it's 1984/Knock, knock at your front door
It's the suede & denim police/They have come for your uncool niece
Come quietly to the camp/You'd look nice as a draw-string lamp
Dont worry it's only a shower/For your clothes here's a pretty flower...
California Uber Alles
Uber Alles California."

... Governor Brown was not a fan!

Their first album 'Fresh Fruit For Rotting Vegetables' (1980), carried the single along with other hardcore anthems such as 'Holidays In Cambodia', 'Kill The Poor' and the very fine 'Nazi Punks, Fuck Off!'. Determined to show the fallacy of free speech in America, the Kennedys released the single 'Too Drunk To Fuck' in 1981, and as anticipated the band received an immediate radio ban followed by all copies of the record being seized by the police on instructions from the state.

The release of their third LP 'Frankenchrist' produced the same results and the group were prosecuted and spent most of 1985 in court defending their right to free speech as guaranteed in the American constitution. Teaming up with Frank Zappa, Biafra took his campaign to Washington and gave evidence against proposed legislation that would have subjected all record lyrics to censorship. Biafra and Zappa's assertions that this type of law making would lead to the suppression of artistic expression and was a step down the slippery slope to a totalitarian state, led to a less repressive version of the law, making it onto the statute books; warning stickers would be attached to the covers of records that contained obscene or blasphemous language.

Fully politicised by these experiences, Biafra recorded a final LP with the Kennedys 'Bedtime For Democracy' (1986), before taking up a solo career and becoming more actively involved in politics - Jello ran for mayor of San Francisco and came fourth out of a field of ten nominations.

The Masque continued to churn out outfits of varying degrees of skill and fire throughout the spring of 1979 - a fine, left field, new wave combo, WALL OF VOODOO, made its debut there, and punk prime movers the MAU-MAUS secured a useful following within its sweat stained walls. Out of towners dropped by, including NY's excellent CRAMPS and Philadelphia's PURE HELL (the first all black punk band) who made the long trip to Hollyweird to play the venue.

Come the summer though, the club was closed down for the second and last time - same problem, fire hazard - and the creative power moved from Hollywood to the LA suburbs. Huntington Beach had given birth to an extreme form of hardcore as exemplified by THE SLASHERS, THE SCREWS, OUTSIDERS and CHINA WHITE.

Long Beach incubated VICIOUS CIRCLE, and from Hermosa Beach came teen punks RED CROSS and the eventual standard bearers for the LA hardcore movement...

BLACK FLAG: The initial line-up of Black Flag included singer Keith Morris, who, having appeared on the band's debut EP 'Nervous Breakdown' (1978), had left to form hardcore heroes the CIRCLE JERKS and was succeeded by the heavily tattooed and angry Henry Rollins. Along with Dez Cadenza and Greg Ginn - guitars, Chuck Dukowski - bass, and Robo - drums, Rollins recorded the first Black Flag LP 'Damaged' in 1981, releasing the record on the quintet's own label SST. The label went on to be a huge success in its own right boasting an eventual catalogue that would include SONIC YOUTH, THE MINUTEMEN, HUSKER DU, THE MEAT PUPPETS and DINOSAUR Jr.

Specialising in a blistering all out sonic assault of a sound over which Rollins would pitch his vitriolic vocals, the band earned themselves a huge West Coast following and made inroads into the UK and European punk markets in the early 1980's. Follow up albums 'My War' (1984), 'Family Man' (1984), 'Loose Nut' (1985) and 'In My Head' (1985) showed diversity and even featured some of Rollins' poetry, though the crux of the band's sound continued to remain firmly in the hardcore arena.

Disbanding in 1986, Rollins took up a solo career and expanded his interests to book writing/publishing, poetry readings and acting. Ginn and Dukowski swapped their instruments for desks at the SST Records office and devoted their energies to the labels continued success.

All of the suburban LA groups had a tougher, angrier and more physically confrontational approach than their Hollywood counterparts.

It was in these hardcore punk communities that a macho martial mutation of the English pogo, the Slam Dance, appeared for the first time among the audience at Black Flag, Vicious Circle, Fear, and Circle Jerks gigs. The whole point of the Slam Dance was to either draw blood

or incapacitate your nearest neighbour in the crowd. Heads low, elbows thrusting out into the ribs of those in striking distance, slam dancers clashed in genuine battle, just in front of their bands, below the stage in an area they called the pit. I once played a San Diego gig with the UK Subs where in a punk rock inspired frenzy the slam dancers tore into each other with sharpened screwdrivers!

Stage diving also became a popular pastime at these shows. This consisted of getting onto the stage to dance for a few seconds before swan diving back into the arms of the audience. The really cool divers could do backflips off the stage onto their feet, and the slightly insane ones would climb fifteen feet or so up a PA system and do a somersault off the top hoping that their comrades below would prove to be brave enough to try to stop them crashing to the venue's hard floor on their heads. I've actually witnessed the messy results of slow reflexes on the part of the catchers.

All this West Coast hardcore activity inspired copyists in other cities in the country. Washington DC produced the superb, super-fast Rastafarian Rockers THE BAD BRAINS along with lesser outfits like MINOR THREAT and IRON CROSS, while New York slammed to KRAUT, THE FEELIES, MISFITS (psychobilly hardcore), and former porn star Wendy O. William's PLASMATICS who took great delight in chainsawing guitars in half and blowing up Cadillac cars on stage to their virulent soundtrack.

By the mid-1980's LA had added to its hardcore roster the likes of SOCIAL DISTORTION, DOA, BAD RELIGION, T.S.O.L and WASTED YOUTH, with San Francisco's Bay area contributing the FUCK UPS, BAD POSTURE, FLIPPER, CODE OF HONOUR and LEWD.

The hardcore movement still continues to attract new adherents to its fast, loud and proud musical tradition in and around the West Coast of the USA. Its contribution to punk history is significant, and its influence on such popular thrash metal and grunge outfits of the late 1980's and 1990's as Nirvana, Metallica, Anthrax, Megadeath and Faith No More is enormous.

A number of the bands, both profiled and mentioned in this chapter, can be seen and heard in action in the definitive movie of the American punk scene, Penelope Spheeris' 'The Decline Of Western Civilisation'.

Left: Henry Rollins (Black Flag) / Illustration © Adam Cansino

10
ENDANGERED SPECIES
THE CHANGING OF THE GUARD

"The realities were already fixed; the illness was understood to be terminal, and the energies of the movement were long since aggressively dissipated by the rush for self-preservation."
Hunter S. Thompson, 'Fear And Loathing In Las Vegas' (1971).

"Our overall impression is optimism, uplift, power, elation which very few acts, like the Who and Springsteen, possess. I believe U2 should be there because there's a lot of dross, a lot of unworthy music in our place. There are a lot of bands who should finish now."
Bono, U2 (1980).

In the first edition of the UK's 'Punk's Not Dead' magazine in the early 1980's, editor Gary Bushell articulated in black and white the importance and aspirations of punk's second wave on its first page. This editorial captured the mood of the movement at that moment in time more than any other I've uncovered in the research for this book, and as such I have decided to transcribe it for you in full...

"Five years ago John Rotten bared his naked rage to the world and lit a fuse that exploded inside the brains of bored teenagers everywhere.
The Sex Pistols were unrelenting, raining musical fire and lyrical brimstone on a shocked adult world that stood for everything punks despised - hypocrisy, complacency, conformity, boredom, a world based on privilege and pomp where the young had little to say, and the working class/dole queue young, even less. And that's why they're still important today. Not as idols to be worshipped from afar, not as a nice, safe, castrated memory hanging on the walls of company executives, but as vital inspiration to the people who are still carrying the punk message on. It hasn't been easy.
One by one the punk 'heroes' sold out. Rock 'n' roll's greatest ever moment was being absorbed by the Entertainment Industry. The 'leaders' were too greedy. The mouthpieces were corrupt, the message distorted. The critics said that punk had died. What they forgot was the thousands of kids who needed

---

and believed in punk as it was supposed to be, a street level movement based on real rock energy.

And these kids formed new bands or found new ones they thought they could trust.

Bands like the UK Subs, Sham, Stiff Little Fingers, the Angelic Upstarts and the Ruts rose up to carry on where the first wave had left off.

The anarchy beat stayed on the streets, growing, changing, transmuting, diversifying, the bands staying true to their roots or getting forgotten, and finally resurging now stronger than ever because punk today has never been more necessary.

Dole Queue Rock is now a grim reality rather than a neat slogan.

And that's why we need Punk - not as a dogma or religion but as rock 'n' roll in its purest form, raw aggressive rebel music, music that screams, rages, demands, excites and always asks why.

Our challenge is to keep it going, keep it challenging and prove it means more than the Fleet Street image of glue-sniffing (sick) and swastika-wearing (sicker).

Punk has got to stay the poison in the machine. So form your own band, write your own fanzine, form your own opinions, expose the people who'd use you.

Prove it to the world: we're the young generation and we've still got something to say."

Less than ten years later, the man who wrote this fine appraisal of 1980's punk had become a Tory supporting journalist for the very tabloid newspaper that had been at the forefront of the attack on the movement - that popular bastion of prejudice and reaction 'The Sun'. Utilising his 'Sun' column to deride left of centre/liberal views, Bushell also provided the paper with one of its ugliest and twisted pieces of anti-Labour Party propaganda during the 1992 British general election.

Under a photograph showing Indian and Pakistani immigrants arriving at Heathrow Airport, Bushell's article insinuated that if Labour leader Neil Kinnock became prime minister, the immigration floodgates would open and the country would be swamped in brown and black faces. The piece deliberately played on the irrational prejudices of the readership towards minorities - the dark side of the British character - and was racist in tone.

Labour lost the election and the Conservatives were returned to government with Bushell's paper claiming a major part in the victory in an editorial entitled 'IT WOZ THE SUN WOT WON IT'.

This is all very strange to me. When I knew Bushell as a UK Sub he

Right: The last of the Mohicans? - Wattie (Exploited) featured on the cover of
'Punk's not dead' magazine - Issue 1 / (1980)

No.1 50p

PUNK's NOT DEAD!

featuring
the
ALL-TIME
PUNK
TOP 100

EXPLOITED
ANTI-PASTI
DISCHARGE
KILLING JOKE
VICE SQUAD
UPSTARTS
UK SUBS
DEAD KENNEDYS
THEATRE OF HATE
CRASS   CLASH
TENPOLE TUDOR
CHRON-GEN
TOYAH

was somewhere politically left of Lev Trotsky, a hardline socialist and friend of some of the Labour party's more radical MP's. What happened to the hatred of *"Hypocrisy"*, *"Conformity"* and *"The punk 'heroes' who sold out"*, his loathing of the tabloid press lies, *"Corrupt mouthpieces"*, *"Distorted messages"* and *"A world based on privilege and pomp"*?

The essential reason behind Bushell's conversion from anti-establishment punk writer to tabloid advocate of a ruling Conservative government is at the very centre of the decline and fall of the punk movement. *"The energies of The Movement were aggressively dissipated by the rush for self-preservation"* wrote Hunter S. Thompson in 1971 about the demise of the 1960's counter-culture revolution - what was true for that failed exercise in world changing was also true for the failure of punk.

But let's not bury punk quite yet, there is still more to tell.

As well as Gary Bushell's Second Wave call to arms, 'Punk's Not Dead' magazine also contained an 'All-Time Punk Top 100' record chart which had been compiled from thousands of votes from readers of the music weekly 'Sounds'. I have also decided to reproduce this in full as it provides an interesting mix of the most popular 1st and 2nd wave songs and bands from that decade.

THE ALL-TIME PUNK TOP 100
AS VOTED BY THE READERS OF 'SOUNDS' (1981).

1) *Anarchy In The UK* - Sex Pistols.
2) *New Rose* - Damned.
3) *No Government* - Anti Pasti.
4) *White Riot* - Clash.
5) *God Save The Queen* - Sex Pistols.
6) *Last Rockers* - Vice Squad.
7) *Holidays In Cambodia* - Dead Kennedys.
8) *Suspect Device* - Stiff Little Fingers.
9) *Alternative Ulster* - Stiff Little Fingers.
10) *Decontrol* - Discharge.
11) *Punk's Not Dead* - Exploited.
12) *Army Life* - Exploited.
13) *Pretty Vacant* - Sex Pistols.
14) *Warhead* - UK Subs.
15) *I'm An Upstart* - Angelic Upstarts.
16) *California Uber Alles* - Dead Kennedys.
17) *Bodies* - Sex Pistols.

18) *Public Image* - Public Image Ltd.
19) *SPG* - Exploited.
20) *Ain't No Feeble Bastard* - Discharge.
21) *Love Song* - Damned.
22) *Hong Kong Garden* - Siouxsie and the Banshees.
23) *Murder Of Liddle Towers* - Angelic Upstarts.
24) *Holidays In The Sun* - Sex Pistols.
25) *Chaos* - 4-Skins.
26) *Big A, Little A* - Crass.
27) *Stranglehold* - UK Subs.
28) *Too Drunk To Fuck* - Dead Kennedys.
29) *Banned From The Roxy* - Crass.
30) *Days Of War* - Exploited.
31) *Smash It Up* - Damned.
32) *Neat, Neat, Neat* - Damned.
33) *Wardance* - Killing Joke.
34) *Resurrection* - Vice Squad.
35) *Complete Control* - Clash.
36) *CID* - UK Subs.
37) *Babylon's Burning* - Ruts.
38) *Bloody Revolutions* - Crass.
39) *Requiem.*
40) *Wasted Life* - Stiff Little Fingers.
41) *Nasty, Nasty* - 999.
42) *My Way* - Sid Vicious.
43) *Fight Back* - Discharge.
44) *Where Have All The Bootboys Gone* - Slaughter and the Dogs.
45) *Fuck A Mod* - Exploited.
46) *No More Heroes* - Stranglers.
47) *Borstal Breakout* - Sham 69.
48) *I Believe In Anarchy* - Exploited.
49) *Party In Paris* - UK Subs.
50) *Police Oppression* - Angelic Upstarts.
51) *White Man In Hammersmith Palais* - Clash.
52) *Love In A Void* - Siouxsie and the Banshees.
53) *Follow The Leader* - Killing Joke.
54) *Kill The Poor* - Dead Kennedys.
55) *Barmy Army* - Exploited.
56) *Do They Owe Us A Living* - Crass.
57) *Blown To Bits* - Exploited.
58) *EMI* - Sex Pistols.
59) *GLC* - Menace.

60) *In A Rut* - Ruts.

61) *Realities Of War* - Discharge.

62) *Teenage* - UK Subs.

63) *Religion Instigates* - Discharge.

64) *Psyche* - Killing Joke.

65) *Royalty* - Exploited.

66) *Ain't Got A Clue* - Lurkers.

67) *Tomorrow's Girls* - UK Subs.

68) *Fascist Dictator* - Cortinas.

69) *A Look At Tomorrow* - Discharge.

70) *Legion* - Theatre Of Hate.

71) *Police Car* - Cockney Rejects.

72) *Young Blood* - Vice Squad.

73) *One Law For Them* - 4-Skins.

74) *Let Them Free* - Anti Pasti.

75) *Wonderful World* - 4-Skins.

76) *Bad Man* - Cockney Rejects.

77) *Securicor* - Crass.

78) *Gary Gilmore's Eyes* - Adverts.

79) *No Feelings* - Sex Pistols.

80) *Remote Control* - Clash.

81) *Playground Twist* - Siouxsie and the Banshees.

82) *So What* - Crass.

83) *Nagasaki Nightmare* - Crass.

84) *Peaches* - Stranglers.

85) *Emotional Blackmail* - UK Subs.

86) *Ready To Ruck* - Cockney Rejects.

87) *Flares 'N' Slippers* - Cockney Rejects.

88) *Clash City Rockers* - Clash.

89) *Never Had Nuthin* - Angelic Upstarts.

90) *C'Mon Everybody* - Sex Pistols.

91) *Army Song* - Abrasive Wheels.

92) *Don't Dictate* - Penetration.

93) *Puppets Of War* - Chron Gen.

94) *I'm Not A Fool* - Cockney Rejects.

95) *Jigsaw Feeling* - Siouxsie and the Banshees.

96) *After The Gig* - Discharge.

97) *Right To Work* - Chelsea.

98) *She's Not There* - UK Subs.

99) *London's Burning* - Clash.

100) *We Outnumber You* - Infa-Riot.

Looking at this punk hit list I notice that the Exploited have nine songs included while the UK Subs managed one less with eight titles in the chart. Even as early as 1981 the Subs' leadership of the second wave was on the wane with the Exploited, Stiff Little Fingers and Killing Joke all looking to take our crown. The need for Charlie Harper, Nicky Garratt, Steve Roberts and I to find a new audience and expand our slowly but perceptibly dwindling fan base became imperative. A case of change or die.

In late 1981 we swapped record companies leaving the GEM label for NEMS Records, sacked our ineffectual, shady and downright corrupt management team, and spent six weeks in a residential studio in deepest Surrey recording an album with a sound and approach unlike any the Subs had recorded before. 'Endangered Species' was a record of contrasting sides: side A consisted of a sequence of hard driving, metallic masterpieces, while the B side exhibited a more reflective and musically elaborate series of tracks that stood the LP apart from the usual one dimensional, hardcore album fare.

Having released a single from the 'Species' collection of cuts, the apocalyptic 'Countdown', we decided to look for American management with a view to taking a crack at that vast market, hopeful of duplicating the Clash's impressive States-side success. The ex-Patti Smith manager Jane Friedman was mentioned to us as a viable candidate and a transatlantic phone call to her NY Broadway office resulted in a USA tour and management offer which we immediately accepted.

Things were looking good. We had a new, fine sounding album to promote, Broadway management, a long tour of America on the horizon - considered by all four members of the Subs to be the Holy Land of rock 'n' roll - and the firm belief that we could find a whole new identity and audience in that remarkable country. But we also had a problem in drummer Steve Roberts.

Steve had taken to very heavy drinking and wild behaviour for some time and though for the first few years I readily joined in with, and even instigated some of his Keith Moon style antics, by the beginning of 1982, his drunken attention seeking buffoonery - regular hotel room destruction, bar brawls and bizarre stage stunts; at one memorable show during that period he played through a whole Subs performance with a large floor tom over his head - had become the cause of real concern. Harper and Garratt saw him as a dangerous liability and became convinced he would end up getting shot if he went to America with us.

I liked Steve, argued against sacking him from the band and giving him one more chance, but in my heart I knew Charlie and Nicky were right and that he would prove to be a major handicap on a long North American tour. Roberts was informed he was no longer a UK Sub and a replacement was found in Chelsea's Sol Mintz - nabbed from his drum seat with Gene October's combo after a Marquee show.

In the February of 1982, after a series of UK warm up dates, the United Kingdom Subversives boarded a Pan Am 747 bound for New York City, looking for adventure and whatever came their way.

FIFTY STATES
AN AMERICAN SOJOURN WITH THE UK SUBS.

Setting up Subs HQ at the Iroquois Hotel, a West 44th St. hostelry with a rock 'n' roll pedigree - both the Clash and Iggy Pop moved out the same day we moved in - we spent a week in the city rehearsing and making plans for the forthcoming tour with our new manager Jane Friedman. After a meal in Chinatown one night, I stopped by the hotel bar to pick up a beer and noticed a man wearing an Arsenal Football Club scarf, alone, sipping on a Guinness, looking up at me from his bar stool. He enquired my name and who I played for, insisted on buying me another brew and asked *"Is that cow Thatcher still fucking up Britain?"* It was the man behind 'The Filth and the Fury', that English establishment's nightmare and punk incarnate, John Lydon, the man formerly known as Johnny Rotten.

Lydon had moved to New York to live and was a regular frequenter of the Iroquois bar, a location that would pretty much guarantee his running into visiting UK musicians from whom he could gleam news of England's ever changing music scene and shoot the breeze with on most nights. We got to talking about our bands, - he was about to go on tour with PIL - politics, the fact that Guinness doesn't travel well and movies, which it turned out Lydon had a passion for.

"I love films, really like to get into a bit of acting and give that a go" he told me.

"Really, what kind of movie would you like to be in then?" I asked him.

"Stuff like 'Mean Streets', 'Taxi Driver', that kind of picture, something gutsy and tough". (A couple of years later Lydon had his movie ambitions come true with a starring role alongside actor Harvey Keitel in the thriller 'Orders Of Death'.)

Later that evening we went to a Manhattan nightclub together, drank beer and continued our conversation, during which time I asked him why he had left London for a life in New York.

"Just look around you" he told me *"It's a better class of movie isn't it?"*
"Let's hope in that case that it's gonna be at a two reeler" I replied.

As the Subs tour progressed I came to appreciate the wisdom of Lydon's observation. For British musicians more used to the horrors of UK touring, of cold and wet weather, bad hotels, surly promoters and motorway food, America with its amazing geographical variety, its fine hostelries and its seeming respect for rock 'n' roll musicians, was indeed 'a better class of movie'.

Our support act for the tour was the Tunbridge Wells hardcore outfit the Anti-Nowhere League. Animal - vocals, Winston Blake - bass, Magoo - guitar and PJ - drums were a biker gang turned punk band dressed in leathers, chains, tattoos and studded belts who had hit the tabloids that year portrayed as yet another evil influence on Britain's youth, their single 'So What' having been removed from store shelves for being obscene. Here's a verse and chorus of 'So What' for your approval...

"Well I've fucked a sheep/And I fucked a goat
I've even stuck my cock/Down their throats
So what, so what... so what, so what you boring little cunt
Who cares about you, who cares what you do!"

They also played a raucous, super-fast version of folk singer Ralph McTell's 'Streets Of London' and had a number of superbly offensive songs with titles such as 'I Hate People (And They Hate Me!)', 'I Cant Stand Rock 'n' Roll' - they particularly enjoyed playing that one a couple of blocks away from Elvis' Graceland gaff in Memphis - and 'Fuck The Law'.

I loved them, thought they were the best rock band I'd seen in ages and within a short space of time the Subs and the League became great friends.

Starting with a two night stint at the Ritz in New York, the 'Hardcore Storms America' tour (Jane's idea) moved to Washington DC where we found we had a big following among the capital city's punk community. We played one of the most satisfying and exciting Subs shows ever at the 9.30 Club on DC's F St. before flying out to Montreal for the Canadian leg of our sojourn.

A bunch of OK mid-West dates followed during which we encouragingly kept hearing the Clash's American hit singles 'Should I Stay Or Should I Go' and 'Rock The Casbah' being played over the airwaves, but with the southern states coming up I was plenty worried that redneck problems could ruin things. As it happened, our gigs in

New Orleans, Atlanta, Memphis, Houston, Dallas and Austin were all excellent, the southern audience having obviously taken punk rock to their hearts somewhat since their exposure to the genre via that Pistols visit of 1978.

After being feted by the hardcore crowds in California - our Los Angeles Country Club appearance was a particularly fine gig - we played one last show with the Anti-Nowhere League at Manhattan's famous Peppermint Lounge before heading back to the UK, much enthused by our impact on America and truly believing we could forge a new career in the land of the free and the brave for ourselves.

Back in Blighty it came as no surprise to find that the Exploited had overtaken our popularity and had become the new supremos of the second generation pack. We shed no tears over that discovery, going into the studio to record a new piece of vinyl, the 'Shake Up The City' EP, with yet another new drummer, my old Brian James and the Brains buddy John Towe, and headed straight back out to the USA again in the Autumn of 1982 for another two month crack at achieving States-side success.

The second tour though proved to be a difficult, spirit breaking affair. In the six months we had been away from the USA, bands such as U2, Simple Minds, Flock Of Seagulls and XTC had made their names in that country with their radio friendly compositions and non-threatening new wave images, monopolising interest away from (perceived) traditional punk outfits and heralding the end of our tentative invasion of America.

Our audience had shrunk across the country apart from the loyal hardcore cities of New York, Los Angeles, Washington DC and San Francisco, and it became obvious that our initial impact and general appeal had evaporated over the months we had been away. We were going backwards not forwards and after three consecutive nights at the Bowery's CBGB's at the end of the tour, we flew back to the UK at the start of 1983, exhausted, dejected and fearing for the UK Subs's future as a viable rock 'n' roll band.

* * * * *

On returning to London, Charlie and I put together a garage-type outfit with the Vibrators' Knox and Hanoi Rocks' Andy McCoy - guitars, and a friend of Captain Sensible's, Matthew 'Turkey' Best - drums, for part time fun and profit. Calling ourselves the Urban Dogs, we played a bunch of UK club dates and made a self-titled LP for the

Left: So what! - The Anti-Nowhere League / (1982) Photograph © Alvin Gibbs

indie Fallout label which featured alcohol fuelled versions of prime New York Dolls and Iggy Pop and the Stooges numbers along with our own original material. But, despite these interesting side line projects, a decision about the future direction of the Subs could not be put off indefinitely.

Garratt, Towe and I wanted to continue moving away from the band's purist past, to become a more commercial sounding rock group, but Harper took the opposite view. He wanted us to regress, to return to our fundamental punk roots - he was afraid of change.

We agreed to give the pure punk option one more chance and set off on a major tour of the UK and Europe - I hated it. The spirit was just not there, it was punk cabaret - yes folks, all your favourite anti-establishment hits of yesteryear... and more! - and I did not enjoy the experience of playing in small clubs to smaller audiences in cities where last time around we had packed out the big venues and punters had to be turned away from the door for lack of space.

As in America, in Britain and Europe our popularity had become devalued as the result of a musical sea change . Our time was up and I realised that being a UK Sub from now on would entail less rewarding work for diminishing returns. I fully intended to quit the Subs after completing the tour, but in the spring of 1983 one last trip presented itself and I was intrigued by its unique opportunities.

The then hard-line communist dictator of Poland, General Jaruzelski had been getting some bad press in the West for his heavy-handed suppression of the pro-democracy Solidarity movement and the imposition of martial law throughout the country. He had decided to try and ditch his autocratic image for that of a cool and groovy guy by inviting some western rock bands over to play for his pop music starved Polish youth.

Now, I still don't know how the name UK Subs came to be mentioned to the ruling class in this (then) Soviet Block State, but mentioned we were and sure enough an invitation came for us to tour Poland along with the lifting of martial law by the General. We readily agreed and became the first punk rock band to play behind the Polski Iron Curtain.

Ironically enough, this proved to be the most decadent tour I ever played with the Subs. We spent two weeks performing to upwards of ten thousand people a night in large ice hockey stadiums across the nation, with two hundred thousand units of the Polish national currency, the Zloty, each in our pockets. The average citizen earned about six thousand Zlotys a month, so by Polish standards we were very rich, but the problem for us was that the Zloty was pretty much worthless outside of the country.

There was no point in taking the stuff back to England, so the only sensible thing to do was spend it all on our travels. Despite the majority of the population having to wait on a daily basis in line, in the cold, for such basics as bread, milk and fuel, all our food requirements were lavishly catered for by our government appointed promoter, and the only freely available goods we could find to spend our huge bundle of Zlotys on was fine Polish Bison brand vodka, Russian champagne and Baltic caviar.

For fourteen days we ate caviar and drank champagne for breakfast, lunch, dinner and supper, threw Zlotys around like confetti and played punk rock for an audience of thousands that had never heard its like before. We were on the national news every night and had an armed guard wherever we went - it was like being in the Goddamn Rolling Stones!

As amazing as these circumstances were, the tour was not the entirely enjoyable experience it should have been due to the deterioration of relations between Charlie, with his insistence on rigid punk compositions and attitude, and Nicky and I, with our desire for musical change and development. I guess Charlie realised that his limited vocal abilities were fine for yelling out punk lyrics over a thrash backing but not for something more commercial and adventurous, and in retrospect he was entirely right to resist our insistance on change. At the time though we thought he was just being stubborn and numerous arguments flared up with Charlie accusing us of selling out, etc., and Nicky and I accusing him of clinging to the past and being too afraid to move into the future, etc. Certainly the gallons of champagne and vodka that flowed daily didn't help matters any.

On the last gig of the tour, the UK Subs played in Warsaw to its biggest ever audience - twenty thousand souls - and flew home. On reaching my apartment I phoned Charlie Harper to inform him I was no longer a UK Sub. My days as a punk rock musician in a punk rock band were over and I looked around to see what I could see.

* * * * *

Parallel to the UK Subs failure as a band to adapt and find a new audience was the evidence of the very failure of punk rock itself in hard commercial terms. On my return from Poland in 1983, the British airwaves were filled with the sounds of new romantic inspired outfits such as Duran Duran, Spandau Ballet and Culture Club. Things had moved on.

In the early 1980's, only a solo Captain Sensible and second wave novelty band Splogenessabounds, had attained number one singles in the UK with 'Happy Talk', Sensible's twee rendition of a Rogers and Hammerstein 'South Pacific' song, and 'Two Pints Of Lager And A Packet Of Crisps Please', respectively. And while U2 were well on their way to being one of the biggest rock bands in the world, even those great white punk hopes the Clash, were unravelling and looking to self-destruct.

Margaret Thatcher, the prime target of punk's hatred and loathing since 1979, won her landslide victory in the 1983 British general election and had begun in earnest to sell her 'greed is good' political philosophy to the populous. Despite continuing opposition to her government from punk, the grim reality was that the movement no longer had what little power it once attained to form and change people's political opinions and perceptions. Despite the *"No Maggie Thatcher and no government"* rhetoric and the empty gestures, Thatcherism continued to hold sway over the masses and the movement went into major retreat.

By the mid 1980's punk was not so much an underground movement as positively subterranean. Its followers had either moved on or become sad caricatures, tourist attractions sporting their Mohawk haircuts and bondage strides for Japanese snappers, and peering out with cartoon sneers from postcards on newsagents shelves. Punk became frozen, stunted, no longer capable of growth or advancement; its troops, the equivalent of those uncomprehending Japanese soldiers on remote Pacific islands who refused to believe their war was lost and fought on long after the rest of their countrymen had surrendered.

Despite the Exploited's insistence to the contrary, punk had acquired a distinctly blue/grey pallor, was cold to the touch and no longer had a pulse.

11
I SPIT ON YOUR RAVE
WINNERS AND LOOSERS

"It was a magical interlude, and like all such interludes, all too brief: 'The things we have never remain: it is the things we have that go'..."
William S. Burroughs, foreword to 'Beat Hotel' (1983).

"Punk? Yeah, it's coming back this week, just for a week and then you'll want something else."
John Richmond, designer (1993).

Punk had its winners and losers. Those who were chewed up bad and spat out by the revolution, and those who used the movement as a springboard for career opportunities and a means of joining the very establishment they once claimed to despise.

One time 'NME' pen pusher Tony Parsons, now writes for the ultimate Tory propaganda sheet 'The Telegraph', while his ex-partner in punk Julie Burchill, makes a nice wad scribbling in favour of the return of capital punishment and harping on about how wonderful Margaret Thatcher and the 1980's were in the pages of 'The Times' - a paper not noted for its rebel credentials.

Vivienne Westwood, having elevated her once seditious fashion designs to the height of 'haute couture', has conformed, curtsied and collected her Order of the British Empire from H. M. the Queen, and gone and traded her once infamous anarchistic philosophy for ruthless elitism: *"Democracy"* she now insists *"panders to the common imbecility."* No doubt we will have a baroness Westwood of Chelsea in the House of Lords by the turn of the century.

In professional and bank balance terms, both Sting and Billy Idol did very well out of punk, and many other first and second wave names continue to have successful careers and make anywhere from reasonable to excellent livings from their associations with the movement - John Lydon's autobiography 'Rotten - No Irish, No Blacks, No Dogs', was a number one best-seller in 1994.

If I'm honest with both myself and you, in a much less high profile and lucrative way, I guess I fit snugly into this category too.

Having moved to Los Angeles for a five year stay in the mid-1980's, I utilised my punk credentials to become the Godfather of the genre Iggy Pop's bass guitarist, during which time I was paid handsomely to traverse the globe with my rock idol and perform all those songs that had played such a major part in influencing punk's raw, raucous and vital sound.

In 1993, Guns N' Roses put one of my UK Subs compositions, 'Down On The Farm', on their multi-million selling 'salute to punk' album 'The Spaghetti Incident', alongside songs by the Damned, Fear, the New York Dolls, the Stooges and the Dead Boys; again my involvement in punk paid hefty dividends and also, incidentally, provided me with my first, maybe only, platinum album. Then, of course, there is this very book!

So, who are the real losers?

Some are too obvious to name, others too numerous to mention. They are of course the dead ones, the failed ones, the lost ones, those who could neither adapt nor advance - those who flew for an all too short space of time on the elevating, liberating power of rebellion and belonging, only to drop like stones back to Earth, into the grey sucking mud of workaday existence once punk's hour had past.

The cashed in and the crashed out - *"Winners and losers"* sings Iggy pop in the song of the same name, *"in love with themselves, no Santa Claus, no happy elves"*... spot on Mr. Osterberg!

NO CHANGE

Now in his fifties, Charlie Harper has continued to front, tour and record with an ever changing line up of the UK Subs since 1976. Only the other day he telephoned me to say he had completed the recording of the thirteenth official Subs studio album and was preparing to play his particular brand of punk, yet again, to audiences in the clubs and pubs of the UK, Europe and the USA. He also assured me that the band had become very big in Argentina!

The Buzzcocks, Sham 69, the Anti-Nowhere League, GBH, Chelsea and the Stranglers have all reformed for another shot at success, while Knox, also now in his fifties, still sings about *"Whips and Furs"* with the Vibrators and the word on the street, man, is that the Clash and the Sex Pistols no less, are about to get back together and open for business.

In recent years, that cavernous London rock venue, the Brixton Academy, has taken to holding an all day and night, punk alternative to the summer Reading Rock Festival which has featured most of these reformed and never-went-aways. I went to last year's bash and was amazed to find thousands of pogoing punks in their bondage and leather finest enjoying the attractions, most of whom would have been wearing nappies rather than bum-flaps when the majority of these bands made their debuts.

And yes, the Exploited were present, still insisting with such admirable conviction to the assembled spiky hordes that *"Punk's Not Dead!"* that for a bizarre moment I found myself almost believing them. Then I looked again with clearer vision, saw the corpse with my own eyes and heard the death rattle over the almost deafening barrage of guitar and drums, and realised it was just a trick of the light, and that Wattie was truly the last of the Mohicans.

NO FUTURE?

Guns N' Roses released an album dedicated to it, Oasis wish to do the same. The late Kurt Cobain used its attitude and attack to inform Nirvana's *"Teen Spirit"*, while his misses used it to fill her remarkable Hole. The UK's Elastica, Manic Street Preachers and Smash are new versions of *it*, as is America's multi-million CD selling outfits Green Day and Rancid - a band that features an ex-UK Sub no less. REM, U2 and Paul Weller, reborn as a politically left of centre, 1970's style rocker, are all products of it, and Billy Idol longs for its return. But punk's influence hasn't solely had a musical dimension.

JOHN PEEL: *"A lot of people would be outraged if you suggested that their lives have been in any way coloured by punk. The fact is, you can tell by looking at them that it very much has been. You'd have to go to a fairly remote part of the world to avoid its influence."*

William Gibson has invented the 'Cyber Punk' genre in his futuristic novels, and writer Will Self has used punk imagery for his compelling and twisted tales. In the movies we had the popular 'Mad Max' trilogy, 'Sid And Nancy' and 'Tank Girl', while Jean Paul Gaultier, Stephen Sprouse and John Richmond are but a few of the many fashion designers who have utilised punk's audacity and wit to enhance their collections.

GIANNI VERSACE: (Designer, 1991) *"Punk has not been out of fashion. It has survived through the years. If we talk about fashion, with a bit of mood and humour, we will find punk for ever."*

In terms of life-styles, it has been a useful prototype for new age travellers, ravers and followers of grunge. From the art world, the K-foundation (a million pounds in cash to burn), and Gavin Turk (Sid Vicious in a box), have both acquired the movement's sense of subterfuge and use of shock tactics to make waves in this field, and if Damien Hirst isn't using Malcolm McLaren's old methods to advance his career I'll eat my mothballed bondage strides. Here's a description of one of his exhibits from 'The Sunday Times' dated August, 1995...

"A Rotting sculpture of a cow and a bull copulating, conceived by Damien Hirst, the 'enfant terrible' of British art, has been banned from New York because health officials fear the exhibit would threaten the wellbeing of the public. The piece, entitled 'Two Fucking (I've replaced the newspaper's deleted expletive), *Two Watching', is the latest controversial work by Hirst, who is famous for his use of dead animals. It involves a hydraulic devise being inserted into a dead cow and bull, inside a glass case, to simulate movement as they gradually rot away. It was due to be shown at a Manhattan gallery next month, but the New York health department has decreed that it would pose a public health risk as it might explode or prompt vomiting among spectators."*

Punk or what!

I believe the true and vital spirit of punk lives on in the likes of Damien Hirst far more than any reformed or never-gave-up, cliché punk cabaret outfit in these 1990's. Only artists of his perverse calibre and courage will ensure the survival of that spirit into what looks increasingly like being a fearfully bland, corporate run and media controlled Twenty First Century.

In this now and future world where mediocrity, uniformity, conformity and the reduction of all human passions and variety will effectively be forced upon us by communication empires via flickering screens. Where TV will, no doubt, be even more effectively used as a tool to control society, to keep the culture credulous and the populous spellbound. In such a world, we will need that very spirit to come again to challenge, to take us by the lapels, to shake the shit out of us and scream *"WAKE UP!"*.

We will have need of the cyber punks... and all other disobedient servants.

Destroy

Boy looked at Johnny / riddin' on a new wave
Johnny got rich / lives Marina Del Rey
Icon face surfin' on the dead sea
Got career opportunities / anything you wanna be

Destroy destroy destroy / is his first principle
Destroy destroy destroy / and we all followed
Destroy destroy destroy / it's elemental
Destroy destroy destroy destroy
There's no sin in that at all

New York City / jumping to a psycho beat
Thunders got a sound / from the heart of its burning streets
Dee Dee's shaking / talking on the telephone
Saying no more Chinese Rocks man / they ain't home grown

Destroy destroy destroy / is his first principle
Destroy destroy destroy / and we all followed
Destroy destroy destroy / it's elemental
Destroy destroy destroy destroy
There's no sin in that at all

20 years down / all change for a new scene
Empty eyes mesmerised by a flickering screen
Fixing up on future junk / back on the Internet
Youth cult, culture shock / bring on the cyber punks

Destroy destroy destroy / is his first principle
Destroy destroy destroy / and we all followed
Destroy destroy destroy / it's elemental
Destroy destroy destroy destroy
There's no sin in that at all

DESTROY © Alvin Gibbs (1996)

ACKNOWLEDGEMENTS

The author and publisher would like to thank the following:

BOOKS
Fear And Loathing In Las Vegas - Hunter S, Thompson (Flamingo)
The Complete Rock Familly Trees - Pete Frame (Omnibus Press)
When The Music's Over - Robin Denselow (Faber and Faber)
Rotten: No Irish, No Blacks, No Dogs - John Lydon (Coronet)
From The Velvets To The Voidoids - Clinton Heylin (Penguin)
The Boy Looked At Johnny - Julie Burchill/Tony Parsons (Pluto Press)
England's Dreaming - Jon Savage (Faber and Faber)
The Guiness Who's Who Of Indie And New Wave Music (Guiness)
30 Years Of Number Ones (BBC Books)
Dictionnary Of Musical Quotations - Derek Watson (Wordsworth)
The Sex Pistols File - Ray Stevenson (Omnibus Press)
The Clash - Miles (Omnibus Press)
Iggy Pop: The Wild One - Pers Nielsen/Dorothy Sherman (Omnibus Press)
New York Dolls - Steven Morrissey (Babylon Books)

NEWSPAPERS / MAGAZINES
New Musical Express, Melody Maker, Sounds, Record Mirror, Q Magazine,
The Sunday Times, Punk's Not Dead Magazine, Sniffin' Glue Fanzine, Mojo.

TELEVISION / VIDEOS
Punk And The Pistols (BBC Arena)

PHOTOGRAPHS
Cover (Rex Features); page 17 (Hoffmann Ltd.); page 23 (Hoffmann Ltd.); page 29
(Rex Features / BMO); page 36 (Rex Features / Pat Enyart); page 43 (unknown);
page 54 (Rex Features); page 76 (Sheila Rock / Rex Features); page 78 (Rex Features);
page 83 (Rex Features); page 88 (Rex Features); page 90 (Rex Features); page 96
(Mark Perry); page 118 (B. Plummer); page 121 (Sheila Rock / Rex Features); page
130 (Ray Stevenson); page 132 (Marc Perry); page 137 (Sheila Rock / Rex Features);
page 144 (Rex Features); page 150 (Rex Features); page 182 (Alvin Gibbs); page 197
(Rex Features); page 206 (Rex Features); page 216 (Alvin Gibbs); page 224 (Alvin
Gibbs); page 227 (Alvin Gibbs); page 234 (Rex Features); page 243 (Rex Features);
page 245 (Bob Gruen); page 265 (Punk's Not Dead Magazine); page 272 (Alvin
Gibbs); page 281 (Rex Features).

ILLUSTRATIONS
All illustrations by Adam Cansino.